新编国际商务英语系列教材

新编国际商法英语教程
New International Business Law

（修订本）

李浚帆　梁　雁　主　编

王如利　副主编

清华大学出版社

北京交通大学出版社

·北京·

内 容 简 介

本书共 10 章，涵盖国际商法导论、合同法、商事组织法、票据法、产品责任法、代理法、反倾销法与反补贴法、竞争法、知识产权法等内容，系统阐述了上述各个领域的重要国际条约、两大法系主要国家的重要法律规定，以及我国的相关法律法规。全书各章（除"国际商法导论"外）都附有相关的真实案件和判例，以帮助读者联系实际，加深理解。

本书既可以用作国际贸易等专业学生的国际商法教材和相关专业教师进行双语教学的参考书，还可以为国际商务及涉外法律等行业的人士提供帮助。

图书在版编目（CIP）数据

新编国际商法英语教程/李浚帆，梁雁主编． — 修订本． — 北京：清华大学出版社；北京交通大学出版社，2009.4（2021.2 修订）

（新编国际商务英语系列教材）

ISBN 978 – 7 – 81123 – 548 – 7

Ⅰ．新…　Ⅱ．① 李…　② 梁…　Ⅲ．国际商法 – 英语 – 高等学校 – 教材　Ⅳ．H31

中国版本图书馆 CIP 数据核字（2009）第 035852 号

新编国际商法英语教程

XINBIAN GUOJI SHANGFA YINGYU JIAOCHENG

责任编辑：张利军

出版发行：清 华 大 学 出 版 社　　邮编：100084　　电话：010 – 62776969　　http://www.tup.com.cn

　　　　　北京交通大学出版社　　邮编：100044　　电话：010 – 51686414　　http://press.bjtu.edu.cn

印 刷 者：艺堂印刷（天津）有限公司

经　　销：全国新华书店

开　　本：203 mm×280 mm　　印张：14.5　　字数：504 千字

版 印 次：2021 年 2 月第 1 版第 1 次修订　　2021 年 2 月第 4 次印刷

印　　数：9 001 ～ 10 000 册　　定价：44.00 元

本书如有质量问题，请向北京交通大学出版社质监组反映。对您的意见和批评，我们表示欢迎和感谢。

投诉电话：010 – 51686043，51686008；传真：010 – 62225406；E-mail：press@bjtu.edu.cn。

前 言

随着当今世界经济全球化的日益加深，对于许多行业，尤其是国际商务领域的从业人员来说，了解并熟悉国际通行的法律及惯例是事业成功的必要前提和重要保障。因此，对于国际商务相关专业的高校学生来说，很有必要熟练掌握相关的专业知识和英语词汇，这样才能够为将来的就业做好充分准备。为了帮助广大学生更好地完成这一任务，特编写这本《新编国际商法英语教程》，作为国际商务相关专业学生的核心专业课教材。

本书参考国际商法经典中文教材编写，内容较为全面，涵盖合同法、商事组织法、票据法等重要内容。本书将专业知识与英语能力紧密地结合起来，旨在帮助读者在熟悉国际商法基础知识的同时提高英语水平。

本书既可以用作国际贸易等专业学生的国际商法教材和相关专业教师进行双语教学的参考书，还可以为国际商务及涉外法律等行业的人士提供帮助。

与其他同类教材相比，本书具有以下特色。

1. 形式丰富新颖

本书每章开篇设有学习目标、开篇案例、热身问答，章末设有小组讨论题和真实案例，并且穿插一些有关重点或热点问题的阅读材料或图表，以帮助读者拓宽视野，加深理解。

2. 注重联系现实

本书力图把握当今的全球化与时代感，就新出现的一些国际商法领域，如反倾销和反补贴法、竞争法、知识产权法、电子商务法等也进行了相应的介绍。全书各章（除"国际商法导论"外）都附有相关的真实案件和判例，以帮助读者更好地将书本理论与法律实践联系起来，并有利于提高学生的学习兴趣。

3. 国际性与中国特色相结合

本书一方面系统阐述国际商务各个领域的重要国际条约，以及两大法系主要国家的重要法律规定；另一方面，始终注重体现中国特色，每一章都对中国的相关法律法规进行介绍，而这一点恰恰是那些国外的商法英文教材所欠缺的。

本书共10章，具体的编写分工如下：李浚帆和梁雁共同编写第1章，李浚帆编写第2、3、4章，张美丽编写第5章，王如利编写第6、7章，梁雁编写第8、9、10章。全书由主编负责大纲制定及统稿等工作。

本书得以面世，有赖于北京交通大学出版社的热情支持，在此深表谢意。

由于作者水平有限，书中难免存在错误与遗漏之处，敬请广大读者批评指正。

作 者
2021 年 2 月

Contents
目　录

Chapter 1　An Introduction to International Business Law ························ (1)
国际商法导论

1. 1　An Overview of International Business Law ······················· (2)
国际商法概述

1. 1. 1　Definition of International Business Law ················· (2)
国际商法的定义

1. 1. 2　Modern International Business Law ················· (3)
现代国际商法

1. 1. 3　Sources of International Business Law ················· (4)
国际商法的渊源

1. 2　Continental Law System ······················· (4)
大陆法系

1. 2. 1　A Brief Introduction to Continental Law System ················· (4)
大陆法系简介

1. 2. 2　Characteristics of Continental Law ················· (5)
大陆法的特点

1. 2. 3　Sources of Continental Law ················· (6)
大陆法的渊源

1. 3　Common Law System ······················· (7)
普通法系

1. 3. 1　A Brief Introduction to Common Law System ················· (7)
普通法系简介

1. 3. 2　Characteristics of Common Law ················· (9)
普通法的特点

1. 3. 3　Characteristics and Sources of English Law ················· (10)
英国法的特点及渊源

1. 3. 4　Characteristics and Sources of American Law ················· (11)
美国法的特点及渊源

1. 4　Comparison of the Two Major Law Systems ······················· (12)
两大法系的比较

1. 4. 1　Differences between the Two Law Systems ················· (12)
两大法系的区别

I

  1.4.2 New Development of the Two Law Systems ·············· (13)
     两大法系的新发展

1.5 International Organizations Relating to International Business Law ······ (14)
  与国际商法有关的国际组织
  1.5.1 International Chamber of Commerce（ICC） ················· (14)
     国际商会
  1.5.2 International Law Association（ILA） ················· (14)
     国际法协会
  1.5.3 United Nations Commission of International Trade Law（UNCITRAL） ··· (14)
     联合国国际贸易法委员会
  1.5.4 International Institute for the Unification of Private Law（UNIDROIT） ··· (14)
     国际统一私法协会

1.6 International Business Law and China ················· (15)
  国际商法与中国

Chapter 2 Contract Law（Ⅰ） ················· (17)
  合同法（一）

2.1 An Overview of Contract Law ················· (19)
  合同法概述
  2.1.1 Definition and Characteristics of a Contract ················· (19)
     合同的定义及特征
  2.1.2 Functions of a Contract ················· (19)
     合同的作用
  2.1.3 A Brief Introduction to the Contract Law of Different Countries ········· (20)
     各国合同法的简要介绍

2.2 Formation of Contract ················· (21)
  合同的成立
  2.2.1 Offer and Acceptance ················· (21)
     要约与承诺
  2.2.2 Consideration and Cause ················· (23)
     对价与约因
  2.2.3 The Parties' Capacity to Contract ················· (24)
     当事人的订约能力
  2.2.4 Form of a Contract ················· (25)
     合同的形式
  2.2.5 Legality of a Contract ················· (25)
     合同的合法性
  2.2.6 Reality of the Mutual Assent ················· (25)
     合意的真实性

2.3 Performance of Contract ················· (26)
  合同的履行

2.3.1   Basic Points ·· (26)
　　　　基本要点

2.3.2   Breach of Contract ··· (27)
　　　　违约

2.3.3   Remedies for Breach of Contract ························ (27)
　　　　违约的救济方法

2.3.4   Change of Circumstances, Frustration of Contract and Force Majeure ······ (32)
　　　　情势变迁、合同落空和不可抗力

2.4   Assignment of Contract ·· (33)
　　　合同的让与

2.4.1   Definition of Assignment of Contract ··················· (33)
　　　　合同让与的概念

2.4.2   Assignment of the Rights under the Contract ············ (33)
　　　　合同债权让与

2.4.3   Transfer of the Obligations under the Contract ·········· (33)
　　　　合同债务承担

2.4.4   Concurrent Assignment and Transfer under the Contract ······ (34)
　　　　合同权利与义务的概括转让

2.5   Discharge of Contract ·· (34)
　　　合同的消灭

2.5.1   Provisions under the Continental Law System ··········· (34)
　　　　大陆法系的规定

2.5.2   Provisions under the Anglo-American Law System ······· (35)
　　　　英美法系的规定

2.5.3   Provisions under the Chinese Law ····················· (36)
　　　　中国法的规定

2.5.4   Limitation of Time ···································· (36)
　　　　时效

CASES ·· (39)
案例

• Battle of Forms ·· (39)
　格式之战

• Past Consideration or Executed Consideration ························· (40)
　过去的对价还是已履行的对价

• Formation of a Contract by Instantaneous Communication between
　Offeror and Offeree ·· (40)
　发盘人与受盘人通过即时通信手段订立合同

• Esso Petroleum Ltd.' Case on Purchase Tax ······················· (41)
　埃索石油公司购买税案

Chapter 3   Contract Law (Ⅱ) ································· (43)
　　　　　合同法（二）

3. 1 UN Convention on Contracts for the International Sale of Goods ··· (44)
　　　《联合国国际货物销售合同公约》
　　3. 1. 1 A Brief Introduction to CISG ·············· (44)
　　　　　《联合国国际货物销售合同公约》简介
　　3. 1. 2 Formation of a Contract for the International Sale of Goods ········ (45)
　　　　　国际货物销售合同的订立
　　3. 1. 3 Obligations of the Buyer and the Seller ········· (47)
　　　　　买卖双方的义务
　　3. 1. 4 Breach of Contract and Remedies ········· (50)
　　　　　违约及其救济
　　3. 1. 5 Passing of Risk ·············· (55)
　　　　　风险的转移
3. 2 Principles of International Commercial Contracts ·········· (56)
　　　国际商事合同通则
　　3. 2. 1 A Brief Introduction to PICC ············· (56)
　　　　　国际商事合同通则简介
　　3. 2. 2 Comparison between PICC and CISG ·········· (57)
　　　　　PICC 与 CISG 的比较

CASES ·············· (61)
案例
· Buyer's Burden of Proof for Lack of Conformity and the Requirements of
　Notice under CISG ·············· (61)
　CISG 之下买方就质量不符的举证责任及通知的要求
· Jurisdiction and Place of Payment ·············· (62)
　管辖权和支付地点
· The Independence of the Remedies of Avoidance of the Contract and
　Price Reduction ·············· (62)
　宣告合同无效与降价两种救济方法相互独立

Chapter 4 Business Organization Law ·············· (64)
　　　　　商事组织法

4. 1 Legal Forms of Business Organizations ·············· (65)
　　　商事组织的法律形式
　　4. 1. 1 Individual Proprietorship ·············· (66)
　　　　　个人企业
　　4. 1. 2 Partnership ·············· (66)
　　　　　合伙企业
　　4. 1. 3 Company ·············· (67)
　　　　　公司
4. 2 Partnership Enterprise Law ·············· (67)
　　　合伙企业法

4.2.1　Definition and Features of Partnership Enterprise ·················· (67)
　　　　合伙企业的概念及特征

4.2.2　Establishment of a General Partnership Enterprise ················· (68)
　　　　普通合伙企业的设立

4.2.3　Relationships inside a General Partnership Enterprise ·············· (69)
　　　　普通合伙企业的内部关系

4.2.4　Relationship between a General Partnership Enterprise and Third Persons ······ (70)
　　　　普通合伙企业与第三人的关系

4.2.5　Dissolution of a General Partnership Enterprise ··················· (70)
　　　　普通合伙企业的解散

4.2.6　Limited Partnership Enterprise ·································· (71)
　　　　有限合伙企业

4.3　Company Law ·· (72)
　　公司法

4.3.1　An Overview of Company ······································ (72)
　　　　公司概述

4.3.2　Stock Limited Company ······································· (74)
　　　　股份有限公司

CASES ·· (83)
案例

•　Dodge v. Ford Motor Company ······························ (83)
　　道奇诉福特公司案

•　Piercing the Corporate Veil ································· (84)
　　揭开公司面纱

•　The Case Not Applied to the Rule of Piercing the Corporate Veil ·········· (85)
　　没有应用揭开公司面纱原则的案例

Chapter 5　Negotiable Instrument Law ······························ (86)
　　　　　　票据法

5.1　An Intruduction to Negotiable Instrument ························ (87)
　　票据概述

5.1.1　Definition of Negotiable Instrument ························· (87)
　　　　票据的概念

5.1.2　Legal Principles of Negotiable Instrument ··················· (88)
　　　　票据的法理

5.1.3　Types of Negotiable Instrument ···························· (89)
　　　　票据的种类

5.1.4　Functions of Negotiable Instrument ························· (89)
　　　　票据的作用

5.1.5　The International Conventions on Negotiable Instrument ········· (90)
　　　　关于票据的国际公约

Ⅴ

5.2　Bill of Exchange ……………………………………………………… (91)
　　　汇票
　　5.2.1　Basic Points ……………………………………………………… (91)
　　　　　　基本要点
　　5.2.2　Drawing ………………………………………………………… (93)
　　　　　　出票
　　5.2.3　Endorsement …………………………………………………… (96)
　　　　　　背书
　　5.2.4　Presentment …………………………………………………… (97)
　　　　　　提示
　　5.2.5　Acceptance …………………………………………………… (98)
　　　　　　承兑
　　5.2.6　Guarantee ……………………………………………………… (99)
　　　　　　保证
　　5.2.7　Payment ……………………………………………………… (100)
　　　　　　付款
　　5.2.8　Dishonor and Recourse ……………………………………… (100)
　　　　　　拒付与追索
　　5.2.9　Forged Signature ……………………………………………… (101)
　　　　　　伪造签名
5.3　Promissory Note and Cheque ………………………………………… (101)
　　　本票与支票
　　5.3.1　Promissory Note ……………………………………………… (101)
　　　　　　本票
　　5.3.2　Cheque ………………………………………………………… (102)
　　　　　　支票

CASES ………………………………………………………………………… (106)
案例
• Whether the Document is a Bill of Exchange? ………………………… (106)
　这样的单据是否是汇票?
• The Promisor's Duty to Indemnify the Guarantor of the Dishonored
　Promissory Notes ……………………………………………………… (106)
　本票被拒付后出票人对保证人的赔偿责任
• Payee Owed No Special Duty to Drawer of Forged Check …………… (107)
　收款人对被伪造签名的支票出票人不承担特殊责任
• Checks Paid by Bank on Which Stop Payment Orders Had Been Placed …… (108)
　已经发出止付指令却被银行支付的支票

Chapter 6　Product Liability Law ……………………………………… (109)
　　　　　　产品责任法

6.1　An Overview of Product Liability Law ……………………………… (111)
　　　产品责任法概述

      6.1.1 Definition of Product Liability ································· (111)
            产品责任的定义
      6.1.2 Development of Product Liability Laws ················· (111)
            产品责任法的发展

  6.2 Product Liability Law in the US ······························· (112)
      美国的产品责任法
      6.2.1 Theories of Product Liability ························· (112)
            产品责任的法学理论
      6.2.2 Defences ··· (115)
            被告的抗辩
      6.2.3 Damages ··· (116)
            损害赔偿
      6.2.4 Impact of Product Liability Law on American Foreign Trade ··········· (117)
            产品责任法对美国对外贸易的影响

  6.3 Product Liability Law in the EU ······························· (118)
      欧盟的产品责任法
      6.3.1 Liability without Fault ······························· (118)
            无过失责任原则
      6.3.2 Definition of Producer ······························· (118)
            生产者的定义
      6.3.3 Definition of Product ······························· (119)
            产品的定义
      6.3.4 Definition of Defective Product ····················· (119)
            有缺陷产品的定义
      6.3.5 Producer's Defences ······························· (119)
            生产者的抗辩
      6.3.6 Damages ··· (120)
            损害赔偿

  6.4 Product Quality Law in China ······························· (120)
      中国的产品质量法
      6.4.1 Responsibilities and Obligations of the Producers for the Quality ······ (120)
            of Their Products 生产者的产品质量责任与义务
      6.4.2 Responsibilities and Obligations of the Sellers ··········· (121)
            销售者的责任与义务
      6.4.3 Liabilities and Time Limitation ····················· (121)
            责任与时效

CASES ··· (123)
案例
 • Escola v. Coca Cola Bottling Company of Fresno ··············· (123)
   艾丝克拉诉可口可乐弗雷斯诺瓶装公司案
 • Henningsen V. Bloomfield Motors, Inc. ························· (124)
   海宁森诉布鲁姆费尔德汽车公司案

Chapter 7   Law of Agency ·· (126)
代理法

7. 1   An Overview of the Law of Agency ································ (127)
代理法概述
    7. 1. 1   Definition of Agency ·· (127)
        代理的定义
    7. 1. 2   Creation of the Authority of Agent ···················· (128)
        代理权的产生
    7. 1. 3   Unauthorized Agency ·· (129)
        无权代理
    7. 1. 4   Termination of Agency ····································· (130)
        代理的终止

7. 2   Internal Relationship of Agency ······························· (131)
代理的内部关系
    7. 2. 1   Duties of the Agent ·· (131)
        代理人的义务
    7. 2. 2   Duties of the Principal ······································ (132)
        本人的义务

7. 3   External Relationship of Agency ······························· (133)
代理的外部关系
    7. 3. 1   Under the Continental Law System ····················· (133)
        大陆法系
    7. 3. 2   Under the Common Law System ························· (133)
        普通法系

7. 4   Agents Assuming Special Liabilities ·························· (134)
承担特别责任的代理人
    7. 4. 1   Agents Assuming Special Liabilities to the Principal ······ (134)
        对本人承担特别责任的代理人
    7. 4. 2   Agents Assuming Special Liabilities to the Third Parties ·········· (134)
        对第三人承担特别责任的代理人

7. 5   Provisions and Regulations Relating to Agency in China ·············· (136)
中国与代理有关的法律法规
    7. 5. 1   Provisions of the General Principles of the Civil Law of the PRC ······ (136)
        《中华人民共和国民法通则》中的规定
    7. 5. 2   Provisions of the Contract Law of the PRC ·············· (136)
        《中华人民共和国合同法》中的规定

CASES ··· (139)
案例
  • Restraining Agent from Misusing Confidential Information ···················· (139)
    限制代理人滥用机密信息

• Duty of Care Owed by Agent ·· (140)
　　代理人应尽的谨慎义务

Chapter 8　Anti-dumping Law and Anti-subsidy Law ····················· (142)
　　反倾销法与反补贴法

　　8.1　Anti-dumping Law ··· (143)
　　　　反倾销法
　　　　8.1.1　Dumping and International Anti-dumping Legislation ········ (143)
　　　　　　倾销及国际反倾销立法
　　　　8.1.2　Major Principles of the Anti-dumping Agreement ············ (145)
　　　　　　反倾销协议的主要原则
　　　　8.1.3　Chinese Laws and Regulations on Anti-dumping ············ (150)
　　　　　　中国有关反倾销的法律法规

　　8.2　Anti-subsidy Law ··· (150)
　　　　反补贴法
　　　　8.2.1　Subsidy and International Anti-subsidy Legislation ·········· (150)
　　　　　　补贴及国际反补贴立法
　　　　8.2.2　Major Principles of SCM ·· (151)
　　　　　　补贴与反补贴措施协议的主要原则
　　　　8.2.3　Chinese Laws and Regulations on Anti-subsidy ············ (153)
　　　　　　中国有关反补贴的法律法规

CASES ··· (155)
案例
• Anti-dumping Duties Imposed by European Council on Electronic Weighing Scales
　Exported by a Chinese Company ·· (155)
　欧洲理事会对某中国公司出口的电子秤征收反倾销税
• US Anti-dumping and Countervailing Duty Cases against Imports of
　Canadian Wheat ··· (156)
　美国对加拿大小麦的反倾销及反补贴税案件
• Chinese Firm Wins Anti-dumping Case on Lighters Brought by the EU ········ (157)
　中国公司打赢欧盟针对打火机的反倾销案件

Chapter 9　Competition Law ·· (160)
　　竞争法

　　9.1　An Overview of Competition Law ·· (161)
　　　　竞争法概述
　　　　9.1.1　A Brief Introduction to Competition Law ····················· (161)
　　　　　　竞争法简介
　　　　9.1.2　Unfair Competition ··· (162)
　　　　　　不正当竞争

      9.1.3   Monopoly ……………………………………………… (164)
            垄断

  9.2   Competition Laws of Some Countries or Regions …………… (165)
      某些国家或地区的竞争法
      9.2.1   Antitrust Law of the US ……………………………… (165)
            美国的反托拉斯法
      9.2.2   Competition Law of the EU …………………………… (166)
            欧盟的竞争法
      9.2.3   Competition Law of China ……………………………… (167)
            中国的竞争法

  9.3   International Legislation Relating to Competition …………… (169)
      与竞争有关的国际立法
      9.3.1   Provisions on Competition of Paris Convention ………… (169)
            《巴黎公约》中有关竞争的规定
      9.3.2   Provisions on Competition of TRIPs …………………… (169)
            《与贸易有关的知识产权协议》中有关竞争的规定
      9.3.3   The UN Set ……………………………………………… (170)
            联合国《关于控制限制性商业做法的公平原则和规则的一揽子多边协议》

CASES ………………………………………………………………………… (174)
案例
- European Union Microsoft Competition Case ……………………… (174)
  欧盟对微软公司的竞争诉讼

- United States Microsoft Antitrust Case …………………………… (176)
  美国对微软公司的反托拉斯诉讼

- Protecting Goodwill and Reputation of a Business in the UK：The Law of
  Passing Off ………………………………………………………… (177)
  英国对企业信誉和声望的保护：仿冒法

Chapter 10   Other laws Relating to International Business ………… (182)
          其他与国际商务有关的法律

  10.1   Law of Intellectual Property ………………………………… (184)
      知识产权法
      10.1.1   An Overview ………………………………………… (184)
            概述
      10.1.2   WIPO ………………………………………………… (186)
            世界知识产权组织
      10.1.3   The Paris Convention ……………………………… (187)
            《巴黎公约》
      10.1.4   The Berne Convention ……………………………… (187)
            《伯尔尼公约》

        10. 1. 5   TRIPs ··· (189)
               《与贸易有关的知识产权协议》
        10. 1. 6   Chinese Intellectual Property Laws ··············· (194)
               中国的知识产权法
  10. 2   Model Law on Electronic Commerce ·························· (196)
      电子商务示范法
        10. 2. 1   An Overview of Electronic Commerce ············ (196)
               电子商务概述
        10. 2. 2   Model Law on Electronic Commerce ··············· (197)
               《电子商务示范法》

CASES ··· (200)
案例

  • Frosty Treats, Inc. v. Sony Computer Entertainment America, Inc. ··········· (200)
    冰冻盛宴公司诉美国索尼电脑娱乐公司案
  • Perfect 10 v. Google, Inc ··· (200)
    完美 10 诉谷歌公司案
  • Questions Raised by Yoga Copyright ··· (202)
    瑜珈著作权引发的问题

Glossary ·· (205)
专业词汇表

References ·· (215)
参考文献

Chapter 1

An Introduction to International Business Law
国际商法导论

Learning Objectives

- ☑ To learn the definition and sources of international business law
- ☑ To learn the basic points about the Continental Law System and the Common Law System
- ☑ To understand the differences between the two major law systems
- ☑ To know the important international organizations relating to international business law

Opening Vignette

History of International Business Law

Formal documents and other evidences of regularized trade practices were first known in Egypt and Babylonia. The Hammurabi Codes[1], the earliest known comprehensive codes of law in the world, have been regarded as the origin of international business law by many researchers.

In fact, in many parts of the ancient world, foreign merchants, through treaty arrangements or other agreements, were allowed to regulate their affairs and adjudicate their own disputes without interference from local authorities. They tended to settle in special sections of business cities where they might follow their own religions, laws, and customs. Roman law incorporated features of the already developed business law, which, however, was no longer handled separately in special courts but was treated simply as part of the whole legal system.

The barbarian invasions of Europe caused such social disruption that it was not until late in the Middle Ages that long-range commerce again became possible in Europe and merchants were once more able to determine the rules and regulations under which they could safely operate. In the cities of north Italy and south France, the merchant class frequently dominated the state and could enact the needed rules as legislation. In other parts of Europe, associations of merchants bought protection from powerful lords or kings who granted them safe conduct and permitted them to conduct fairs and to establish rules and methods of enforcement. The merchant class established special courts where summary judgment was granted with little regard for the technicalities of procedure and doctrine in the regular courts, and without the necessity for lawyers.

The term "law merchant[2]" was applied to the substantive principles that eventually emerged from this quasi-judicial[3] activity. The law merchant developed later in England than in continental Europe, and it was not completely established there until the mid-16th century, when English trade with the New World began to assume the most importance. In England the law was administered by special courts having jurisdiction only over those engaged in trade; these were the courts of *piepoudre* (French, means dusty foot, an allusion to the dusty shoes of merchant judges who perhaps had been trudging the roads).

The English royal courts in early days refused to hear merchants' suits, but in the 17th century they reversed this position and obtained exclusive jurisdiction. At first, however, the litigants were required to present proof of the law merchant in each case. In the 18th century lord chief justice[4] Mansfield made the law merchant a part of the common law[5] and abolished the requirement of special proof. The United States (after its foundation) adopted the principles prevailing in England in the late 18th century.

Warm-up Questions

1. What do you think international business law is?
2. What is the relation between trade practices and business law?
3. What is the difference between business law and international business law?

1.1　An Overview of International Business Law
国际商法概述

1.1.1　Definition of International Business Law　国际商法的定义

International business law, or international commercial law, refers to the body of rules and norms governing international business transactions and commercial organizations (except those relating to the maritime transportation of goods which is known as maritime law). In particular, it regulates the legal relationships of international business[6].

Every country has its business or commercial law. However, international business law is to be examined particularly herein. The "international" here means that there has to be at least one of the three factors of the legal relationship (subject, object, legal fact) relating to foreign countries.

The following three cases may be considered to be international:

(1) The two parties (or more) to the legal relationship have different nationalities, or have their places of business in different nations;

(2) The object of the legal relationship belongs to foreign countries, and the object may be tangible goods or intangible property;

(3) The fact of creation, alteration and termination of the legal relationship occurs in foreign countries.

1.1.2　Modern International Business Law　现代国际商法

Traditional international business law includes contract law, company law, negotiable instruments law and etc. With the rapid development of international business, modern international business law, in comparison with the traditional law, covers much more extensively and set foot in many new commercial activities, such as intellectual property right transfer, international finance, international trade in services, etc.

As the increasing involvement of most countries in economic globalization, the line between domestic commercial law and international business law is becoming confusable. The domestic commercial laws of those countries and regions which play very important roles in international business (such as the US and the EU) might be regarded as international business law by the rest of the world.

With the further progress of economic globalization, it can be said that international business law has become the most important aspect of international law, and should be paid much attention to by the merchants, transnational corporations and others who engage in international business.

Reading Material

Modern Commercial Law in Western Countries

Commercial law or business law is the body of law which governs business and commerce and is often considered to be a branch of civil law and deals both with issues of private law and public law. Commercial law regulates corporate contracts, hiring practices, and the manufacture and sales of consumer goods. Many countries have adopted civil codes which contain comprehensive statements of their commercial law.

In the US, commercial law is the province of both the Congress under its power to regulate interstate commerce, and the states under their police power. Efforts have been made to create a unified body of commercial law in the US: the most successful of these attempts has resulted in the general adoption of the Uniform Commercial Code (1970).

On the continent of Europe, commercial law remains a separate subject matter with its special courts. Within the EU, the European Parliament and the legislatures of member nations are working to unify their various commercial codes.

1.1.3 Sources of International Business Law 国际商法的渊源

1. International treaties and conventions

Legally, international treaties are binding agreements between two or more states, whereas international conventions are those binding agreements entered into by different states (normally more than two states) sponsored by international organizations, such as the United Nations.

Both international treaties and conventions relating to international business are important sources of international business law. The General Agreement on Tariffs and Trade (GATT)[7] and the United Nations Convention on Contracts for the International Sale of Goods (CISG)[8] are famous examples.

2. International business customs and usages

International business customs and usages refer to the general rules and practices in international commercial activities that have become generally adopted through unvarying habit and common use.

International business customs and usages are not law, yet, they are also very important sources of international business law, and play a significant role in international business practice. For example, the International Commercial Terms (INCOTERMS)[9] and the Uniform Customs and Practice for Documentary Credits (UCP)[10], have been used widely in international trade and finance for decades.

3. National commercial law

National commercial law refers to all the rules and norms made by a state to regulate commercial activities in its territory. Since there is no uniform international business law which is adopted by all the states, sometimes, an international business transaction may be conducted under a state's jurisdiction which relates to this transaction. Furthermore, state legislature is usually needed to assure the efficient enforcement of international business law. Therefore, national commercial law is generally considered as another important source of international business law.

The national laws of most countries in the present world, especially those of the developed countries, can be categorized into two major law systems: Continental Law System[11] and Common Law System[12].

1.2 Continental Law System
大陆法系

1.2.1 A Brief Introduction to Continental Law System 大陆法系简介

The Continental Law System (also called Civil Law System or Romano-Germanic Law System), originated in the European Continent, is the most widespread system of law in the present world.

The central sources of continental law are codifications in a constitution or statute passed by legislature that is recognized as authoritative to amend a code. The continental laws mainly derive from the Roman Empire, and more particularly, the Corpus Juris Civilis issued by the Emperor Justinian[13]. This was an extensive reform of the law in the Eastern Roman Empire, bringing it together into codified documents.

The continental law today, in theory, is interpreted rather than developed or made by judges. Only legislative enactments (rather than judicial precedents) are considered legally binding. However, in reality, courts do pay attention to previous decisions, especially from higher courts.

In the present world, many states and regions base their law systems on the continental law, such as:

(1) The European Continental countries, especially France and Germany;

(2) All the Latin American countries and some African countries;

(3) Japan, Thailand, Indonesia and Turkey in Asia;

(4) Louisiana in the US, Scotland in the UK, Quebec in Canada.

1.2.2   Characteristics of Continental Law   大陆法的特点

1. Codification

The concept of codification developed especially during the 17th and 18th century, as an expression of both natural law and the ideas of the enlightenment. The political ideal of that era was expressed by the concepts of democracy, protection of property and the rule of law. That ideal required the certainty of law, through the recording of law and through its uniformity. So, the mix of Roman law and customary and local law ceased to exist, and the road opened for law codification, which could contribute to the aims of the above-mentioned political ideal.

Another reason that contributed to codification was the notion of the nation state, which was born during the 19th century and required the recording of the law that would be applicable to particular state.

The continental law lays such a strong emphasis on codification that some authors tend to consider it as written law[14]. The Romans categorized their law into *jus scriptum* (written law) and *jus non scriptum* (unwritten law[15]). By "unwritten law" they meant custom; by "written law" they meant not only the laws derived from legislation but also, literally, laws based on any written source.

Nevertheless, not everyone likes law codification. The proponents of codification regarded it as conducive to certainty, unity and systematic recording of the law; whereas its opponents claimed that codification would result in the ossification of the law.

2. Public law & private law

Almost all the continental law countries divided their law into public law and private law[16], which also rooted in Roman law. Public law is the branch of law that deals with the state or government and its relationships with individuals or other governments. It refers to the constitutional, statutory, or judicial law developed by governments and applied equally to the general public, including the constitutional law, administrative law, criminal law and procedural law[17]. In contrast, private law is the branch of law that deals with the legal rights and relationships of private individuals. It governs relationships between two or more private individuals, companies, or organizations. The civil law, commercial law and marriage law are examples of private law.

Here, the distinction between public international law and private international law[18] has to be stressed and it is not as clear as that between domestic public and private law. Public international law is sometimes called the "law of nations[19]". It should not be confused with private international law, which is concerned with conflict of laws.

Public international law establishes the framework and the criteria for identifying states as the principal actors in the international legal system (international laws). This system deals with the acquisition of territory, state immunity and the legal responsibility of states in their conduct with each other. It is similarly concerned with the treatment of individuals within state boundaries. There is thus a comprehensive regime dealing with group rights, the treatment of aliens, the rights of refugees, international crimes, nationality problems, and human rights generally. International law further includes the important functions of the maintenance of international peace and security, arms control, the pacific settlement of disputes and the regulation of the use of force in international relations. Although the law is not able to stop the outbreak of war, it has developed principles to govern the conduct of hostilities and the treatment of prisoners. International law is also used to govern issues relating to the global commons such as global environment, international waters, outer space, global communications, and world trade.

Private international law is a branch of jurisprudence arising from the diverse laws of various nations that applies when private citizens of different countries interact or transact business with one another. It refers to that part of the law that is administered between private citizens of different countries or is concerned with the definition, regulation, and enforcement of rights in situations where both the person in whom the right inheres and the person upon whom the obligation rests are private citizens of different nations. It is a set of rules and regulations that are aiming to eliminate differences between laws of different nations and established or agreed upon by citizens of different nations who privately enter into a transaction and that will govern in the event of a dispute. In this respect, private international law differs from public international law which is the set of rules entered into by the governments of various countries that determine the rights and regulate the intercourse of independent nations.

Reading Material

Roman Law & Continental Law

The Continental Law system (Civil Law system) is based on Roman law, especially the Corpus Juris Civilis of Emperor Justinian, as later developed by medieval legal scholars.

However, the acceptance of Roman law had different characteristics in different countries, even in the European Continent. In some of them its effect resulted from legislative act, i.e. it became positive law, whereas in other ones it became accepted by way of its processing by legal theorists.

Consequently, Roman law did not completely dominate in Europe. Roman law was a secondary source of European laws, which was applied only as long as local customs and local laws lacked a pertinent provision on a particular matter. However, local rules were interpreted primarily according to Roman law (it being a common European legal tradition of sorts), resulting in its influencing the main source of law also.

Another characteristic, beyond Roman law foundations, is the extended codification of the adopted Roman law, i.e. its inclusion into civil codes.

1.2.3 Sources of Continental Law 大陆法的渊源

1. Written law

Written laws are main sources of continental law, including constitutions, codes and statutes.

The constitutional law is at the top of the whole legal system in every continental law country and all other laws must be established according to the principles of it.

The legal systems in many continental law countries are based around one or several codes of law, which set out the main principles that guide the law. The most famous example is perhaps the French Civil Code[20]. Exceptionally, the civil laws of Scotland and South Africa are uncodified, and the civil laws of Scandinavian countries remain largely uncodified.

There are also many statutes established by the administrative departments in continental law countries, which are regarded as written laws too.

2. Custom

Most European Continental countries consider customs as one of the sources of law. Customs still play an important role in these counties and some laws can be understood only when associated with customs.

3. Cases

Normally, continental law countries do not put the cases the same effectiveness as laws and the prejudications are only efficient on the particular cases. However, since the beginning of 20th century, the attitude of continental law countries towards cases has changed to some extent, many judges will refer to previous cases when making judge.

4. Jurisprudence and doctrines

First, jurisprudence and doctrines provide the legislators with theories of law, terminologies and concepts, which contribute much to legislation. Second, jurisprudence and doctrines can help to explain the laws and analyze the cases. Third, jurisprudence and doctrines can be used to train lawyers and judges who will affect the law enforcement.

1.3   Common Law System
普通法系

1.3.1   A Brief Introduction to Common Law System   普通法系简介

1. Common Law System

The term Common Law System came to be used of the English legal system and, generally, to describe a system where the law is based on court decisions and precedent. The Common Law System prevails in England, the US, and other countries ever colonized by England, such as Canada, Australia, New Zealand, Ireland, India, Pakistan, Malaysia, Singapore, Burma, Libya, Liberia, Nigeria, Chinese Hong Kong. It is distinct from the Continental Law System, which predominates in Europe and in areas historically colonized by France and Spain.

The Common Law System originated and developed in England and based on court decisions, on the doctrines implicit in those decisions, and on customs and usages rather than on codified written laws.

Many of the legal concepts in use today, including the law of contracts, are derived from common law.

During the colonialism times, the English common law was taken by emigrants from the Old Country to the English colonies, especially the America. After the American Revolution, English common law became the foundation of legal procedures in the US. Today, the law system in every American state, except Louisiana, is based on the Common Law System. In Louisiana, once a French colony, many French legal practices and customs (based on the Continental Law System) have been maintained.

Since the Common Law System is typically represented in England and the US, it is also known as the Anglo-American Law System.

2. Common law

There are three important connotations to the term of common law.

1) Common Law System as opposed to Continental Law System

The first connotation differentiates the Common Law System from the Continental Law System. Modern Common Law System primarily descends from the English Law. Common Law System places great weight on court decisions, which are considered as law. By contrast, the Continental Law System mainly descends from the Roman law.

2) Common law as opposed to statutory law or written law

The second connotation differentiates the authority that promulgated a particular proposition of law. For example, in most areas of law in most jurisdictions in the US, there are statutes enacted by a legislature, regulations promulgated by executive branch agencies pursuant to a delegation of rule-making authority from a legislature, and common law decisions issued by courts (or quasi-judicial tribunals within agencies).

This connotation can be further differentiated into:

(1) Laws that arise purely from the common law without express statutory authority, for example, most of the criminal law and procedural law before the 20th century, and even today, most of contract law and the law of torts;

(2) Decisions that discuss and decide the fine boundaries and distinctions in written laws promulgated by other bodies, such as the constitution, statutes and regulations.

3) Law as opposed to equity

The third connotation differentiates common law from equity[21]. Before 1873, England had two parallel court systems, courts of law (courts of common law) that could only award money damages and recognized only the legal owner of property, and courts of chancery[22] (courts of equity) that recognized trusts of property and could issue injunctions[23] (orders to do or stop doing something).

Although the separate courts were merged long ago in most jurisdictions, or at least all courts were permitted to apply both common law and equity (though probably under different laws of procedure), the distinction between common law and equity remains significant in:

(1) Categorizing and prioritizing rights to property;

(2) Determining whether the guarantee of a jury trial[24] applies (a determination of a fact necessary to resolve a common law claim) or whether the issue can only be decided by a judge (issues of equity);

(3) The principles that apply to the grant of equitable remedies by the courts.

1.3.2 **Characteristics of Common Law   普通法的特点**

The distinctive feature of common law is that it represents the law of the courts as expressed in judicial decisions. The grounds for deciding cases are found in precedents provided by past decisions, as contrasted to the Continental Law System, which is based on statutes and prescribed texts. Therefore, some authors refer to common law as case law[25] or unwritten law.

Common law courts base their decisions on prior judicial pronouncements rather than on legislative enactments. Where a statute governs the dispute, judicial interpretation of that statute determines how the law applies. Common law judges rely on their predecessors' decisions of actual cases, rather than on abstract codes or texts, to guide them in applying the law. Common law judges find the grounds for their decisions in law reports, which contain decisions of past cases. Under the doctrine of *stare decisis* (Latin, means stand by the decided matter), common law judges are obliged to adhere to previously decided cases, or precedents, where the facts are substantially the same. A court's decision is binding authority for similar cases decided by the same court or by lower courts within the same jurisdiction. The decision is not binding on courts of higher rank within that jurisdiction or in other jurisdictions, but it may be considered as persuasive authority.

Besides the system of judicial precedents, other characteristics of common law are trial by jury and the doctrine of the supremacy of the law. Originally, supremacy of the law meant that not even the king was above the law; today it means that acts of governmental agencies are subject to scrutiny in ordinary legal proceedings. In the common law counties, all citizens, including the highest-ranking officials of the government, are subject to the same set of laws, and the exercise of government power is limited by laws. The judiciary may review legislation, but only to determine whether it conforms to the requirements of the constitutional law.

Anglo-American Common Law System traces its roots to the medieval idea that the law as handed down from the king's courts represented the common custom of the people. It evolved chiefly from three English Crown Courts of the 12ᵗʰ and 13ᵗʰ centuries: the Exchequer, the King's Bench, and the Common Pleas. These courts eventually assumed jurisdiction over disputes previously decided by local or manorial courts, such as baronial, maritime, guild, and forest courts, whose jurisdiction was limited to specific geographic or subject matter areas. Equity courts, which were instituted to provide relief to litigants in cases where common law relief was unavailable, also merged with common law courts. This consolidation of jurisdiction over most legal disputes into several courts was the framework for the modern Anglo-American judicial system.

Because common law decisions deal with everyday situations as they occur, social changes, inventions, and discoveries make it necessary for judges sometimes to look outside reported decisions for guidance in a case of first impression (previously undetermined legal issue). The Common Law System allows judges to look to other jurisdictions or to draw upon past or present judicial experience for analogies to help in making a decision. This flexibility allows common law to deal with changes that lead to unanticipated cases. At the same time, *stare decisis* provides certainty, uniformity, and predictability and makes for a stable legal environment.

Both England and the US base their laws on judicial precedents, and divide their laws into common law and equity. But English law and American law are not identical, and they respectively have some particular features.

1.3.3　Characteristics and Sources of English Law　英国法的特点及渊源

1. Characteristics of English law

English law is divided into common law and equity, which represents the primary characteristic of it.

The origins of the English common law lay in the justice of the king, exercised through his curiae, together with the customary law exercised in the old communal courts of shire and hundred, and the feudal law exercised by the lord in relation to his own vassals. As overlord of all subjects, the king had a residual right to give justice to all, and as feudal lord of the tenants-in-chief[26] he had the right and the duty to sit in his curiae to hear their disputes. Until the time of Henry II, royal justice was available to subjects who were not tenants-in-chief only in exceptional cases. However, in the reign of Henry II, access to the king's justice was extended by the enactment of a principle that "no man need answer for his freehold land without the king's writ being obtained". As these royal writs became popular with litigants, they increasingly sought the justice of the king's courts rather than the local or feudal courts, which slowly declined.

The king's justice was dispensed by the itinerant justices of the curiae. When the courts of Common Pleas, King's Bench, and Exchequer developed as separate entities, the law they applied was the common law. By the time of Edward I there was in existence a "common law"—the law administered in the king's courts throughout the land and therefore "common" to the whole kingdom.

As early as the 15th century, people started petitioning the King for relief against unfair judgments and as the number of petitioners rapidly grew, the King delegated the task of hearing petitions to the Lord Chancellor[27]. The Chancellors were required to pass judgment guided by conscience and based on morals and equality. It has been suggested that ecclesiastics were chosen for this position as they belonged to the small class of people who were able to read and write. Since these early Chancellors had no formal legal training, and were not guided by precedent, their decisions were often widely diverse. In 1529, a lawyer, Sir Thomas More, was appointed as the Lord Chancellor, marking the beginning of a new era. After this time, all future Chancellors were lawyers, and from around 1557 onwards, records of proceedings in the courts of chancery were kept, leading to the development of a number of equitable doctrines.

However, as the law of equity developed, it began to rival and conflict with the common law. Litigants would go "jurisdiction shopping" and often would seek an equitable injunction prohibiting the enforcement of a common law court order. The penalty for disobeying an equitable "common injunction" and enforcing a common law judgment was imprisonment.

Consequently the Judicature Acts of 1873 and 1875 was established, which combined the common law and equity, and from then on there would no longer be different procedures for seeking equitable and common law remedies. It is important to note, however, that the Judicature Acts did not fuse common law and equity, only their administration. There is still a body of rules of equity which is quite distinct from that of common law rules, and acts as an addition to it. Although they are implemented by the same courts, the two branches of the law are separate. Where there is conflict, equity still prevails.

2. Court structure of England

English courts can be categorized into the superior courts and justice courts[28].

There are three subcategories of superior courts: the High Court, the Crown Court and the Court of Appeals[29]. The High Court has three divisions: the Queen's Bench Division[30] responsible for the admiralty and commercial litigation, the Chancery Division for the corporation and insolvency lawsuits, and the Family Division hearing the familial cases. The Crown Court is responsible for criminal cases. The Court of Appeals, of course, is the court of second instance[31]. Some exceptional cases having been decided by the Court of Appeals, may be further appealed to the House of Lords[32].

The justice courts include county court and magistrate court[33]. The county court is responsible for hearing civil cases, especially those involving small sums of money and the cases may be appealed to the Court of Appeals. The cases of venial misdeeds are heard by the magistrate court and may be appealed to the Queen's Bench Division of the High Court or the Crown Court.

3. Sources of English law

(1) Case law — Case laws, or judicial precedents, are the primary source of English law.

(2) Statute — Statutes, (or statutory laws, written laws, codes), are another important source of English law.

(3) Custom — Custom was the most important source of ancient English law, but it plays a less important role in modern English law.

1.3.4　Characteristics and Sources of American Law　美国法的特点及渊源

1. Characteristics of American law

American law roots in English law, and is also divided into common law and equity. However, the US is a federal country and its legal systems include two major parts of federal system and state system, which make its law differ much from the English law.

In the US, normally, the states have the legislative powers. In another word, the states' legislation is the principle, while the federal legislation is exceptional. The federal legislation only cover the areas relating to national defense, diplomacy, emigration, maritime, international trade, intellectual property rights and etc. Even in these areas the states' legislations are not excluded, and the states can establish supplementary and additional laws. However, the federal laws are superior to the state laws, the federal laws prevail when there is a conflict.

Reading Material

Questioning the Common Law

Many outside the legal system saw the common law differently. Those outsiders in the US consider the common law not as the perfection of reason but as the perfection of nonsense.

In speeches and newspapers, outsiders to the legal system—usually adherents of the Democratic Party—attacked the common law as the creation of judges, who were making law to protect property against democracy. These debates occurred at a time when judges were using common-law doctrines to outlaw union organizing, to require the return of fugitive slaves, and to protect merchants and creditors at the expense of consumers and debtors.

The critics of the common law ridiculed it as an arbitrary collection of abstruse rules. William Sampson's attack was among the most vitriolic. He thought Americans "had still one pagan idol to which they daily offered up much smokey incense. They called it by the mystical and cabalistic name of common law." Some principles were ancient, others recent, but in all instances, the common law sat "cross-legged and motionless upon its antique altar, for no use or purpose but to be praised and worshiped by ignorant and superstitious votaries."

2. Court structure of the US

There are two parallel systems of courts in the US: the US courts and the state courts[34].

The US courts include the US District Court, the US Circuit Court, the US Supreme Court[35].

Most state courts have two levels: courts of first instance[36] and appellate courts. The courts of first instance can be subclassified as the limited jurisdiction courts (generally are the county or municipal courts), and the general jurisdiction courts[37] (hear the general civil and criminal cases relating to the state). The state appellate courts usually include the state appellate court and the state supreme court.

It should be noted that the US courts and the state courts are two parallel and separate systems, and the state supreme court's decisions are final to the cases within the state.

3. Sources of American law

(1) Case law — Case laws, or judicial precedents, are the primary source of American law. No matter the US courts or the state courts, the precede decisions of the superior courts are bind on the lower courts. However, the US Supreme Court and the state supreme courts are not subject to their own judicial precedents, and they have the power to make cassations on precedents and establish new doctrines through new cases. This may be the so-called "Judges make laws".

(2) Statute — Statutes (or statutory laws, written laws, codes), are another important source of American law. The Federal Constitution takes the most significant part in the American written laws, and it is regarded as the source of all other American laws.

1.4　Comparison of the Two Major Law Systems
两大法系的比较

1.4.1　Differences between the Two Law Systems　两大法系的区别

The original difference is that, historically, the common law was developed by custom, beginning before there were any written laws and continuing to be applied by courts after there were written laws, whereas the continental law developed out of Roman law.

In later times the continental law became codified as *droit coutumier*[38] or customary law that were local compilations of legal principles recognized as normative. Sparked by the age of enlightenment, attempts to codify private law began during the second half of the 18th century, but civil codes with a lasting influence were promulgated only after the French Revolution, in jurisdictions such as France (with its Napoleonic Code). However, codification is not a defining characteristic of the Continental Law System, e. g. the civil laws of Scandinavian countries remain largely uncodified, whereas common law jurisdictions have frequently codified parts of their laws, e. g. the Uniform Commercial Code[39] of the US. There are also some jurisdictions of mixed law system, such as the laws of Scotland, the Philippines, Namibia and South Africa.

Thus, the difference between continental law and common law lies not just in the mere fact of codification, but also in the methodological approach to codes and statutes. In continental law countries, legislation is seen as the primary source of law. By default, courts thus base their judgments on the provisions of codes and statutes, from which solutions in particular cases are to be derived. Courts thus have to reason extensively on the basis of general rules and principles of the codes, often drawing analogies from statutory provisions to fill lacunae and to achieve coherence. By contrast, in the common law jurisdictions, cases are the primary source of law, while statutes are only seen as incursions into the common law and thus interpreted narrowly.

The underlying principle of separation of powers is seen somewhat differently in continental law and common law countries. In some common law countries, especially the US, judges are seen as balancing the power of the other branches of government. By contrast, the original idea of separation of powers in France was to assign different roles to legislation and to judges, with the latter only applying the law ("the mouth of the law"). This translates into the fact that many continental law jurisdictions reject the formalistic notion of binding precedent (although paying due consideration to settled case law)

There are, however, certain sociological differences. In some continental law countries judges are trained and promoted separately from lawyers, for example, France has a specialized graduate school for judges; whereas common law judges are usually selected from accomplished and reputable lawyers.

1.4.2 New Development of the Two Law Systems 两大法系的新发展

It is clear that the Continental Law System and the Common Law System are two different systems. The chief principles of the two systems, however, have been coming so close in recent years that some legal doctrines can hardly be distinguished from each other. The important reasons for this are the growing similarity of economic, political and even cultural systems of most nations, which resulted from the increasing globalization.

In the past decades, there have been respective new developments of the Continental Law and Common Law Systems, which blur the line between the two.

In continental law countries, case law has been playing an increasing important role in their legal systems in recent years. Most judges and juries, under continental law jurisdiction, pay much consideration to precedential cases before they make decisions, especially when the case is difficult to adjudicate if only judged by the statutory law.

On the other hand, there are more and more statutory laws in common law countries. Early common law was somewhat inflexible; it would not adjudicate a case that did not fall precisely under the purview of a judicial precedent and had an unwieldy set of procedural rules. Judicial precedents derive their force from the doctrine of *stare decisis* and the previous decisions of the highest court in the jurisdiction are binding on all other courts in the jurisdiction. However, changing conditions soon make most decisions inapplicable except as a basis for analogy, and a court must therefore often look to the judicial experience of the rest of the English-speaking world. This gives the system flexibility, while general acceptance of certain authoritative materials provides a degree of stability. Nevertheless, in many instances, the courts have failed to keep pace with social developments and it has become necessary to enact statutes to bring about needed changes; indeed, in recent years statutes have superseded much of common law, notably in the fields of commercial, administrative, and criminal law.

1.5　International Organizations Relating to International Business Law　与国际商法有关的国际组织

1.5.1　International Chamber of Commerce（ICC）　国际商会

The International Chamber of Commerce is a famous INGO (International Non-governmental Organization)[40] in international business. It is a worldwide commercial organization founded in 1919 and headquartered in Paris, which make efforts to compile and publish international business practices. The most famous publications of it are INCOTERMS (International Commercial Terms), UCP (Uniform Customs and Practice for Documentary Credits) and etc.

1.5.2　International Law Association（ILA）　国际法协会

The International Law Association is also an INGO, which was founded in 1873 and headquartered in London. Its aims are to research and develop international law, and resolve the conflict of law and put forward suggests on international uniform laws. One of the examples of its achievements is Warsaw-Oxford Rules 1932[41].

1.5.3　United Nations Commission of International Trade Law（UNCITRAL）　联合国国际贸易法委员会

The United Nations Commission of International Trade Law is generally regarded as the most authoritative and important international organization in international trade. It was established in 1966, which is affiliated with the United Nations (UN) and aiming to harmonize and unify international trade law. The United Nations Convention on Contracts for the International Sale of Goods (CISG) is one of its famous achievements.

1.5.4　International Institute for the Unification of Private Law（UNIDROIT）　国际统一私法协会

The International Institute for the Unification of Private Law was founded as an INGO in 1962, and later was transformed into a separate international governmental organization by its member nations. It aims to promote the harmony of private law of the members and establish a whole set of principles on private law which could be accepted by all the members. The Principles of International Commercial Contracts (PICC)[42] is one of the examples of its achievements.

1.6   International Business Law and China
国际商法与中国

China has a legal history of several thousands of years, but owning to various historical and political reasons, little business (commercial) rules and norms can be found in the Chinese legal system before the 20th century.

China started to introduce international business law during the late period of Qing Dynasty, and enacted some commercial law (such as company law, negotiable-instrumental law, insurance law, bankruptcy law, and etc) in the early-half of the 20th century. However in fact, such laws are executed practically only in those big cities like Shanghai.

After the founding of the People's Republic of China, especially after the implementation of the policy of reform and open-up, Chinese government began to establish the new commercial legal system which referring to the developed legal systems of other countries as well as keeping the Chinese features. Till now, the Chinese legislatures have promulgated a number of business rules and norms, such as the Contract Law of the People's Republic of China and the Foreign Trade Law of the People's Republic of China.

Today China has a whole set of business law which keeps pace with the development of the international business law. Chinese business law will certainly help to enhance the international business relationship between China and the other countries, and further push forward China's progress to a prospering modern country.

Group Discussion ▶▶▶

1. State the sources of international business law.
2. Talk about the characteristics and sources of both continental law and common law.
3. Compare the Continental Law System and the Common Law System.
4. Discuss the respective merits and deficiencies of the two major law systems.
5. Say something about Chinese commercial law.

NOTES ▶▶▶

1   Hammurabi Codes   《汉谟拉比法典》
2   law merchant   商业习惯法，商人法
3   quasi-judicial   准司法性的
4   lord chief justice   最高法院的首席法官
5   common law   普通法（有时也指习惯法）
6   legal relationships of international business   国际商事法律关系
7   General Agreement on Tariffs and Trade (GATT)   《关税与贸易总协定》

8　United Nations Convention on Contracts for the International Sale of Goods（CISG）
　　《联合国国际货物销售合同公约》

9　International Commercial Terms（INCOTERMS）　　《国际贸易术语解释通则》

10　Uniform Customs and Practice for Documentary Credits（UCP）　　《跟单信用证统一惯例》

11　Continental Law System　大陆法系（亦称为 Civil Law System，即民法法系，或 Romano-
　　Germanic Law System，即罗马－日耳曼法系）

12　Common Law System　普通法系（亦称为 Anglo-American Law System，即英美法系）

13　Corpus Juris Civilis issued by the Emperor Justinian　东罗马帝国皇帝优士丁尼安颁布的《民
　　法大全》（亦称为《优士丁尼安法典》）

14　written law　成文法，制定法（亦用 statutory law, statute, positive law）

15　unwritten law　不成文法（有时也译为"习惯法"）

16　public law　公法；private law　私法

17　constitutional law　宪法；administrative law　行政法；criminal law　刑法；procedural laws
　　诉讼法，程序法

18　public international law　国际公法；private international law　国际私法

19　law of nations　万国公法，国际法

20　French Civil Code　《法国民法典》

21　equity　衡平法（有时也译为"平衡法"）

22　courts of chancery　（英国）枢密大臣法庭，大法官法庭（现为英国高等法院的部门之一）

23　injunction　禁令

24　jury trial　陪审团

25　case law　判例法（亦用 judge-made law）

26　tenants-in-chief　总佃户，直接从国王那里获得土地的地主（有时也译为"领主"）

27　Lord Chancellor　英国封建时代的枢密大臣（今指大法官）

28　superior court　高级法院；justice court　低级法院

29　High Court　高等法院；Crown Court　王冠法院；Court of Appeals　上诉法院

30　Queen's Bench Division　王座庭

31　court of second instance　二审法院

32　House of Lords　（英国）上议院

33　county court　郡法院；magistrate court　治安法院

34　US court　美国联邦法院；state court　州法院

35　US District Court　美国联邦地方法院；US Circuit Court　美国联邦巡回法院（即上诉法
　　院）；US Supreme Court　美国联邦最高法院

36　court of first instance　一审法院

37　limited jurisdiction court　有限管辖权法院；general jurisdiction court　普通管辖权法院

38　droit coutumier　（法语）法律汇编

39　Uniform Commercial Code　（美国）《统一商法典》（缩写为 UCC）

40　INGO（International Non-governmental Organization）　国际非政府间组织

41　Warsaw-Oxford Rules 1932　《1932 年华沙－牛津规则》

42　Principles of International Commercial Contracts（PICC）　　《国际商事合同通则》

Chapter 2

Contract Law（Ⅰ）
合同法（一）

Learning Objectives

☑ To know the definition and characteristics of contract
☑ To understand the necessary conditions for the valid formation of a contract
☑ To learn the legal provisions on breach of contract under two major law systems
☑ To know about the relevant legal provisions on assignment and discharge of contract
☑ To learn about the important provisions in Chinese contract law

Opening Vignette

The Elements of a Valid Contract

Contracts are part of everyone's every day life. For example, when a person leases an apartment, buys a home or makes a charge purchase, a contract is often involved. But what on earth is a contract? A contract has many definitions, but one of the simplest definitions for a valid contract is a "promise enforceable by law".

Typically, in order to be enforceable (or valid, legal), a contract must involve the following elements:

1. A "Meeting of the Minds" (Mutual Consent)

The parties to the contract should have a mutual understanding of what the contract covers. For example, in a contract for the sale of a "mustang", the buyer thinks he will obtain a car while the seller believes he is contracting to sell a horse, there is no meeting of the minds and the contract will likely be held unenforceable. Moreover, the meeting of the minds must be real.

2. Offer and Acceptance

The contract usually involves an offer (or more than one offer) to another party, who accepts the offer. For example, in a contract for the sale of a piano, the seller may offer the piano to the buyer for $1000. The buyer's acceptance of that offer is a necessary part of creating a binding contract for the sale of the piano.

3. Mutual Consideration (The Mutual Exchange of Something of Value)

In order to form a valid contract, the parties to a contract must exchange something of value. In the case of the sale of a piano, the buyer receives something of value in the form of the piano, and the seller receives money.

4. Competent Parties

Anyone can enter into a contract, except minors, certain felons and people of unsound mind or intoxicated persons. The contract must identify who the parties are; usually names are sufficient, but sometimes addresses or titles may be used. In sales contracts, for example, in addition to names, "seller" and "buyer" are sometimes used to further describe the parties.

5. Legal Object

The thing being agreed to in a contract is also known as the object or subject. It must be lawful, possible and definite. A court, for example, will not enforce a contract to perform an illegal act. For example, drug deals are illegal and often go wrong, and therefore a person who pays for drugs that aren't delivered can't seek the help of a court in getting the money back.

6. Proper Form

Contracts should be in the forms in line with the legal provisions. Even though in some countries courts may enforce an oral contract, some categories of contracts must be in writing to be legal.

Additionally, other elements, such as good faith, may also factor into the enforceability of a contract.

It is implicit within all contracts that the parties are acting in good faith. For example, if the seller of a "mustang" knows that the buyer thinks he is purchasing a car, but secretly intends to sell the buyer a horse, the seller is not acting in good faith and the contract will not be enforceable.

In order to be enforceable, the contract must be performed according to the terms of it, or else the contract may be rendered void. For example, if the purchaser of a piano does not pay the $1,000 purchase price, he can not enforce the contract to require the delivery of the piano. Similarly, again depending upon the contract terms, the seller may not be able to enforce the contract without delivering the piano. In a typical "breach of contract" action, the party alleging the breach will recite that it performed all of its obligations under the contract, whereas the other party failed to perform its obligations.

Contract law is a product of the modern commercial civilization. It is changing with time and different from country to country. The above is just a general explanation of the elements of a contract. For a detailed contract to be drafted or interpreted, a local attorney's help is advisable.

 Warm-up Questions

1. Please give your own definition of contract.
2. Why is a contract required by law to involve these elements?
3. What do you know about the legal requirements on elements of a contract in China?

2.1　An Overview of Contract Law
合同法概述

2.1.1　Definition and Characteristics of a Contract　合同的定义及特征

Everyone may agree that a contract is an agreement. However, not every agreement is a contract. In most countries, a contract is strictly and explicitly defined by law.

According to the article 2 of the Contract Law of the People's Republic of China[1], a contract refers to an agreement establishing, modifying and terminating the civil rights and obligations between parties of equal footing, such as natural persons, juristic persons[2] or other organizations.

On the basis of the above definition, three important characteristics of a contract can be summarized as follows:

（1）A contract is a manifestation of the mutual assent of the parties;

（2）A contract is between two or more parties;

（3）Concluding a contract is for the purpose of certain civil legal effects.

2.1.2　Functions of a Contract　合同的作用

Contracts play very important roles in the modern economic society. In the present world, it can be said that no business transaction, domestic or international, can be made without contracts. In most cases, more than one contracts should be concluded to carry out one transaction. For example, an international sales transaction normally involves an international sales contract, a transportation contract and an insurance contract.

Contracts help to smooth the transactions and keep them in proper order, and protect the parties involved. Contracts can also promote the optimum distribution of resources.

Reading Material

An Agreement to agree

In the US, an "agreement to agree" is not a contract. This type of agreement is frequently employed in industries that require long-term contracts to ensure a constant source of supply and an outlet of production. Mutual manifestations of assent in themselves sufficient to form a binding contract are not deprived of operative effect by the mere fact that the parties agree to prepare a written reproduction of their agreement.

In determining whether, on a given set of facts, there is merely an "agreement to agree" or a sufficiently binding contract, the courts apply certain rules. If the parties express their intention — either to be bound or not bound until a written document is prepared — that intention controls. If they have not expressed their intention, but they exchange promises of a definite performance, and agree upon all essential terms, then the parties have a contract even though the written document is never signed. If the expressions of intention are incomplete — as, for example, if a material term such as a price or quantity has been left to further negotiation — the parties do not have a contract. The designation of the material term for further negotiation is interpreted as demonstrating the intention of the parties not to be bound until a complete agreement is reached.

2.1.3   A Brief Introduction to the Contract Law of Different Countries
各国合同法的简要介绍

1. Contract law under the Continental Law System

In continental law countries, such as France, Germany, Italy and Japan, contracts are categorized into the sources of obligations, and the laws relating to contracts are included in the law of obligations, which is one of the component private law elements of the civil law, and usually contained in the civil code as one chapter with the title of "Obligations".

2. Contract law under the Common Law System

In most common law countries except India, such as England, the US, Canada and Australia, the basic legal principles of contract are mainly represented by the case law. Although some common law countries enacted certain laws relating to contracts in statutory law, for instance, the Sale of Goods Act 1979[3] of the UK and the Uniform Commercial Code of the US, these written laws do not cover the primary legal principles of contracts, but only govern the commercial contracts.

3. Contract law of China

The Contract Law of the People's Republic of China was adopted at the Second Session of the Ninth National People's Congress on March 15, 1999. This law comprises two parts: the general provisions, which includes 8 chapters, covering conclusion, effectiveness, performance of contracts, modification and assignment of contracts, termination of the right and obligations of contracts and liability of breach of contracts; the specific provisions, which includes 15 chapters, governing the contracts for sales and other 14 categories of contracts.

2.2   Formation of Contract
合同的成立

According to the contract law in most countries, the followings are the necessary conditions for the valid formation of a contract:

(1) The parties shall conclude a contract in the form of an offer and acceptance;

(2) The contract shall be based upon a consideration or a cause;

(3) The parties shall have the legal capacity to contract;

(4) The form of the contract shall be in accordance with the provisions of laws;

(5) The contract must be legal;

(6) The mutual assent between the parties must be real.

2.2.1   Offer and Acceptance   要约与承诺

1. Offer

1) Definition of an offer

In light of article 14 of the Contract Law of the People's Republic of China, an offer is a proposal for concluding a contract if it is sufficiently definite and indicates the intention of the offeror to be bound in case of acceptance. A proposal constituting an offer may be made in writing or orally, or by other conduct of the offeror.

It is important to distinguish an offer and an invitation for offer[4]. An invitation for offer is a proposal for requesting other parties to make offers to the principal, such as price lists and catalogues mailed, public notices of auction and tender, commercial advertisements, etc.

While in most countries commercial advertisements directed to the public are deemed as invitations for offer, some prejudications in common law countries held that an offer may be addressed to a particular offeree, or a group of persons, or even people all over the world, and an advertisement with its content definite enough to constitute a promise can be regarded as an offer. For example, in an English case in 1856, an advertisement of train rates was held to be a valid offer. By contrast, in the Nordic countries an offer is emphasized to be addressed to specific persons.

2) Effectiveness of an offer

An offer becomes effective when it reaches the offeree. An offer may be withdrawn before and revoked after it takes effect.

The Chinese contract law provides that an offer may be withdrawn, if the withdrawal notice reaches the offeree before or at the same time when the offer arrives; an offer may be revoked, if the revocation reaches the offeree before it has dispatched an acceptance; however an offer can not be revoked if the offeror indicates a fixed time for acceptance or otherwise explicitly states that the offer is irrevocable, or the offeree has reasons to rely on the offer as being irrevocable and has made preparation for performing the contract.

Under the Common Law System, an offer in principle is not binding on the offeror and may be revoked at any time before it is accepted, even if it indicates a specified period of validity. Such a principle may not protect the proper interest of the offeree, therefore some improvements have been made in common law countries. For example, the Uniform Commercial Code of the US provides that an offer can not be revoked, if it is offered by a merchant in written form and signed by the offeror, within the stated valid period of time or a reasonable time not to exceed 3 months.

The continental law holds that an offer is binding on the offeror unless otherwise stated in the offer and can not be revoked within the indicated expiry time. Some civil codes in continental law countries, such as Germany, Switzerland, Greece and Brazil, even go further to provide that an offer without stated expiry time may not be revoked within the period of time for the offeree's acceptance to arrive in normal cases.

In most countries, an offer terminates under any of the following circumstances:

(1) The notice of rejection reaches the offeror;

(2) The offeror withdraws or revokes its offer in accordance with law;

(3) The offer expires;

(4) The offeror or the offeree loses the legal capacity of conduct[5].

2. Acceptance

1) Definition of an acceptance

In light of article 21 of the Contract Law of the PRC, an acceptance is a statement made by the offeree indicating assent to an offer. A contract is established when the acceptance becomes effective.

An acceptance must be made by the offeree and manifest assent to the offer, within the time the offeror has fixed or within a reasonable time having regard to the circumstances.

The offeree may make an acceptance orally or by mail or fax, or even by performing an act, if by virtue of the offer or as a result of practices which the parties have established between themselves or of usage.

As to the contents of an acceptance, there is a strict principle of "the mirror image rule" at common law, which means that the content of the acceptance must be identical with the offer or else it may be deemed as a counter-offer. Most continental law countries employ similar principles. Such principles are too rigid to conclude contracts and smooth transactions. The Uniform Commercial Code of the US improved on this aspect and provides that between merchants a reply to an offer containing additions may be regarded as an acceptance, unless the offeror definitely excluded any additions in the offer, or the additions materially alter the content of the offer, or the offeror objects to the additions within a reasonable time after receiving the reply.

2) Effectiveness of an acceptance

The article 26 of the Contract Law of the PRC states that an acceptance becomes effective when its notice reaches the offeror.

The attitudes towards this issue differ much in Western countries. Most common law countries employ the "mail-box rule[6]", which means an acceptance takes effective when it is addressed out. However, in Germany an acceptance is held to become effective after the offeror receives it. Based upon the German rule, the contract can not be formed if the letter of acceptance loses in transmission. French Civil Code does not give definite provisions on this issue, but in practice the acceptances are often construed to become effective when addressed.

An acceptance may be withdrawn if the withdrawal reaches the offeror before or at the same time as the acceptance would have become effective. Under the German civil law, an acceptance can be withdrawn if the notice of withdrawal reaches the offeror before or at the same time when the acceptance reaches the offeror; whereas under the common law, on the basis of the "mail-box rule", an acceptance can not be withdrawn since it becomes effective once it is addressed and simultaneously the contract is formed. In most countries, an acceptance can not be revoked anyway, because of the formation of the contract after its taking effect.

2.2.2　Consideration and Cause　对价与约因

1. Consideration

Consideration is a distinctive concept at common law, which means a bargained-for exchange, that is, the existence of mutuality of obligation. It may be defined as some right, interest, profit or benefit accruing to one party or some forbearance, detriment, loss or responsibility given, suffered or undertaken by the other.

Reading Material

Motive is Not a Consideration

The court reviewed a verbal promise made by a dying man, which ran contrary to his will. The executors gave effect to the wish by putting the spouse of the deceased (the plaintiff) in possession of the home. But was there a valid consideration to make the promise enforceable?

No, said the court:

"A pious respect for the wishes of the testator does not in any way move from the plaintiff. Motive is not the same thing with consideration. Consideration means something which is of some value in the eye of the law, moving from the plaintiff."

Under the common law, contracts are categorized into the two types of deed contract under seal and simple contract[7]. Consideration is a necessary condition for the validity of simple contracts in the common law jurisdictions.

Consideration must be legal, sufficient and reciprocal, and of value, but need not to be adequate or equivalent. Consideration must move from the promisee, and be executory or executed, but not past consideration. A preexisting obligation or legal compulsory duty or obligation can not constitute a consideration.

The traditional rule of consideration at common law is not very feasible in modern society and has come under increasing criticism. So at present most judges in common law countries tend to apply the rule in a flexible way.

2. Cause

French Civil Code provides that the obligation cause[8] is a prerequisite for the validity of contract. The obligation cause, having the similar meaning of the consideration under the common law, may be defined as the immediate and direct end that the party undertakes the obligation to pursue. According to French civil law, a valid contract should base on two causes. For example, in a sales contract, the seller's delivery is the cause of the buyer's undertaking the obligation of payment; contrarily the buyer's payment is the cause of the seller's undertaking the obligation of delivery.

Due to the fact that the obligation cause is deeply rooted in the Civil Law System, the obligation cause does have its place in German law. However, German civil law does not hold the cause as the requirement for the validity of contract.

There is a doctrine of unjust enrichment[9] in German civil law, which means that if a person receives money or other property from another without a legal cause, the recipient should return the property to the rightful owner, even if the property was not obtained illegally. For example, if a cattle raised by the farmer A itself ran into the farm owned by the farmer B, this is a unjust enrichment for the farmer B and he should return the cattle to the farmer A.

Legal doctrine similar to unjust enrichment also exists in other countries. It is referred to as "quasi contract" in common law and French law, and some times called "law of restitution[10]" in the US. Although the names differ, the legal effects are the same; that is, the court will order the property to be returned to the rightful owner if he brings a lawsuit.

2.2.3   The Parties' Capacity to Contract   当事人的订约能力

1. Natural person's capacity to contract

Under Chinese civil law, there are three types of civil capacity[11]: full, limited and devoid civil capacity. The contracts entered into by persons devoid of civil capacity, including the minors under the age of 10 and the mental patients who can not understand the nature and consequences of his/her own acts, of course, are void. A person with limited civil capacity may independently enter into a pure profit-making contract or a contract which is appropriate to his/her age, intelligence or mental state; other contracts made by such a person shall be enforceable upon ratification by his/her legal agent.

In Germany, the legal requirements on capacity to contract are similar to those in China. The children under the age of 7, adults with mental disability and the interdicted persons[12] are devoid of capacity for conduct, and the contracts concluded by them are void. The minors above the age of 7 are with limited capacity, and the contracts entered into by them shall become effective after being retrospective approval by their legal agents, or by themselves when they grow up.

French civil law provides no differentiation of capacity for conduct, but does interdict certain persons concluding contracts independently. These persons are the minors, the adults with disabled senses and those who got into poverty because they were extravagant in living or idled away their time. Contracts entered into by these persons will be declared to be void by the courts, if without the consent of their guardians or custodians.

In most common law counties, such as the US, contracts concluded by minors, drunkards, drug addicts and mental patients will generally be held to be void or voidable. But an exception is that a contract entered into by a minor who paid reasonable price for necessaries can be enforceable.

2. Juristic person's capacity to contract

A juristic person is an artificial entity lawfully established through which a group of natural persons act as if it were a single composite individual for certain purposes. This concept goes by many names, including legal person, juridical person, corporate personhood, fictitious person, artificial person, or legal entity (although the last term is sometimes understood to include natural persons as well).

The most common juristic person is a company. In most countries, the company is required by law to conclude a contract through its authorized agent, not beyond his/her authority.

2.2.4　Form of a Contract　合同的形式

In the light of the article 10 of the Contract Law of the PRC, a contract may be concluded in written, oral, or other forms. A contract shall be made in written form if a relevant law or administrative regulation so requires, or the parties have so agreed.

In most countries, there is no legal requirement for a formal contract, except for some special contracts. This is the so-called "principle of informality[13]".

In Germany only the sales contracts for lands are required to be in legal forms, and in another continental law country — France, the contracts for dotation, for establishment of mortgage and the contracts relating to marital property system are so required.

In the UK, the bills of exchange and the promissory notes, marine insurance contracts, bill of sale[14], contracts for acknowledgement of obligation should be made in written forms. Additionally, other contracts, such as insurance contracts, sales contracts for lands and contracts for money loans, are required to be evidenced by written documents. In the US, almost every state promulgated the Statute of Frauds[15], which followed the English Statute of Frauds 1667 and required the sales contracts of lands, the contracts which can not be performed within 1 year from the concluding time, the guarantees for other's obligation and the sales contracts with the amount above US\$ 500, to be evidenced by written forms.

2.2.5　Legality of a Contract　合同的合法性

The Article 7 of the Contract Law of the PRC states that in concluding and performing a contract, the parties shall abide by the laws and administrative regulations, observe social ethics. Neither party may disrupt the socio-economic order or damage the public interests.

Although the Western countries place emphasis on the so-called "Freedom of Contract", they also require the contracts to be legal and illegal contract shall be void.

According to the French civil law, the contracts with illegal subject matter[16] or illegal cause constitute illegal contracts. But the German civil law focuses on the legality of conducts and the contents of contract.

At common law, there are normally three types of illegal contracts: the contracts break the statutes or the public policy, or the immoral contracts.

2.2.6　Reality of the Mutual Assent　合意的真实性

Most countries require the mutual assent between the parties to a contract must be real. The contract may be held to be void or voidable, if there is mistake, fraud or duress in concluding a contract.

The Chinese contract law provides that a party shall have the right to request the people's court or an arbitration organization to modify or revoke the following contracts:

(1) Those concluded as a result of serious misunderstanding (which refers to misunderstanding to the nature of the contract, the other party, the quantity and quality, the assortment and specification of the contracted object);

(2) Those that are obviously unfair at the time when concluding the contract.

If a contract is concluded by one party against the other party's true intentions through the use of fraud, duress or exploitation of the other party's unfavorable position. The aggrieved party shall have the right to request the people's court or an arbitration organization to modify or revoke it.

1. Mistake

Mistake usually means the misunderstanding between the parties to a contract.

The French Civil Code provides that, a mistake on the nature of the contracted object or the other party, may cause the contract to be void; while the German civil law holds that a mistake relating to the content or the formality of the expression of the intentions, may make the contract to be voidable.

Under common law, the unilateral mistake can not cause a contract to be void; only when the parties made mutual mistakes on the vital matters of the contract, the contract may be held to be void.

2. Fraud

Fraud refers to the misrepresentation committed by one party deliberately and knowingly, intending to cause the other party to make mistakes.

The common law and the civil law jurisdictions all provide that if a contract is concluded by the use of fraud, the aggrieved party may revoke the contract, or request the court to do so.

As for silence on some facts, most laws hold that silence may not constitute fraud, unless the party has the obligation to represent the facts.

3. Duress

Duress refers to the deliberate acts done by one party intending to cause the other party to be scared.

The common law and the civil law jurisdictions all provide that if a contract is concluded by the use of duress, the aggrieved party may revoke the contract, or request the court to do so.

Under common law, duress also includes the undue influence which means a party uses a position of influence to persuade the other party to enter into a contract for the purpose of benefits.

2.3　Performance of Contract
合同的履行

2.3.1　Basic Points　基本要点

Performance of contract normally means the parties to a contract perform their obligations in compliance with the contract.

The article 60 of the Contract Law of the PRC states that the parties shall completely perform their respective obligations in accordance with the contract. The parties shall abide by the principle of good faith, and perform obligations such as notification, assistance, confidentiality, and etc., in light of the nature and purpose of the contract and in accordance with the relevant practices.

In modern civilization, all laws require the contract to be performed by the parties thoroughly according to the terms of the contract. If any party fails to perform its contractual obligations, it may be held responsible for breach of contract.

2.3.2 Breach of Contract 违约

1. Under the Continental Law System

The continental law countries employ the principle of fault liability[17] on civil liability, which finds its root in Roman law. It means that the contractual obligor shall not be liable for breach of contract unless it is responsible for a fault. In other words, only the nonperformance of the obligor may not amount to a breach of contract; it should be also proved or construed to be at fault.

French law classifies breaches of contract into two types of nonperformance and delayed performance, and German law similarly divides breaches of contract into supervening impossibility of performance and delay in performance[18]. As to delayed performance, there is a rule of "putting in default[19]" under the Continental Law System, which means that the obligor shall assume the liability for delayed performance only after the obligee exhorts the obligor to perform the contract.

2. Under the Common Law System

In common law countries there is no need to prove the obligor to be at fault to judge a breach of contract. This is known as the principle of no-fault liability[20]. The common law holds that all contracts are warranties or promises, the party who failed to fulfill its promise shall be held liable for breach of contract.

Under the English law, there are two types of breaches of contract: breach of condition and breach of warranty[21]. The condition and the warranty respectively refers to the vital (or essential) and the subsidiary (or collateral) terms of the contract.

In the US, the contractual obligation is referred to as promise that may be unconditional or conditional. Failure to fulfill the unconditional promises constitutes a breach of contract. In addition, the American law also categorizes breaches of contract into the two types of minor breach and material breach[22]. This categorization is similarly to the classification in England which is mentioned in the above paragraph.

2.3.3 Remedies for Breach of Contract 违约的救济方法

In the event of a breach of contract, the nonbreaching party, as provided by law, may resort to some remedies to protect its interest. Generally speaking, the remedies for breach of contract in common use are specific performance, damages, rescission, injunction and liquidated damages[23].

1. Specific performance

Specific performance means the obligee requests of the obligor, or a court order requiring performance exactly as specified in the contract.

The Chinese contract law provides that where a party fails to perform, or rendered nonconforming performance of, a nonmonetary obligation, the other party may require specific performance, except where:

(1) Performance is impossible in law or in fact;

(2) The subject matter of the obligation is unfit for compulsory performance or the cost of performance is excessive;

(3) The obligee fails to require the specific performance within a reasonable time.

The continental law holds specific performance as a primary remedy for breach of contract. The obligee has the right to require specific performance when there is a breach but the court may not decide for it unless it is possible for the obligor to perform its obligation.

However, at common law, there is no provision of specific performance as one of the remedies for breach of contract. Under the Common Law System, specific performance is regarded as an exceptional and equitable remedy in some particular cases.

2. Damages

The article 112 of the Contract law of the PRC says that where a party failed to perform or rendered nonconforming performance, if notwithstanding its subsequent performance or cure of nonconforming performance, the other party has sustained other loss, the breaching party shall pay damages.

Damages may be the most commonly used judicial remedy for breach of contract in the present world, which can be defined as compensation or indemnity that may be recovered in the courts by any person who has suffered loss, detriment, or injury to person, property, or rights through the unlawful act or negligence of another.

Reading Material

Foreseeablity of Damages

The English case of *Hadley v. Baxendale* (1854) is the mostly cited case of all time when it comes to damages. A broken shaft was given to a carrier to bring to a repair shop. The carrier was not told that the absence of the shaft meant complete work stoppage for the owner. The carrier was in breach of contract by being several days late in delivery. Then the owner brought an action against the carrier for damages.

The court held that the plaintiff can recover on damages arising naturally, or that a reasonable man should have foreseen, whether or not the defendant foresaw them. Therefore the carrier was not liable to compensate for the loss of profit that would have been generated during the work stoppage.

1) Liability for damages

Under continental law, in normal cases, there shall be three conditions for holding the obligor to be liable for damages:

(1) The fact of damage;

(2) The obligor is responsible for the damage;

(3) There is a causality between the former two conditions.

In common law countries, the only condition for the nonbreaching party to sue for damages is the existence of breach of contract. The nonbreaching party may claim for nominal damages if the breach does not cause actual damage to it.

2) Means of damages

There are two means of damages: restitution and monetary damages. The German civil law holds restitution as principle while monetary damages as exception. By contrast, the French civil law takes the monetary damages as principle and restitution as exception

In the common law jurisdictions, damages are all monetary, which is referred to as pecuniary (or monetary) restitution[24].

3) Measurement of damages

Chinese contract law provides that the amount of damages payable shall be equivalent to the injured party's loss resulting from the breach, including any benefit that may be accrued from performance of the contract, provided that the amount shall not exceed the likely loss resulting from the breach which was foreseen or should have been foreseen by the breaching party at the time of conclusion of the contract.

The continental law holds that damages shall recover both the actual damage and the loss of benefit. The actual damage refers to the loss directly caused by the breach of contract, and the loss of benefit means that, the obligee would get some benefit if the contract is performed but it loses the benefit because of the obligor's breach of contract. For example, if the seller fails to deliver the goods then the loss of the goods is the actual damage to the buyer; the profit that the buyer would make by reselling the goods may be regarded as the loss of benefit.

The basic principle of measuring damages at common law is that the damages shall restore the aggrieved party to the same economic position as if the contract had been fully performed. The common law provides for the duty of the aggrieved party to mitigate, or minimize, the amount of damage to the extent reasonable. Damages cannot be recovered for losses that could have been reasonably avoided or substantially ameliorated after the breach occurred. The aggrieved party's failure to use reasonable diligence in mitigating the damage means that any award of damages will be reduced by the amount that could have been reasonably avoided.

3. Rescission

Rescission refers to exemption or termination of contractual obligations of the parties to a contract. In light of article 94 of the Contract Law of the PRC, if one party delayed performance of its main obligations and failed to perform within a reasonable time after receiving demand for performance, or otherwise breached the contract, thereby frustrating the purpose of the contract, the other party may terminate the contract.

1) Establishment of rescission right

Under continental law, the obligee may rescind the contract if the obligor was liable for breach of contract. In the cases of delayed performance and incomplete performance, the obligee should exhort the obligor to perform within a period of time, and then the obligee may make the rescission if the obligor still failed to perform within the period.

As mentioned previously, the English common law divided breaches of contract into breach of condition and breach of warranty, and the American common law divided them into material breach and minor breach. In the common law countries, the nonbreaching party may rescind the contract only when there is a breach of condition or a material breach.

2) Exercise of rescission right

There are two means for the nonbreaching party to exercise rescission right. One is to sue to court for rescission, and the other is just to express the intention of rescission to the breaching party.

French civil law requires the obligee to sue to court for rescission unless an express clause of rescission prescribed in the contract, whereas German civil law provides that the entitled party may rescind the contract just by the expression of such intention.

The common law holds that rescission is a right the nonbreaching party entitled to have because the breach of contract by the other party and the nonbreaching party may be exempted of its contractual obligation by the means of declaring rescission.

Most countries legally allow the nonbreaching party to claim for damages at the same time when it rescinds the contract with an exception of Germany. The Germany Civil Code provides that the obligee can choose only one of the two rights.

3) Effect of rescission

The Chinese contract law provides that upon termination of a contract, a performance which has not been rendered is discharged; if a performance has been rendered, a party may, in light of the degree of performance and the nature of the contract, require the other party to restore the subject matter to its original condition or otherwise remedy the situation, and is entitled to claim damages; and discharge of contractual rights and obligations does not affect the validity of contract provisions concerning settlement of account and winding-up.

The provisions on effect of rescission of contract at continental law are similar to the Chinese provisions; that is, the parties are released from the obligations unperformed and the performed obligations shall be restituted because of nonexistence of the legal cause.

English common law holds that rescission only causes the contract to be void in future but not from the beginning and therefore the future performance is exempted while the performed rights and obligations need not to be restituted. However, American law differs from English law in this regard, and requires the parties to make restitution to rescind a contract (such as returning the goods, property, or money received from the other party). Such a requirement is similar to that under continental law.

4. Injunction

Injunction is an equitable remedy under the Anglo-American Law System which can be used in some breaching cases where a direct order of court is required to stop a party from continuing an ongoing breach.

It is developed as the main remedy in equity, and used especially where money damages would not satisfy a plaintiff's claim. It is an extraordinary remedy, reserved for special circumstances in which the temporary preservation of the status quo is necessary. An injunction usually is issued to prohibit an action.

5. Liquidated damages

Liquidated damages refers to a sum of money agreed upon by the parties to a contract, to be paid by the breaching party to the nonbreaching party in the event of a breach of contract.

The article 114 of the Contract Law of the PRC states that the parties may prescribe that if one party breaches the contract, it shall pay a certain sum of liquidated damages to the other party in light of the degree of breach, or prescribe a method for calculation of damages for the loss caused by the breach; where the amount of liquidated damages prescribed is below the loss, a party may petition the People's Court or an arbitration organization to increase it; conversely where the amount of liquidated damages prescribed exceeds the loss, a party may petition the People's Court or an arbitration organization to make an appropriate reduction. Where the parties prescribed liquidated damages for delayed performance, the breaching party shall pay the liquidated damages and also render performance.

French civil law and German civil law differs on the nature of liquidated damages. The liquidated damages in Germany are punitive and regarded as a penalty to be paid by the obligor. Therefore, German civil law allows the obligee to claim not only compensatory damages for the loss it suffered but also liquidated damages, if the obligor failed to perform its obligation. However, French civil law holds that liquidated damages are the anticipatory damages for the possible nonperformance. In principle, French law does not permit the obligee to request specific performance or damages at the same time when it claims liquidated damages. Both French law and German law provides that the amount of liquidated damages shall be adjusted by the court if it is evidently below or above the actual loss caused by the breach of contract.

Reading Material

Categories of Damages in the USA

Three major categories of damages are recognized in the United States: compensatory damages, which are intended to restore what a plaintiff has lost as a result of a defendant's wrongful conduct; nominal damages, which consist of a small sum awarded to a plaintiff who has suffered no substantial loss or injury but has nevertheless experienced an invasion of rights; punitive damages, which are awarded not to compensate a plaintiff for injury suffered but to penalize a defendant for particularly egregious, wrongful conduct.

In specific situations, two other forms of damages may be awarded by the court: treble damages and liquidated damages.

In common law countries, liquidated damages may be used when it would be difficult to prove the actual harm or loss caused by a breach and can not be punitive. The amount of liquidated damages must represent a reasonable estimate of the actual damage that a breach would cause. A contract clause fixing unreasonably large or disproportionate liquidated damages may be held to be void by the court because it constitutes a penalty, or punishment for default. Furthermore, if it appears that the parties have made no attempt to calculate the amount of actual damage that might be sustained in the event of a breach, a liquidated damages clause will be deemed unenforceable. In determining whether a particular contract provision constitutes liquidated damages or an unenforceable penalty, a court will look to the intention of the parties, even if the terms liquidated damages and penalty are specifically used and defined in the contract.

2.3.4 Change of Circumstances, Frustration of Contract and Force Majeure 情势变迁、合同落空和不可抗力

1. Change of circumstances

Change of circumstances means that enforcement of a contract should be modified, by increasing or decreasing obligations, or even avoided, on condition that the underlying circumstances of the contract have changed unexpectedly, and maintaining the original enforcement may give rise to an effect obviously unfair and running contrary to the principle of good faith.

The continental law acknowledges the doctrine of change of circumstances but the civil laws in most counties do not make specific provisions on it. Only the Italian Civil Code explicitly states that the court may order to avoid the contract, under the contracts to be performed after long time or in installments, if a party argues that some unexpected and extraordinary events have occurred and made it overburdened to perform its obligations.

2. Frustration of contract

Frustration of contract is a concept at common law, similar to the change of circumstances under continental law. It means that the contract may be avoided and the contractual obligations may be released from the parties by operation of law, if an event occurs, not reasonably foreseeable when the contract was made and not under the direct control of either party, which renders impossible further performance of the contract in the way envisaged by the parties to it.

In common law countries, frustration of contract is very rarely considered by the courts. In order for frustration to be used as a defense for nonperformance, the value of the anticipated counter-performance must have been substantially destroyed and the frustrating occurrence must have been beyond the contemplation of the parties at the time the contract was made.

3. Force majeure

In practice, it is very difficult to judge whether a frustration did occur or the doctrine of change of circumstances can be applied, so the parties is advised to prescribe a force majeure clause in the contract, especially in international business.

Force majeure refers to such an event occurring after the conclusion of contract, which is not caused by either party's faulty and beyond the control of both parties.

The article 117 of the Contract Law of the PRC provides that a party who was unable to perform a contract due to force majeure is exempted from liability in part or in whole in light of the effect of the event of force majeure, except otherwise provided by law. Where an event of force majeure occurred after the party's delay in performance, it is not exempted from liability. Force majeure in this law means any objective circumstance which is unforeseeable, unavoidable and insurmountable.

2.4　Assignment of Contract
合同的让与

2.4.1　Definition of Assignment of Contract　合同让与的概念

An assignment of contract is the transfer to a new party of rights and/or obligations under the contract with the contractual subject matter remaining intact.

Contracts were not assignable in early Roman law, but today most contracts are assignable unless the nature of the contract or its provisions demonstrates that the parties intend to make it personal to them and therefore incapable of assignment.

Assignment of contract includes assignment of the rights and transfer of the obligations under the contract.

2.4.2　Assignment of the Rights under the Contract
合同债权让与

Assignment of the rights under the contract means that a party（assignor）partly or wholly transfers by agreement its contractual rights to a new party（assignee）.

The Chinese contract law provides that the obligee may assign its rights under a contract in whole or in part to a third person, except where such assignment is prohibited in light of the nature of the contract, or by agreement between the parties, or by law. Where the obligee assigns its rights, it shall notify the obligor or else the assignment shall be not binding upon the obligor. Upon receipt of the notice of assignment the obligor may, in respect of the assignee, avail itself of any defense it has against the assignor.

The continental law allows the obligee assigns its obligatory rights to a third party without the consent of the obligor and such an assignment is regarded as a new contract between the assignor and the assignee. French law requires such an assignment contract to be based on a legal cause while German law does not so required. Besides, German law does not require the assignor to give the notice of the assignment to the obligor, whereas French law holds the notice of assignment as the necessary condition for its enforceability to the obligor.

Under modern English law, there are two types of assignment: statutory assignment and equitable assignment. A statutory assignment must be made in written form and signed by the assignor; the assignor must absolutely and unconditionally assign the rights under the contract in whole; and the obligor shall be given a written notice of assignment. An equitable assignment need not to be noticed to the obligor.

American law provides that a party may assign its rights except where the assignment would materially change the duty of the other party, or increase materially the burden or risk imposed on it, or impair materially its chance of obtaining return performance.

2.4.3　Transfer of the Obligations under the Contract　合同债务承担

Transfer of the obligations under the contract means that the contractual obligations are transferred from the original obligor to a third party (the new obligor), by the agreement between the original obligor (or the obligee) and the new obligor.

The Chinese contract law allows the obligor delegates its obligations under a contract in whole or in part to a third person with the consent of obligee.

German civil law deems transfer of obligations as a contractual relation which may be made by two means. The one is the obligee conclude a new contract, without the consent of obligor, with a third party to whom is delegated the obligations of the original obligor under the original contract. The other is the original obligor conclude a new contract with a third party who is to replace the original obligor to perform its obligations and such a transfer must be retrospective approved by the obligee.

French civil law does not permit obligations to be transferred but allows novation of obligations. Novation is the replacement of one contract between two parties with another contract, either between the same parties or others. Thus the original contractual obligation is discharged and the new obligation under a new contract is established. Similarly, under English common law, one party's obligations can only transfer to a third party through novation and such a novation must be subject to the consent of the obligee.

In the US, contractual obligations, in principle, are also held not to be transferred to a third party. Under particular circumstances a third party is allowed to perform the contractual obligations on the behalf of the original party. But the original party shall be held liable if the third party does not fulfill the obligations in accordance with the contract.

2.4.4 Concurrent Assignment and Transfer under the Contract 合同权利与义务的概括转让

Concurrent assignment and transfer means that a party transfers all its rights and obligations arising out of a contract to a third party and then it will be completely released from the contract. In other words, it is the assignment of the whole contract.

The article 88 of the Contract Law of the PRC says that upon consent by the other party, one party may concurrently assign its rights and delegate its obligations under a contract to a third person.

In Western countries, sometimes an assignment may operate under law in the case of a bankruptcy where a trustee comes in and takes over all the contractual rights and obligations of the insolvent party. Another example is upon death, where the legal successor assumes the position of the deceased and to whom all contracts of the deceased are assigned. However, such an assignment normally governed by the insolvency law or the law of succession, and may not be equated with what is provided in the article 88 of the Contract Law of the PRC.

2.5 Discharge of Contract 合同的消灭

2.5.1 Provisions under the Continental Law System 大陆法系的规定

In the continental law jurisdictions, contracts are regarded as one type of obligation, and there is no special provision on discharge of contract which is included in discharge of obligation. Under continental law, discharge of obligation commonly results from payment, deposit, set-off, release and merger[25].

1. Payment

Payment refers to the fulfillment of the obligation and is the primary reason for discharge of obligation.

2. Deposit

Deposit means that the obligor may consign the due money or other articles to a legal institution for deposit, if the obligee defers taking over, or it is yet not clear that who is the obligee. Deposit is deemed as fulfillment of obligation and results in discharge of obligation.

3. Set-off

For two parties under mutual obligations with the same type and expiry time, the mutual obligations can be set off as against each other. If amounts of the two obligations are equivalent, both obligations are discharged simultaneously; if not, the lesser obligation will be extinguished. For example, If Party A owes Party B ¥100 and Party B owes Party A ¥105, the two sums are set off and replaced with a single obligation of ¥5 assumed by Party B to Party A.

4. Release

Discharge of obligation may be also resulted from the release by the obligee, which means that the obligee waived his right. In certain jurisdictions, such as France and Germany, the release is subject to the assent of the obligor.

5. Merger

Merger means that both the obligatory right and the obligatory liability are assumed by the same party, that is, the party who is the obligee is also the obligor. For example, a creditor company acquired the debtor company indebted to it. In such a case, it is not necessary for the obligation to exist, and therefore it shall be discharged.

2.5.2 Provisions under the Anglo-American Law System 英美法系的规定

In common law countries, contract law is one of the basic laws. Under the Anglo-American Law System, a contract may be discharged by agreement of the two parties, performance, breach or legal provisions.

1. Agreement of the two parties

The two parties may agree to discharge the contract by rescission, or substituting it with a new contract. It will be referred to as novation if such a new contract is not concluded between the origin parties. A contract can also be discharged according to the terms and conditions of itself which were agreed upon by the parties in advance. In addition, a contract may be discharged by waiver of either party.

2. Performance

Performance is the primary reason for discharge of contract. The performance shall be complete or substantial, or else it may constitute a breach of contract.

3. Breach

The nonbreaching party may be entitled the right to rescind the contract in the case of a breach to the root of the contract. Such a breach is referred to as breach of condition in the UK while material breach in the US.

4. Legal provisions

Under the Anglo-American Law System, there are some legal provisions which may cause to discharge of contract.

1) Merger

Where the duty to pay and the right to receive unite in the same person, the contract may be discharged.

2) Bankruptcy

After going through the legal procedure, all the contractual liabilities of the bankrupt may be discharged by the order of court.

3) Unilateral modification of written contract

The other party may be discharged from contractual obligations if one party modified the material parts of the written contract without the assent of the other party.

2.5.3 Provisions under the Chinese Law　中国法的规定

The article 91 of the Contract Law of the PRC provides that the rights and obligations under a contract are discharged in any of the following circumstances:

(1) The obligations were performed in accordance with the contract;

(2) The contract was legally terminated or rescinded;

(3) The obligations were set off against each other;

(4) The obligor placed the subject matter for deposit in accordance with the law;

(5) The obligee released the obligor from obligations;

(6) Both the obligatory rights and obligatory liabilities were assumed by one party;

(7) Any other discharging circumstance provided by law or prescribed in advance by the parties occurred.

2.5.4 Limitation of Time　时效

Most countries provided limitation of time as one of the reasons for discharge of contracts or obligations.

1. Limitation of time under the Continental Law System

Under the Continental Law System, there are two types of limitation of time: the positive prescription[26]— the process of acquiring title to property by reason of uninterrupted possession of specified duration and the negative prescription[27]— the limitation of time beyond which an action, obligation, or crime is no longer valid or enforceable. The latter is relevant to discharge of contractual obligations and differently provided in different countries.

2. Limitation of time under the Anglo-American Law System

In the common law jurisdictions, limitation of time only refers to the limitation of action[28], which means that any claim for breach of contract must be brought before the court within a certain period of time otherwise the contract will be discharged. In the UK, the limitation of action is 6 years in case of simple contracts and 12 years in case of deed contracts under seal. In the US, the UCC provides the limitation of action for sales contracts to be 4 years.

3. Limitation of time under the Chinese law

According to the article 129 of Chinese contract law, for a dispute arising from a contract for international sale of goods or for technology transfer, the time limit for bringing an action or applying for arbitration is four years, commencing on the date when the party knew or should have known that its rights were harmed. For a dispute arising from any other type of contract, the time limit shall be governed by the relevant law.

Group Discussion ▶▶▶

1. What do you think about the importance of contracts?
2. Discuss the necessary conditions for the valid formation of a contract.
3. Compare the provisions on breach of contract under the two major law systems.
4. Explain the definition of assignment of contract.
5. Tell the major differences of discharge of contract between the two major law systems.
6. Talk about some important provisions of the Contract Law of the PRC.

NOTES ▶▶▶

1   Contract Law of the People's Republic of China　《中华人民共和国合同法》（也有的外国文献译为 the Chinese Code of Contract Law）

2   juristic person　法人（亦用 legal person, juridical person, artificial person, fictitious person）

3   Sale of Goods Act 1979　（英国）《1979 年货物买卖法》

4   invitation for offer　要约邀请（亦用 invitation to treat）

5   legal capacity of conduct　法律行为能力（亦用 legal capacity）

6　mail-box rule　投邮主义

7　deed contract under seal　签字蜡封合同；simple contract　简式合同

8　obligation cause　债之约因

9　unjust enrichment　不当得利

10　quasi contract　准合同；law of restitution　偿还法

11　civil capacity　民事行为能力（亦用 civil capacity for/of conduct）

12　interdicted person　禁治产者（大陆法的术语，指因精神疾病或酗酒而不能处理自己的事务，或因浪费成性而有败家之虞者，经其亲属向法院提出请求，由法院宣告禁止其治理财产）

13　principle of informality　不要式原则

14　bill of sale　卖方继续保持占有的动产权益转让合同

15　Statute of Frauds　欺诈法

16　subject matter　标的物（有时也用 subject 或 object）

17　fault liability　过错责任，过失责任

18　supervening impossibility of performance　给付不能；delay in performance　给付延迟

19　putting in default　催告

20　no-fault liability　无过错责任，无过失责任

21　breach of condition　违反条件（也译为"违反要件"）；breach of warranty　违反担保

22　minor breach　轻微违约；material breach　重大违约

23　specific performance　实际履行；damages　损害赔偿；rescission　解除合同；injunction　禁令；liquidated damages　违约金，约定的赔偿金

24　pecuniary restitution（monetary restitution）　金钱上的恢复原状

25　payment　清偿；deposit　提存；set-off　抵销；release　免除；merger　混同

26　positive prescription　取得时效

27　negative prescription　消灭时效

28　limitation of action　诉讼时效

Battle of Forms
格式之战

At common law, a purported acceptance containing terms which did not "mirror" those of the offer operated as a rejection thereof and amounted to a counteroffer.

The mirror image rule requires that an acceptance be unconditional and that it not attempt to change any of the terms proposed in the offer. These requirements present special problems when parties exchange preprinted, standardized forms to finalize their bargain and the forms tend to use "boilerplate language" and omit material terms. Each party usually has printed form drafted by his attorney, containing as many terms favorable to him as may be envisioned. A typical situation involves memoranda or acknowledgement confirming oral agreement or letter intended as confirmation of agreement which adds further minor suggestions or proposals when each party uses his own form, and it is to be expected that acceptance will not correspond to terms of offer in all respects. Then problems and disputes which are commonly known as "battle of forms" may arise.

The following American case is an example of battle of forms.

In early 1993, the claimant, Columbia Hyundai, Inc. (Hereafter: Gibbes), negotiated with respondent, Carll Hyundai (Hereafter: Carll) to purchase Carll's Hyundai automobile dealership. After several months of negotiations between the parties and their attorneys, and numerous revisions to drafts of a proposed contract, Carll submitted an "Agreement for Purchase and Sale of Assets" to Gibbes on July 20, 1993. The contract contained a provision to the effect that "This Agreement may not be amended, changed or modified except by instrument in writing signed by the parties to be charged." Paragraph 1(a) of the agreement, concerning the assets to be transferred, reads "All of Seller's right title and interest in and to all saleable new Hyundai vehicles in existence at the close of business on the last business day before final closing date ..." Gibbes signed the agreement but added the words "current year" such that the paragraph 1(a) of agreement now reads "all saleable current year new Hyundai vehicles . . . " Upon receipt of the agreement from Gibbes one week later, Carll advised the "counter-offer" was rejected. Then Gibbes instituted this suit for breach of contract and specific performance. The trial judge submitted the issue to the jury which found there was no contract. Gibbes appealed. The appellate court affirmed the judgement of first trial.

Past Consideration or Executed Consideration
过去的对价还是已履行的对价

At common law, consideration is essential for formation of a contract. One of the important rules governing consideration is said that "Past consideration is no consideration." However, in practice, it is not easy to differentiate past consideration from executed consideration that is a lawful consideration. Compare the following two English cases.

1. Re McArdle (1951)

A woman and her three grown-up children lived together in a house. The wife of one of the children did some decorating and later the children promised to pay her £488 and they signed a document to this effect. But she did not get the money and then sued at law.

It was held by the court that the promise was unenforceable as all the work had been done before the promise was made and was therefore past consideration.

2. Re Casey's Patent (1892)

A and B owned a patent and C was the manager who had worked on it for two years. A and B then promised C a one-third share in the invention for his help in developing it. The patents were transferred to C but A and B then claimed their return.

It was held by the court that C could rely on the agreement. Even though C's consideration was in the past, it had been done in a business situation, at the request of A and B and it was understood by both sides that C would be paid and the subsequent promise to pay merely fixed the amount.

Formation of a Contract by Instantaneous
Communication between Offeror and Offeree
发盘人与受盘人通过即时通信手段订立合同

If the offeror and offeree negotiate by instantaneous communication, whether contract concluded where and when telex sent or received is an issue of great legal significance.

See the following English case.

After negotiations between the parties for the sale of a quantity of steel bars to be delivered by C&F Alexandria in Egypt, the buyer, an English company located in London, accepted, by sending a telex to Vienna, the terms of sale offered by the seller, an Austrian company. The contract was never performed and the buyer, in accordance with the English law, issued a writ claiming damages against the seller for breach of contract. It obtained leave to serve notice of the writ on the seller, who applied to the court to have the service set aside. The judge dismissed the seller's application but on appeal the Court of Appeals held that the service should be set aside because the contract had not been made within the court's jurisdiction. The buyer appealed to the House of Lords, contending that it was entitled to leave to serve notice of the writ on the seller on the ground that the contract "was made within the jurisdiction" on the basis that, by analogy with the rules relating to the acceptance of an offer by post or telegram, acceptance of an offer by telex concluded a contract at the time and place the telex was sent; alternatively, the writ was "in respect of a breach committed within the jurisdiction".

The House of Lords held: Where there was instantaneous communication between the offeror and the offeree the formation of a contract between the parties was governed by the general rule that a contract was concluded where and when acceptance of the offer was received by the offeror. Since the telex communication from the buyer in London to the seller in Austria was instantaneous the contract was made in Austria, and since it was not made within the jurisdiction of the court the buyer could not rely on the English law to obtain leave to serve notice of the writ on the seller. Neither could the buyer obtain because the contract was to have been performed entirely outside the jurisdiction and the breach had therefore occurred outside the jurisdiction. The appeal would accordingly be dismissed.

Esso Petroleum Ltd.' Case on Purchase Tax
埃索石油公司购买税案

In 1970 the taxpayers ("Esso") devised a petrol sales promotion scheme. The scheme involved the distribution of millions of coins to petrol stations which sold Esso petrol. Each of the coins bore the likeness of one of the members of the English soccer team which went to Mexico in 1970 to play in the World Cup competition. The object of the scheme was that petrol station proprietors should encourage motorists to buy Esso petrol by offering to give away a coin for every four gallons of Esso petrol which the motorist bought. The coins were of little intrinsic value but it was hoped that motorists would persist in buying Esso petrol in order to collect the full set of 30 coins. The scheme was extensively advertised by Esso in the press and on television with phrases such as: "Going free, at your Esso Action Station now", and: "We are giving you a coin with every four gallons of Esso petrol you buy." Folders were also circulated by Esso to petrol stations which stated, inter alia: "One coin should be given to every motorist who buys four gallons of petrol - two coins for eight gallons and so on." 4,900 petrol stations joined the scheme. Large posters were delivered by Esso to those stations, the most prominent lettering on the posters stating: "The World Cup coins", "One coin given with every four gallons of petrol".

The Customs and Excise Commissioners claimed that the coins were chargeable to purchase tax under the English Purchase Tax Act 1963 on the ground that they had been "produced in quantity for general sale".

The court held (Lord Fraser of Tullybelton dissenting): The coins had not been "produced for sale", and were not therefore chargeable to purchase tax for the following reasons.

(1) On the basis that the posters and other advertising material constituted an offer by the garage proprietors to enter into a contract with each customer to supply a coin with every four gallons of petrol sold, the contract envisaged was not a contract of "sale", since the consideration for the transfer of the coins was not a money payment but the undertaking by the customer to enter into a collateral contract to purchase the appropriate quantity of Esso petrol.

(2) (per Viscount Dilhorne and Lord Russell of Killowen, Lord Wilberforce and Lord Simon of Glaisdale dissenting) Furthermore, in the circumstances, and in particular in view of the fact that the coins were of little intrinsic value to customers, it could not be inferred that either Esso or the petrol station proprietors on the one hand, or the customers on the other, intended that there should be a legally binding contract to supply the coins to customers who bought the appropriate quantity of petrol. It followed that the coins had been produced for distribution by way of gift and not by way of sale.

Chapter 3

Contract Law (Ⅱ)

合同法（二）

Learning Objectives

☑ To understand the role of CISG in international business law
☑ To learn the major provisions of CISG
☑ To learn about the major provisions of PICC
☑ To compare CISG with PICC

Opening Vignette

United Nations Convention on Contracts for the International Sale of Goods

The United Nations Convention on Contracts for the International Sale of Goods (CISG) is a treaty offering a uniform international sales law that, as of Jan. 1, 2008, had been ratified by 70 countries that account for 75% of all world trade.

CISG was signed in Vienna in 1980 and so is sometimes referred to as the Vienna Convention (but is not to be confused with other treaties signed in Vienna). It came into force as a multilateral treaty on January 1, 1988, after being ratified by ten countries. Countries that have ratified CISG are referred to as "Contracting States[1]". Unless excluded by the express terms of a contract, CISG is deemed to be incorporated into (and supplant) any otherwise applicable domestic laws with respect to a transaction in goods between parties from different Contracting States.

CISG is one of the very successful international conventions, due in no small part to its flexibility in allowing Contracting States the option of taking exception to specified articles. This flexibility was instrumental in convincing states with disparate legal traditions to subscribe to an otherwise uniform code. A key point of controversy had to do with whether or not a contract requires a written memorial to be binding. China declared the exclusion of those articles relating to oral contracts when ratified the convention in 1986. However, oral contracts for international sales of goods were accepted in China after the Contract Law of the PRC was promulgated in 1999.

It should be stressed that CISG does not apply to the sales：a）of goods bought for personal, family or household use, unless the seller, at any time before or at the conclusion of the contract, neither knew nor ought to have known that the goods were bought for any such use；b）by auction；c）on execution or otherwise by authority of law；d）of stocks, shares, investment securities, negotiable instruments or money；e）of ships, vessels, hovercraft or aircraft；f）of electricity.

Notably, the UK is not among the countries that have ratified CISG, despite being a leading jurisdiction for the choice of law in international commercial contracts.

Countries that have ratified CISG as of Jan. 1, 2008 are：Argentina, Australia, Austria, Belarus, Belgium, Bosnia-Herzegovina, Bulgaria, Burundi, Canada, Chile, China, Colombia, Croatia, Cuba, Cyprus, Czech Republic, Denmark, Ecuador, Egypt, El Salvador, Estonia, Finland, France, Gabon, Georgia, Germany, Greece, Guinea, Honduras, Hungary, Iceland, Iraq, Israel, Italy, Kyrgyzstan, Latvia, Lesotho, Liberia, Lithuania, Luxembourg, Macedonia, Mauritania, Mexico, Moldova, Mongolia, Montenegro, Netherlands, New Zealand, Norway, Paraguay, Peru, Poland, Romania, Russia, Saint Vincent and the Grenadines, Serbia, Singapore, Slovakia, Slovenia, South Korea, Spain, Sweden, Switzerland, Syria, Uganda, Ukraine, United States, Uruguay, Uzbekistan, Zambia

Most recently, in July 2008, Japan, as the developed country second to the US, accedes to CISG.

 Warm-up Questions

> 1. What do you think about the role that CISG plays in international business?
> 2. What are the relations between CISG and the domestic laws in the Contracting States?
> 3. What contracts may be applied to CISG?

3.1 UN Convention on Contracts for the International Sale of Goods 《联合国国际货物销售合同公约》

3.1.1 A Brief Introduction to CISG 《联合国国际货物销售合同公约》简介

CISG is comprised of four parts.

Part Ⅰ: Sphere of Application and General Provisions (Articles 1 – 13), provides that CISG covers the international sale of most commercial goods. CISG does not cover sales of goods bought for personal use, sales of ships or aircraft, or contracts for the sale of labor or services, nor does it govern the validity of the contract, the effect which the contract may have on the property in the goods sold, or liability for death or personal injury caused by the goods.

Reading Material

Declarations and Reservations of China on CISG

Upon approving CISG in 1986, China declared that it did not consider itself bound by sub-paragraph（b）of paragraph（1）of article 1（about the applicability of the Convention）and article 11（about the form of contracts for the international sale of goods）, nor the provisions in the Convention relating to the content of article 11. China insisted that CISG is only applicable to sales contracts between parties whose places of business are in different Contracting States and such contracts shall be concluded in written form.

Although the present Contract Law of the PRC which took effective on Oct. 1, 1999 does not require the international sales contracts to be concluded in written form, the declarations and reservations of the article 11 of CISG have not been revoked officially.

Part Ⅱ: Formation of the Contract（Articles 14 – 24）, provides rules on offer and acceptance.

Part Ⅲ: Sale of Goods（Articles 25 – 88）, covers obligations of the seller, such as delivery of goods, handing over of documents, conformity of the goods, third-party claims, and remedies for breach of contract by the seller, as well as obligations of the buyer, such as payment of the price, taking delivery, remedies for breach of contract by the buyer, and rules governing damages and the passing of risk.

Part IV: Final Provisions（Articles 89 – 101）, covers the right of a country to disclaim certain parts of the convention, and accessions and denunciations in respect of the convention.

3.1.2　Formation of a Contract for the International Sale of Goods 国际货物销售合同的订立

Like the provisions on formation of contracts in most domestic jurisdictions, under CISG, a contract for the international sale of goods is to be formed through offer and acceptance[2].

1. Offer

1）Definition of an offer

According to the article 14 of CISG, an offer is a proposal for concluding a contract addressed to one or more specific persons if it is sufficiently definite and indicates the intention of the offeror to be bound in case of acceptance.

A proposal is sufficiently definite if it indicates the goods and expressly or implicitly fixes or makes provision for determining the quantity and the price.

If a proposal other than one addressed to one or more specific persons is to be considered merely as an invitation to make offers, unless the contrary is clearly indicated by the person making the proposal.

2) Effectiveness of an offer

The first paragraph of article 15 of CISG says that an offer becomes effective when it reaches the offeree. This is in conformity with the relevant provisions in most domestic jurisdictions.

3) Withdrawal and revocation of an offer

The second paragraph of article 15 states that an offer, even if it is irrevocable, may be withdrawn if the withdrawal reaches the offeree before or at the same time as the offer.

The first paragraph of article 16 says that until a contract is concluded an offer may be revoked if the revocation reaches the offeree before he has dispatched an acceptance. This is similar to the relevant provisions in the common law jurisdictions.

However, in order to bridge the gap between continental law and common law, the second paragraph of article 16 provides that an offer can not be revoked if it indicates, whether by stating a fixed time for acceptance or otherwise, that it is irrevocable; or if it was reasonable for the offeree to rely on the offer as being irrevocable and the offeree has acted in reliance on the offer.

4) Termination of an offer

The article 17 of CISG says that an offer, even if it is irrevocable, is terminated when a rejection reaches the offeror.

2. Acceptance

1) Definition of an acceptance

The first paragraph of article 18 says that a statement made by or other conduct of the offeree indicating assent to an offer is an acceptance. Silence or inactivity does not in itself amount to acceptance.

However, in order to keep pace with the development of international trade practices and promote the international sales transactions, CISG makes additional provisions in the third paragraph of article 18 that if by virtue of the offer or as a result of practices which the parties have established between themselves or of usage, the offeree may indicate assent by performing an act, such as one relating to the dispatch of the goods or payment of the price, without notice to the offeror, the acceptance is effective at the moment the act is performed, provided that the act is performed within the period of time fixed by the offeror or a reasonable time.

2) Effectiveness of an acceptance

As to when an acceptance takes effective, CISG rules are largely consistent with those of continental law but differ from common law.

According to the second paragraph of article 18, an acceptance of an offer becomes effective at the moment the indication of assent reaches the offeror within the time he has fixed or, if no time is fixed, within a reasonable time, due account being taken of the circumstances of the transaction, including the rapidity of the means of communication employed by the offeror. An oral offer must be accepted immediately unless the circumstances indicate otherwise.

In order to make the above-mentioned "fixed time" clear, the article 20 further provides that a period of time for acceptance fixed by the offeror in a telegram or a letter begins to run from the moment the telegram is handed in for dispatch or from the date shown on the letter or, if no such date is shown, from the date shown on the envelope. A period of time for acceptance fixed by the offeror by telephone, telex or other means of instantaneous communication, begins to run from the moment that the offer reaches the offeree. Official holidays or nonbusiness days occurring during the period for acceptance are included in calculating the period. However, if a notice of acceptance can not be delivered at the address of the offeror on the last day of the period because that day falls on an official holiday or a nonbusiness day at the place of business of the offeror, the period is extended until the first business day which follows.

3) A reply to an offer containing additions, limitations or other modifications

The article 19 of CISG states that a reply to an offer which purports to be an acceptance but contains additions, limitations or other modifications is a rejection of the offer and constitutes a counter-offer. However, a reply to an offer which purports to be an acceptance but contains additional or different terms which do not materially alter the terms of the offer constitutes an acceptance, unless the offeror, without undue delay, objects orally to the discrepancy or dispatches a notice to that effect. If he does not so object, the terms of the contract are the terms of the offer with the modifications contained in the acceptance. Additional or different terms relating, among other things, to the price, payment, quality and quantity of the goods, place and time of delivery, extent of one party's liability to the other or the settlement of disputes are considered to alter the terms of the offer materially.

4) A late acceptance

It will be a late acceptance[3] if the acceptance reaches to the offeror after the fixed time or a reasonable time. In most countries, a late acceptance is not regarded as an effective acceptance but a new offer. But in CISG, there are some different provisions.

The article 21 of CISG says that a late acceptance is nevertheless effective as an acceptance if without delay the offeror orally so informs the offeree or dispatches a notice to that effect. If a letter or other writing containing a late acceptance shows that it has been sent in such circumstances that if its transmission had been normal it would have reached the offeror in due time, the late acceptance is effective as an acceptance unless, without delay, the offeror orally informs the offeree that he considers his offer as having lapsed or dispatches a notice to that effect.

5) Withdrawal of an acceptance

The article 22 of CISG provides that an acceptance may be withdrawn if the withdrawal reaches the offeror before or at the same time as the acceptance would have become effective. This is in conformity with the relevant legal provisions in Germany.

3.1.3 Obligations of the Buyer and the Seller 买卖双方的义务

The Part Ⅲ — Sales of Goods, which mainly deals with the obligations of the buyer and the seller, is the heart of CISG.

1. Obligations of the seller

1) Time and place of delivery

Normally, the time and place of delivery will be stipulated by the parties in the sales contract and the seller shall deliver the goods in accordance with such stipulations. However, in international trade practice, there might be a few cases where no specified time and place of delivery are agreed in the contract. The article 31 and article 33 of CISG make detailed provisions for such cases.

In addition, the article 37 provides that if the seller has delivered goods before the date of delivery specified in the contract, he may, up to that date, deliver any missing part or make up any deficiency in the quantity of the goods delivered, or deliver goods in replacement of any nonconforming goods delivered or remedy any lack of conformity in the goods delivered, provided that the exercise of this right does not cause the buyer unreasonable inconvenience or unreasonable expense. However, the buyer retains any right to claim damages as provided for in this Convention.

2) Handing over the relevant documents

In general, the seller of an international transaction is required to deliver not only the goods but also the relevant documents to the buyer. The article 34 of CISG says that if the seller is bound to hand over documents relating to the goods, he must hand them over at the time and place and in the form required by the contract. If the seller has handed over documents before that time, he may, up to that time, cure any lack of conformity in the documents, if the exercise of this right does not cause the buyer unreasonable inconvenience or unreasonable expense. However, the buyer retains any right to claim damages as provided for in this Convention.

3) Conformity of the goods with the contract

Delivering the goods that are in conformity with the contract is one of the basic obligations of the seller. According to the article 35 of CISG, the seller must deliver goods which are of the quantity, quality and description required by the contract and which are contained or packaged in the manner required by the contract.

The second paragraph of this article lists the requirements for the conformity of the goods with the contract as follows. Except where the parties have agreed otherwise, the goods shall: a) be fit for the purposes for which goods of the same description would ordinarily be used; b) be fit for any particular purpose expressly or impliedly made known to the seller at the time of the conclusion of the contract, except where the circumstances show that the buyer did not rely, or that it was unreasonable for him to rely, on the seller's skill and judgement; c) possess the qualities of goods which the seller has held out to the buyer as a sample or model; and d) be contained or packaged in the manner usual for such goods or, where there is no such manner, in a manner adequate to preserve and protect the goods.

The article 36 provides that the seller is liable for any lack of conformity which exists at the time when the risk passes to the buyer, even though the lack of conformity becomes apparent only after that time; and the seller is also liable for any lack of conformity which occurs after that time and is due to a breach of any of his obligations, including a breach of any guarantee that for a period of time the goods will remain fit for their ordinary purpose or for some particular purpose or will retain specified qualities or characteristics. For example, if a machine sold with a contractual period of guarantee for 5 years went wrong after being used for 2 years, the seller shall be held liable even though the risk had passed to the buyer.

4) The right to sell the goods

A very important prerequisite for a seller to sell some goods is that he ought to make it assured that he does have the right to sell the goods. In other words, his sale of the goods will not infringe the rights of any third party. CISG also places emphasis on this point. According the article 41, the seller must deliver goods which are free from any right or claim of a third party, unless the buyer agreed to take the goods subject to that right or claim. However, if such right or claim is based on industrial property or other intellectual property, the seller's obligation is governed by article 42.

The first paragraph of the article 42 says that the seller must deliver goods which are free from any right or claim of a third party based on industrial property or other intellectual property, of which at the time of conclusion of the contract the seller knew or could not have been unaware, provided that the right or claim is based on industrial property or other intellectual property: a) under the law of the country where the goods will be resold or otherwise used, if it was contemplated by the parties at the time of conclusion of the contract that the goods would be resold or otherwise used in that country; b) in any other case, under the law of the country where the buyer has his place of business.

However, in some cases, the seller may not deliberately deliver the goods infringing the rights of a third party. Taking this point into account, the second paragraph of the article 42 says that obligation of the seller under the preceding paragraph does not extend to cases where: a) at the time of conclusion of the contract the buyer knew or could not have been unaware of the right or claim; b) the right or claim results from the seller's compliance with technical drawings, designs, formulae or other such specifications furnished by the buyer.

2. Obligations of the buyer

1) Inspection of the goods

In international sales transactions, it is necessary for the buyer to inspect the goods delivered by the seller to determine whether they are in conformity with the contract. The first paragraph of the article 38 of CISG states that the buyer ought to examine the goods, or cause them to be examined, within as short a period as is practicable in the circumstances.

The succeeding two paragraphs of this article provide the place of inspection by the buyer. If the contract involves carriage of the goods, examination may be deferred until after the goods have arrived at their destination. If the goods are redirected in transit or redispatched by the buyer without a reasonable opportunity for examination by him and at the time of conclusion of the contract the seller knew or ought to have known of the possibility of such redirection or redispatch, examination may be deferred until after the goods have arrived at the new destination.

The buyer is advised to inspect the goods delivered and, if any, claim for the unconformity of the goods as soon as possible. According to the article 39 of the GISG, the buyer loses the right to rely on a lack of conformity of the goods if he does not give notice to the seller specifying the nature of the lack of conformity within a reasonable time after he has discovered it or ought to have discovered it; in any event, the buyer loses the right to rely on a lack of conformity of the goods if he does not give the seller notice thereof at the latest within a period of 2 years from the date on which the goods were actually handed over to the buyer, unless this time-limit is inconsistent with a contractual period of guarantee.

2) Effecting payment of the price

Effecting payment is undoubtedly the most important obligation of the buyer in international trade. CISG makes more detailed provisions on this issue than most domestic laws.

As to the procedures of payment, the article 54 states that the buyer's obligation to pay the price includes taking such steps and complying with such formalities as may be required under the contract or any laws and regulations to enable payment to be effected.

If there is no clause in the contract requiring the buyer to pay the price at any particular place, according to the article 57, he shall pay it to the seller at the seller's place of business; or at the place where the handing over of the goods or of the documents takes place, if the payment is to be made against such a handing over. The seller must bear any increases in the expenses incidental to payment which is caused by a change in his place of business subsequent to the conclusion of the contract.

The time of making payment is very important to the parties to a sales contract and usually specified in the contract. If it is not specified in the contract, the article 58 of CISG is to be referred to as follows. The buyer must make the payment when the seller places either the goods or documents controlling their disposition at the buyer's disposal in accordance with the contract and this Convention. The seller may make such payment a condition for handing over the goods or documents and if the contract involves carriage of the goods, the seller may dispatch the goods on terms whereby the goods, or documents controlling their disposition, will not be handed over to the buyer except against payment of the price. The buyer is not bound to make payment until he has had an opportunity to inspect the goods, unless the procedures for delivery or payment agreed upon by the parties are inconsistent with his having such an opportunity.

Moreover, the article 59 states that the buyer must pay the price on the date stipulated in the contract and this Convention without the need for any request or compliance with any formality on the part of the seller, or else he will be held to be in default. This differs from the rule of "putting in default" under the Continental Law System, which means that the buyer will not be held liable for deferred payment before the seller exhorts him to make payment.

3) Taking delivery

In addition to make payment, taking delivery is also an important obligation of the buyer. The article 60 of CISG provides that the buyer's obligation to take delivery consists in doing all the acts which could reasonably be expected of him in order to enable the seller to make delivery and taking over the goods.

3.1.4 Breach of Contract and Remedies 违约及其救济

It may constitute a breach of contract if either party to the sales contract fails to fulfill its obligations in accordance with the contract. The Part III of CISG also makes detailed provisions on breach of contract and remedies.

1. Fundamental breach of contract

According to the article 25 of CISG, a breach of contract committed by one of the parties is a fundamental breach[4] if it results in such detriment to the other party as substantially to deprive him of what he is entitled to expect under the contract, unless the breaching party did not foresee and a reasonable person of the same kind in the same circumstances would not have foreseen such a result.

2. Remedies for breach of contract by the seller

In trade practice, the seller may breach the contract by nonperformance, deferred performance, or nonconformity of the goods. Under CISG, the buyer may apply to the following remedies for breach of contract by the seller.

1) Specific performance

According to the first paragraph of the article 46 of CISG, the buyer may require performance by the seller of his obligations unless the buyer has resorted to a remedy which is inconsistent with this requirement.

However, in light of the article 28, if one party is entitled to require performance of any obligation by the other party, a court is not bound to enter a judgement for specific performance unless the court would do so under its own law in respect of similar contracts of sale not governed by this Convention. CISG makes such a provision because of the important difference between the common law and the continental law on this issue.

At common law, specific performance is regarded as an exceptional remedy for breach of contract, whereas the primary remedy at continental law. So the GISG has to allow the courts to decide under the jurisdictions of their domestic laws.

2) Substitution and repair

The second paragraph of the article 46 provides that if the goods do not conform with the contract and the lack of conformity constitutes a fundamental breach of contract, the buyer may require the delivery of substitute goods. Such a request for substitute goods shall be made either in conjunction with notice given under the article 39 (the article 39 has been mentioned in the previous part of "Obligations of the buyer" in the previous section) or within a reasonable time thereafter.

The last paragraph of the article 46 states that if the goods do not conform with the contract, the buyer may require the seller to remedy the lack of conformity by repair, unless this is unreasonable having regard to all the circumstances. A request for repair is also to be made either in conjunction with notice given under article 39 or within a reasonable time thereafter.

It should be stressed that although the two remedies of substitution and repair are provided for in the same article, the former can only be employed against fundamental breach of contract while the latter applied to the cases where no fundamental breach involved.

3) Reduction of the price

In light of the article 50, if the goods do not conform with the contract and whether or not the price has already been paid, the buyer may ask for reduction of the price in the same proportion as the value that the goods actually delivered had at the time of the delivery bears to the value that conforming goods would have had at that time.

However, if the seller remedies any failure to perform his obligations in accordance with the provisions of this Convention, or if the buyer refuses to accept the above-mentioned performance of remedy by the seller, the buyer may lose the right to reduce the price.

4) Damages

According to the article 45 of CISG, if the seller fails to perform any of his obligations under the contract or this Convention, the buyer may claim damages and his right to claim damages is not deprived of by exercising his right to other remedies.

The article 74 provides the calculation of the damages. Damages for breach of contract by one party consist of a sum equal to the loss, including loss of profit, suffered by the other party as a consequence of the breach. Such damages may not exceed the loss which the party in breach foresaw or ought to have foreseen at the time of conclusion of the contract, in the light of the facts and matters of which he then knew or ought to have known, as a possible consequence of the breach of contract.

The article 75 provides that if the contract is avoided and if, in a reasonable manner and within a reasonable time after avoidance, the buyer has bought goods in replacement or the seller has resold the goods, the party claiming damages may recover the difference between the contract price and the price in the substitute transaction as well as any further damages recoverable under article 74.

The article 76 states that if the contract is avoided and there is a current price for the goods, the party claiming damages may, if he has not made a purchase or resale under article 75, recover the difference between the price fixed by the contract and the current price at the time of avoidance as well as any further damages recoverable under article 74. If, however, the party claiming damages has avoided the contract after taking over the goods, the current price at the time of such taking over shall be applied instead of the current price at the time of avoidance. The current price mentioned here refers to the price prevailing at the place where delivery of the goods should have been made or, if there is no current price at that place, the price at such other place as serves as a reasonable substitute, making due allowance for differences in the cost of transporting the goods.

The article 77 requires the party who relies on a breach of contract must take reasonable measures to mitigate the loss, including loss of profit, resulting from the breach. If he fails to take such measures, the party in breach may claim a reduction in the damages in the amount by which the loss should have been mitigated.

5) Refuse to take delivery

According to the article 51, if the seller delivers only a part of the goods or if only a part of the goods delivered is in conformity with the contract, in respect of the part which is missing or which does not conform, the buyer may apply to the remedies above-mentioned (such as requiring substitution or repair, claiming for damages), or refuse to take delivery of the defective part. However, he may declare the contract avoided in whole only if the incomplete delivery or unconformity with the contract amounts to a fundamental breach of contract.

The first paragraph of the article 52 provides that if the seller delivers the goods before the date fixed, the buyer may take delivery or refuse to take delivery. The second paragraph states that if the seller delivers a quantity of goods greater than that prescribed in the contract, the buyer may take delivery or refuse to take delivery of the excess quantity. If the buyer takes delivery of all or part of the excess quantity, he must pay for it at the price agreed upon in the contract.

6) Declare the contract avoided

In light of the article 49, the buyer may declare the contract avoided under the following circumstances:

(1) If the failure by the seller to perform any of his obligations under the contract or this Convention amounts to a fundamental breach of contract;

(2) In case of nondelivery, if the seller does not deliver the goods within the additional period of time fixed by the buyer in accordance with provisions of this Convention, or declares that he will not deliver within the additional period so fixed.

Normally, the buyer is not entitled to declare the contract avoided as long as the seller has delivered the goods. However, there are some exceptional cases. In the event of late delivery, the buyer may avoid the contract within a reasonable time after he has become aware that delivery has been made; In the cases of any fundamental breach other than late delivery, the buyer may declare the contract avoid within a reasonable time after he knew or ought to have known of the breach, or after the expiration of any additional period of time fixed by him for the seller to perform his obligation, or after the seller has declared that he will not perform his obligations within such an additional period, or after the buyer has declared that he will not accept performance by the seller in such an additional period.

Reading Material

Fundamental Breach of Contract under CISG

The following two hypothetic cases will help to understand the fundamental breach of contract under CISG.

In the case of an international sale of iced turkey for Thanksgiving Day, the seller deferred the delivery for one week, and then the buyer incurred substantial losses because the Thanksgiving Day is past and the demand for turkey fell off. According to CISG, this is to be regarded as a fundamental breach of contract, and the buyer may exercise the right to declare the contract avoided.

If the goods sold in the above case changes to chicken and the delivery date required by the buyer is not any festival, and the price of chicken did not fluctuate during this week, according to CISG, this will not constitute a fundamental breach of contract and the buyer may not declare the contract avoided.

3. Remedies for breach of contract by the buyer

The breach of contract by the buyer may be nonpayment or deferred payment, not or deferred taking delivery. Under CISG, the seller may apply to the following remedies for breach of contract by the buyer.

1) Specific performance

According to the article 61, the seller may require performance by the buyer of his obligations unless the seller has resorted to a remedy which is inconsistent with this requirement.

As stated previously, because of the different provisions at continental law and common law, the article 28 of CISG points that, if one party is entitled to require performance of any obligation by the other party, a court is not bound to enter a judgement for specific performance unless the court would do so under its own law in respect of similar contracts of sale not governed by this Convention.

2) Make the specification of the goods himself

As usual practices, the parties will make detailed clauses on the specification of the goods to be delivered by the seller. But sometimes the buyer may not be very sure of specification of the goods when the contract is concluded. Then the contract may not have the stipulations on specification but state that the buyer shall make such specification and inform to the seller on the date agreed upon or within a reasonable time after receipt of a request from the seller. According to the article 65 of CISG, if the buyer fails to do so, the seller may, without prejudice to any other rights he may have, make the specification himself in accordance with the requirements of the buyer that may be known to him.

In order to maintain the relations between the parties and promote successful transactions, this article further provides that if the seller makes the specification himself, he must inform the buyer of the details thereof and must fix a reasonable time within which the buyer may make a different specification; if, after receipt of such a communication, the buyer fails to do so within the time so fixed, the specification made by the seller is binding.

3) Damages

According to the article 61 of CISG, if the buyer fails to perform any of his obligations under the contract or this Convention, the seller may claim damages and is not deprived of any right he may have to claim damages by exercising his right to other remedies.

As for the calculation of the damages and the recovery of the losses, the seller shall also apply to the articles 74 to77, which have been mentioned previously in the section of "Remedies for breach of contract by the seller".

If the buyer fails to pay the price on time, the seller is entitled to claim for interest on it, without prejudice to any claim for damages recoverable under article 74.

4) Declare the contract avoided

In light of the article 64 of CISG, the seller may declare the contract avoided under the following circumstances:

(1) If the failure by the buyer to perform any of his obligations under the contract or this Convention amounts to a fundamental breach of contract;

(2) If the buyer does not pay the price or take delivery of the goods within the additional period of time fixed by the seller in accordance with provisions of this Convention, or declares that he will not do so within the additional period so fixed.

In general, the seller loses the right to declare the contract avoided if the buyer has paid the price. Exceptionally, in respect of late performance by the buyer, the seller may declare the contract avoided before he has become aware that performance has been rendered; in respect of any fundamental breach other than late performance by the buyer, the seller may avoid the contract within a reasonable time or after he knew or ought to have known of the breach, or after the expiration of any additional period of time fixed by him for the buyer to perform his obligations in accordance with the provisions of CISG, or after the buyer has declared that he will not perform within such an additional period.

4. Anticipatory breach

Anticipatory breach[5] means that prior to the agreed date for performance of the contract, there have been grounds for one party to anticipate that the other party will not perform his obligations. The articles 71 and 72 of GISG make special provisions on anticipatory breaches.

A party may suspend the performance of his obligations if, after the conclusion of the contract, it becomes apparent that the other party will not perform a substantial part of his obligations as a result of a serious deficiency in his ability to perform or in his creditworthiness, or his inappropriate conduct in preparing to perform or in performing the contract.

If the seller has already dispatched the goods before the anticipatory breach by the buyer becomes evident, he may prevent the handing over of the goods to the buyer even though the buyer holds a document which entitles him to obtain them. Such a provision relates only to the rights in the goods as between the buyer and the seller.

The party who anticipates the other party to be in breach and suspends the performance of his obligations, whether before or after dispatch of the goods, must immediately give notice of the suspension to the other party and must continue with performance if the other party provides adequate assurance of his performance.

If prior to the date for performance of the contract, it is clear that one party will commit a fundamental breach of contract, the other party may declare the contract avoided. If time allows, the party intending to declare the contract avoided must give reasonable notice to the other party in order to permit him to provide adequate assurance of his performance, unless the other party has declared that he will not perform his obligations.

5. Breach under the instalment contract

An instalment contract refers to the contract for delivery of goods by instalments. The article 73 of CISG says that in respect of any individual instalment, if the failure of one party to perform any of his obligations constitutes a fundamental breach of contract, the other party may declare the contract avoided with respect to that individual instalment. If one party's failure to perform any of his obligations in respect of any individual instalment gives the other party good grounds to conclude that a fundamental breach of contract will occur with respect to future instalments, he may declare the contract avoided for the future within a reasonable time.

If the deliveries by instalments are interdependent and any individual instalment could not be separately used for the purpose contemplated by the parties at the time of concluding the contract, the buyer who declares the contract avoided in respect of any individual instalment may, at the same time, declare it avoided in respect of deliveries already made or of future deliveries.

3.1.5   Passing of Risk   风险的转移

The parties may agree on the conditions of passing of risk in the sales contract. If they did not do so, the following provisions of CISG may be applied to.

1. Effect of passing of risk

The article 66 provides that loss of or damage to the goods arising after the risk has passed to the buyer does not discharge him from his obligation to pay the price, unless the loss or damage is due to an act or omission of the seller.

2. In the case of carriage involved in the sales contract

If the sales contract involves carriage of the goods, according to the article 67, if the seller is not required by the contract to hand them over at a particular place, the risk passes to the buyer when the goods are handed over to the first carrier for transmission to the buyer in accordance with the sales contract; If the seller is bound to hand the goods over to a carrier at a particular place, the risk does not pass to the buyer until the goods are handed over to the carrier at that place. The fact that the seller is authorized to retain documents controlling the disposition of the goods does not affect the passing of the risk.

Nevertheless, the risk does not pass to the buyer until the goods are clearly identified to the contract, whether by markings on the goods, by shipping documents, by notice given to the buyer or otherwise.

3. In the case of goods sold in transit

In light of the article 68, the risk in respect of goods sold in transit passes to the buyer from the time of conclusion of the contract. However, if the circumstances so indicate, the risk is assumed by the buyer from the time the goods were handed over to the carrier who issued the documents embodying the contract of carriage.

Nevertheless, if at the time of concluding the sales contract the seller knew or ought to have known that the goods had been lost or damaged and did not disclose this to the buyer, the loss or damage is assumed by the seller.

4. In other cases

The article 69 makes provisions on passing of risk in other cases. In cases not falling within articles 67 and 68, the risk passes to the buyer when he takes over the goods; if he does not do so in due time, the risk passes to him from the time when the goods are placed at his disposal and he commits a breach of contract by failing to take delivery on time.

If the buyer is required by the contract to take over the goods at a place other than the place of business of the seller, the risk passes when delivery is made in due time and the buyer is aware of the fact that the goods have been placed at his disposal at that place. However, the goods are considered not to be placed at the disposal of the buyer until they are clearly identified to the contract.

5. Passing of risk and fundamental breach of contract

According to the article 70 of CISG, if the seller has committed a fundamental breach of contract, the passing of risk under articles 67, 68 and 69 do not impair the remedies available to the buyer relying on the breach.

3. 2   Principles of International Commercial Contracts
国际商事合同通则

3. 2. 1   A Brief Introduction to PICC   国际商事合同通则简介

Principles of International Commercial Contracts (PICC) was first published by the UNIDROIT[6] in 1994 and revised in 2004. The second edition is the newest version up to now.

The UNIDROIT Principles 2004 consist of the Preamble and 185 articles divided into ten chapters.

- Chapter 1: General Provisions.
- Chapter 2:

Section 1   Formation;

Section 2   Authority of Agents.
- Chapter 3：Validity.
- Chapter 4：Interpretation.
- Chapter 5：

Section 1   Content；

Section 2   Third Party Rights.
- Chapter 6：

Section 1   Performance in General；

Section 2   Hardship.
- Chapter 7：

Section 1   Nonperformance in General；

Section 2   Right to Performance；

Section 3   Termination；

Section 4   Damages.
- Chapter 8：Set-off.
- Chapter 9：

Section 1   Assignment of Rights；

Section 2   Transfer of Obligations；

Section 3   Assignment of Contracts.
- Chapter 10：Limitation Periods.

The UNIDROIT PICC sets forth general rules for international commercial contracts. They may be applied when the parties have agreed that their contract be governed by them, or when the parties have agreed that their contract be governed by general principles of law, the *lex mercatoria*⁷ or the like, or to settle the disputes relating to the contract when the parties have not chosen any law to govern their contract. They may be used to interpret or supplement international uniform law instruments and domestic law. They may also serve as a model for national and international legislators.

3.2.2   Comparison between PICC and CISG   PICC 与 CISG 的比较

In comparison with CISG, PICC is not an international convention and need not to be signed and ratified by countries. It can be applicable to any international commercial contract by virtue of the agreement of the parties.

Although being different in status from CISG, the major rules of PICC were established on the basis of the contents of CISG. In other words, PICC has the primary and essential provisions in common with CISG.

Nevertheless, there are some important differences between PICC and CISG. The major differences are listed as follows.

1. Sphere of application

Provided that the parties so agreed, PICC may be applicable to all sorts of commercial contracts, including contracts for sale, investment, technology license or trade in service; whereas CISG only applies to contracts for international sale of goods.

2. Freedom of contract

The first article of PICC states the basic rule of "freedom of contract", on which is placed much emphasis in many domestic law jurisdictions but not mentioned in CISG. It means that the parties are free to enter into a contract and to determine its content.

3. Good faith and fair dealing

The article 1.7 of PICC provides that each party must act in accordance with good faith and fair dealing in international trade and the parties can not exclude or limit this duty. In comparison, CISG just mentioned the observance of good faith in the interpretation of CISG.

4. Definition of offer

PICC defines the offer in the article 2.1.2 and, unlike CISG, does not require an offer to be addressed to specific persons.

5. Authority of agents

The section 2 of the chapter 2 of PICC deals with authority of agents which is not covered in CISG. Such provisions make PICC applicable to commercial agency agreements if the parties so agreed.

6. Validity of contract

The whole chapter 3 of PICC makes detailed provisions on validity of contract whereas CISG declares expressly in the article 4 that it is not concerned with validity of contract. Thus PICC makes up for this deficiency of CISG.

7. Hardship

Hardship[8] is a new legal term which is put forward in PICC. It refers to such circumstances where the occurrence of events fundamentally alters the equilibrium of the contract either because the cost of a party's performance has increased or because the value of the performance a party receives has diminished, and:

(1) The events occur or become known to the disadvantaged party after the conclusion of the contract;

(2) The events could not reasonably have been foreseen by the disadvantaged party at the time of concluding the contract;

(3) The events are beyond the control of the disadvantaged party;

(4) The risk of the events was not assumed by the disadvantaged party.

According to the article 6.2.3 of PICC, in case of hardship the disadvantaged party is entitled to request renegotiations. The request shall be made without undue delay and shall indicate the grounds on which it is based. However the request for renegotiation does not in itself entitle the disadvantaged party to withhold performance.

Either party may resort to the court upon failure to reach agreement within a reasonable time by renegotiation. If the court finds hardship it may, if reasonable, terminate the contract at a date and on terms to be fixed, or adapt the contract with a view to restoring its equilibrium.

8. Agreed payment for nonperformance

The article 7.4.13 of PICC particularly provides for the agreed payment for nonperformance, which is similar to the liquidated damages in many domestic law jurisdictions.

According to this article, where the contract provides that a party who does not perform is to pay a specified sum to the aggrieved party for such nonperformance, the aggrieved party is entitled to that sum irrespective of its actual harm. However, notwithstanding any agreement to the contrary the specified sum may be reduced to a reasonable amount where it is grossly excessive in relation to the harm resulting from the nonperformance and to the other circumstances.

9. Set-off

The chapter 8 of PICC deals with set-off in detail, which is deemed in many counties as one of the means by which a contract may be discharged. But CISG does not mention it at all.

Similar to some domestic laws, PICC provides that set-off may be exercised by paying money or notice, and it discharges the obligations. If the obligations differ in amount, set-off discharges the obligations up to the amount of the lesser obligation.

10. Assignment

The chapter 9 of PICC provides for assignment in detail, including three sections respectively about assignment of rights, transfer of obligations and assignment of a contract (concurrent assignment of rights and obligations arising out of a contract).

11. Limitation periods

In order to conciliate the different provisions of time limitation from one country to another, PICC makes particular provisions on limitation periods in Chapter 10.

According to PICC, the general limitation period is 3 years beginning on the day after the day the obligee knows or ought to know the facts as a result of which the obligatory right can be exercised. In any event, the maximum limitation period is 10 years beginning on the day after the day the obligatory right can be exercised.

PICC allows the parties to modify the limitation periods. However they may not shorten the general limitation period to less than 1 year; shorten the maximum limitation period to less than 4 years, or extend it to more than 15 years.

Group Discussion ▶ ▶ ▶

1. State the major provisions of CISG on formation of the contract.
2. Discuss the main obligations of the parties to an international sales contract.
3. Compare the provisions on breach of contract of CISG with continental law and common law.
4. Will you choose CISG or PICC to govern your contract if you are doing international business? Why?

NOTES ▶▶▶

1　Contracting States　缔约国
2　offer and acceptance　发盘与接受（为了与普通合同的成立相区别，通常将订立国际货物销售合同的"要约与承诺"译为"发盘与接受"）
3　late acceptance　逾期接受
4　fundamental breach（of contract）　根本性违约
5　anticipatory breach（of contract）　预期违约
6　UNIDROIT　国际统一私法协会（参见第1章第1.5.4节）
7　lex mercatoria　（拉丁语）商业习惯法，商人法（相当于英语中的 law merchant）
8　hardship　艰难情形，履行艰难

CASES

Buyer's Burden of Proof for Lack of Conformity and the
Requirements of Notice under CISG
CISG 之下买方就质量不符的举证责任及通知的要求

The claimant, a Hungarian company, entered into two contracts of sale FOB Budapest Sepal dated 10 and 16 October 2001 with the defendant, a buyer from Germany, for the delivery of Hungarian wheat. The defendant's carrier took the first delivery on 19 October and the second on 25 October. In a letter dated 14 November 2001 the defendant gave notice of lack of conformity, arguing that the wheat had been contaminated with excessive lead content and vomitoxin. The defendant also argued that the falling number of the wheat was only 210 sec or 215 sec although a falling number of 230 sec was agreed in the contract. The defendant relied on the right of price reduction under article 50 of CISG and claimed damages under articles 45 (1)(b), 74 of CISG which it set off against the claim for the purchase price. The claimant denied the nonconformity of the wheat delivered by him and sued the defendant for payment of the purchase price and damages due to delay in taking the first delivery. The Regional Court Mannheim granted the claimant the full purchase price plus interest and compensation for storage costs. The defendant appealed.

The Higher Regional Court dismissed the defendant's appeal against the judgement of the Regional Court Mannheim. With reference to a consolidated line of decisions, the Higher Regional Court held that the buyer has to prove the lack of conformity if he takes the goods without complaining about defects. In the court's opinion the defendant failed to prove the contamination with lead as well as with vomitoxin. Concerning the differing falling number the court stated that the buyer had lost the right to rely on the lack of conformity because it had failed to give notice in compliance with article 39 of CISG. The notice under article 39 of CISG must show the intention to object and identify the lack of conformity exactly. These requirements are not met if the nonconformity is only mentioned incidentally among other such notices and if it is stated that this specific nonconformity is no longer of importance. Therefore the court denied the defendant's right to reduce the price under article 50 of CISG and to claim damages under article 45（1）（b）, 74. On the contrary, it granted the claimant the purchase price plus interest and storage charges, with the rate of interest following from the respective provisions of the Hungarian law applicable according to the parties' agreement.

Jurisdiction and Place of Payment
管辖权和支付地点

The seller, an Italian corporation with its place of business in Italy, agreed to sell women stockings to the buyer, an Austrian company, whose place of business was in Austria. Since the buyer had failed to pay the whole price, the seller brought an action for payment of the price before the Italian judge, alleging the breach of contract for partial performance. The defendant claimed that the Italian judge did not have the authority to decide the issue in controversy, as its place of business was in Austria. The issue before the Italian Supreme Court was therefore whether the Italian court had the power to adjudicate the case.

The Supreme Court held that the relevant rule was to be found in article 57 of CISG, a Convention that both states had ratified at the time of the litigation. On the basis of article 57 （1） of CISG, if the buyer is not bound to pay the price at any other particular place, it must pay it to the seller at the seller's place of business or, if the payment is to be made against the handing over of the goods or of documents, at the place where the handing over takes place. The Court stated that since the parties had not determined different rules in their contract, the general principle provided for by the aforesaid article 57 applies. According to this, the payment for the supplied commodities was to be performed by the buyer at the seller's place of business, therefore Italy may be designed as the forum for solution. The Court ruled that the Italian judge had jurisdiction over the case in light of both article 57 of CISG and article 4 of Italian Civil Procedure Code, which states that the foreigner can be sued before an Italian judge if the action implies obligations to be fulfilled in the territory of Italy.

The Independence of the Remedies of Avoidance of the
Contract and Price Reduction
宣告合同无效与降价两种救济方法相互独立

The claimant, an Italian manufacturer of wine bottles, sued the buyer, a customer from Germany, for payment of the purchase price of several shipments of bottles, after the defendant had declared that it would not pay. The defendant argued that due to defective packaging by the claimant the bottles had been either broken or had lost their sterility and therefore became unsuitable for further use. The contract obliged the claimant only to deliver "ex factory" while it was up to the defendant to take delivery.

On first instance, the Regional Court in Germany partly rejected the claim, on the ground that the buyer had declared the contract avoided pursuant to article 49 (1)(a) of CISG and declared its unwillingness to pay. The Higher Regional Court dismissed the claimant's appeal against the judgement of the Regional Court.

The Higher Regional Court held that the claimant had failed to perform its obligation, pursuant to article 35 (2)(d) of CISG, to provide packaging for the bottles in a manner adequate for transport by truck. Therefore the court regarded the seller to be liable for the damage to the bottles under articles 36 (2) and 66 of CISG, although the risk of loss or damage passed to the buyer, when the bottles were taken over by the buyer's carrier. However, contrary to the Regional Court's reasoning in first instance, the Higher Regional Court stated that the requirement of article 49 (2)(b) of CISG to declare the contract avoided within a reasonable time does not allow to consider the buyer's refusal of payment to be an implied declaration of avoidance.

The court considered the buyer's refusal to be a declaration of reduction of the purchase price to zero. Explicitly the court pointed out that the buyer may reduce the price according to article 50 of CISG even if it had lost its right to avoid the contract for instance as a result of missing the deadline pursuant to article 49 (2)(b) of CISG. According to the court the right to reduce the price may also be used as an objection against a claim for the payment of the purchase price.

As for the interpretation of article 50 of CISG itself the court stated that the wording "at the time of delivery" means the time the goods are available to the buyer after having arrived at their destination. The failure of the claimant to provide adequate packaging for the bottles to preserve them and to ensure their arriving in a marketable condition was deemed as a fundamental breach of contract by the court under article 25 of CISG.

Chapter 4

Business Organization Law
商事组织法

Learning Objectives

- ✔ To understand the three main legal forms of business organization
- ✔ To learn about the partnership enterprise law
- ✔ To compare the company laws under the two major law systems
- ✔ To know the important provisions of Chinese company law

 Opening Vignette

Starting a Business Organization in the US

If you are the type of person that conventional wisdom calls the "entrepreneur", you might be very eager to "roll up your sleeves and just get started". However, conventional wisdom also suggests that many new businesses fail within the first five years. If you truly want to start a business organization which will succeed for the long term, then there really is some preliminary thinking that you really should do. The following may be taken into consideration.

1. Business Ideas

To start a business, you will need to choose or create a business idea. Many people who want their own business don't have an idea, just the desire to be an entrepreneur. For the budding entrepreneur, there are many options: buying a franchise or an existing business, or looking to others for ideas for a start-up business. Once you have decided on the business you wish to start, the real work begins.

2. Business Plan

Writing a business plan is a necessary step, this is how you and others will evaluate your business. When seeking financing, the investors or lenders will want to read your plan before they supply you with funding. If you are able to finance the business yourself, you will still want to have a written plan to develop business strategies and financial projections. A key element of the business plan is the marketing plan, which explains marketing strategies that will be used to advertise and promote the products or services. The goal setting steps of the plan will help you to analyze the success of the business in future years and clearly illustrate the capital needed to operate the company to survive.

3. Financing

With your business plan in hand, you are ready to go find some capital. Most small businesses have three options for financing: friends & family, investors or bank loans. Each of these options has different considerations for the business. Investors and even friends & family usually want ownership and control of their portion of the business. Bank loans burden the business with an additional expense of the interest payment, which can erode the business profits.

4. Legal Concerns

First you should choose a legal form: sole proprietorship, partnership, or corporation. It is best to consult a lawyer to determine which form of business organization will be best for you. Your financing decisions will have an effect on what legal form you choose. Then you can file with the state to incorporate and obtain a federal identification number. Finally, do not forget taxes. You should be aware that what taxes you have to pay and how you shall pay them.

Note that the laws and regulations that your business must follow depend very much on what state you live, the legal form of your business and the nature of your product or service. Consequently, there is no comprehensive, up-to-date checklist of laws and regulations that you can "walk through". To identify the laws and regulations your business will have to follow, contact your state's Attorney General's[1] office.

Warm-up Questions

1. What do you think a business organization is?
2. What is the most important step to start a business in the US?
3. Do you know how to start a business organization in China?

4.1 Legal Forms of Business Organizations
商事组织的法律形式

A business organization is an entity formed for the purpose of carrying on commercial enterprise.

Such an organization is predicated on systems of law governing contract and exchange, property rights, and incorporation.

Business enterprises commonly take one of the following three forms: individual proprietorships, partnerships, or companies.

4.1.1 Individual Proprietorship 个人企业

The individual proprietorship[2] referred to a business entity which is established and invested in by one natural person and the property of which is personally owned by the investor.

An individual proprietorship enterprise is not a legal person. The investor himself is the owner who operates the enterprise all by himself; he shall assume the operating risks solely and take full responsibility for the debts and obligations of the enterprise with his own property, which is known as unlimited liability[3].

In general, individual proprietorship enterprises are small enterprises and their business scope are strictly limited by law. For instances, in many countries, individual proprietorship enterprises can not engage in banking, insurance and other financial business.

The Individual Proprietorship Enterprise Law of the PRC was promulgated in 1999, which makes provisions to regulate the activities of individual proprietorship enterprises in China.

4.1.2 Partnership 合伙企业

A partnership is an agreement in which two or more persons combine their resources in a business with a view to making a profit. In order to establish the terms of the business and to protect partners in the event of disagreement or dissolution of the business, a partnership agreement should be drawn up, usually with the assistance of a lawyer. Partners share in the profits according to the provisions of the agreement.

Reading Material

Should You Have a Partner?

It is best to make your decision concerning whether to have a partner in business by preparing a "for" and "against" list.

The most common reasons for joining with another person to start a partnership business: There is safety in numbers. In other words, you have two heads instead of one to discuss and make decisions. You will not need to be at the business at all times. You will have someone else who will be there to share the load and permit you to take a vacation and have sick time. You will also have a highly motivated co-worker, not just someone who is earning a paycheck. Partners can also be advantageous when they have complementary skills. It may be necessary to have a partner to contribute capital and share the risks when things do not proceed as planned.

Some of the arguments against having a partner: You will have to share the rewards if the business is successful. You will have to share the recognition that will come if the business is successful. You will lose total control over the business, particularly if you and your partner have difficulty in making decisions. A partner can be a disaster if his or her judgment is not good. You run the risk of a falling out and perhaps the necessity of one partner buying the other out if dissention arises.

4.1.3 Company 公司

A company is a legal entity which is created according to the legal conditions and procedures and for the purpose of making profit. Since a company is a legal person separate and distinct from its owners, the death or withdrawal of any owner will not affect the existence of the company. Companies enjoy most of the rights and responsibilities that an individual possesses; that is, a company has the right to enter into contracts, loan and borrow money, sue and be sued, hire employees, own assets and pay taxes.

The most important aspect of a company is limited liability. That is, the owners have the right to participate in the profits, through dividends and/or the appreciation of stock, but are not held personally liable for the company's debts.

Companies are the most important and common forms of business organizations in modern countries.

4.2 Partnership Enterprise Law
合伙企业法

4.2.1 Definition and Features of Partnership Enterprise
合伙企业的概念及特征

1. Definition

A partnership enterprise is an enterprise created and operated jointly by 2 or more partners who share in the profits or losses of the business undertaking in which all have invested.

2. Features

In general, a partnership enterprise has the following legal features:

(1) A partnership enterprise is formed on the basis of the partnership contract/agreement which stipulates the rights and obligations of all the partners;

(2) In principle a partnership enterprise does not have the status of a juristic person;

(3) All the partners take unlimited liabilities for the debts and obligations of the partnership enterprise;

(4) All the partners are equally and personally responsible for the operation of the partnership enterprise unless otherwise agreed upon in the partnership contract;

(5) A partnership enterprise is the association of all the partners and the death, bankruptcy or retirement of any partner may cause the enterprise to dissolve.

3. Different definitions in different jurisdictions

1) Under the Continental Law System

Under the Continental Law System, there are civil partnerships and commercial partnerships[4]. However, the partnerships discussed here are all commercial partnerships. In some civil law jurisdictions partnership agreements may be registered and available for public inspection. In certain countries such as France, Belgium, Holland and Japan, a partnership may be considered to be a juristic person.

2）Under the Common Law System

In the UK, the Partnership Act 1890[5] is still in force now. It defines partnership as the relation which subsists between persons carrying on a business in common with a view of profit.

Many particular provisions of partnership law, which firstly adopted as part of the English Partnership Act of 1890, were subsequently adopted as part of the Uniform Partnership Act[6] of the US, which has been the basis of the partnership law in the US since the 1940s.

3）In China

The Partnership Enterprise Law of the PRC newly revised in 2006 provides that partnership enterprises may be established within China by natural persons, legal persons and other organizations in accordance with the law and categorizes partnership enterprises into two types of general partnership enterprise and limited partnership[7] enterprise. A general partnership enterprise is formed by general partners who bear unlimited joint and several liability[8] for the debts of the partnership while a limited partnership is formed by general partners and limited partners where the limited partners bear the liabilities for the partnership's debts to the extent of their capital contributions.

This law provided a new type of partnership in China — the special general partnership[9]. According to this law, a professional service institution offering services requiring professional knowledge and special skills may be formed as a special general partnership. In such a special partnership, a partner shall take unlimited liabilities while all other partners take limited liabilities for the debts or obligations incurred to the partnership enterprise because of his intentional or serious wrongful act. However, for other debts or obligations of the partnership enterprise, all the partners shall bear unlimited liabilities. Such a special general partnership is similar to the limited liability partnership (LLP)[10] in some western countries.

4.2.2 Establishment of a General Partnership Enterprise
普通合伙企业的设立

A general partnership is to be formed by general partners who bear unlimited joint and several liability for the debts of the partnership. A partnership contract concluded by the partners is the basis of the establishment of a general partnership enterprise.

1. Partnership contract

In normal cases, a partnership contract shall be in written form and have the following important matters:

（1）Name and address of the partnership enterprise and names of the partners;

（2）Nature, purpose and business scope of the partnership enterprise;

（3）Duration of the partnership;

（4）Capital contributions of each partner;

（5）Profit and loss allocation;

（6）Management authority;

（7）Admission to and withdrawal from partnership;

（8）A course of action in case a partner dies.

2. Registration

In most countries, the legal procedure for registration of a partnership enterprise is considerably simple. But there are different requirements from one country to another.

In the US, a partnership may be established in accordance of the agreement of the partners without the approval by the government, provided that it has a legal purpose.

The English partnership law makes strict requirements on the name of a partnership enterprise. A partnership shall be named after the partners and the word "Firm" or "Company" may be added in the end but the word "Limited" may not be added. If the names of the partners are not involved in the name of the partnership enterprise, the partners must register with the authoritative agency to legally establish the partnership.

In Germany, in order to establish a partnership enterprise, all the partners shall make a written application together for legal registration.

To establish a partnership enterprise in China, the applicant shall submit to the relevant registration agency a registration application, the partnership agreement, identity certificates of the partners and other documents. If the business scope of a partnership enterprise contains any item which is subject to approval prior to registration under other laws or administrative regulations, and the approval documents shall also be submitted for registration.

4.2.3 Relationships inside a General Partnership Enterprise 普通合伙企业的内部关系

The relationships within a general partnership enterprise are based on the partnership contract, which provides for the rights and obligations of the partners.

1. Rights of the partners

1) To share profit

The profit made by the operation of the partnership enterprise is owned by all the partners and each partner has the right to share the profit.

2) To take part in the management of partnership enterprise

In theory, the partners enjoy equal rights to the management of partnership enterprise. But in practice, the partnership agreement usually stipulates one or several partners to execute the partnership affairs on behalf of the partnership enterprise.

3) To supervise the execution of partnership affairs

Each partner has the right to supervise the execution of partnership affairs and to consult the account books and other financial materials of the partnership enterprise.

4) To get compensation

In some cases, in order to maintain the normal operation or protect the interests of the partnership enterprise, a partner may make extra payments or suffer losses of his own property. Consequently, the partnership enterprise or other partners shall compensate to him for such payments or losses.

2. Liabilities of the partners

1）**To make capital contribution**

Each partner shall make capital contribution according to the stipulation of the partnership agreement. If the noncontribution of capital by a partner makes the partnership fail to establish as agreed, or causes losses to other partners, other partners have the rights to claim for compensation.

2）**To be loyal and faithful**

When executing the partnership affairs, each partner shall be absolutely loyal and faithful to other partners, must not cheat, hide the facts or figure for self-interest.

3）**Not to operate any business competing with the partnership enterprise.**

No partner may, solely or jointly with others, operate any business competing with the partnership enterprise, or engage in any activity which may impair the interests of this partnership enterprise.

4）**Not to assign the share of properties of the partnership enterprise without the consent of all other partners**

No partner may assign to a third person his entire or partial share of properties of the partnership enterprise, unless he acquired the unanimous consent of all other partners.

4.2.4　Relationship between a General Partnership Enterprise and Third Persons 普通合伙企业与第三人的关系

In most jurisdictions, there is a primary rule about the relationship between a partnership enterprise and third persons. That is — any restriction of a partnership enterprise on the partners' execution of partnership affairs as well as on their right to represent the partnership enterprise in the face of outsiders shall not challenge any bona fide[11] third party. For example, a partner had been prohibited by the partnership agreement from concluding contracts on the behalf of the partnership enterprise; but a third party did not know this and entered into a contract relevant to the partnership enterprise with the said partner; then such a contract may be considered to be enforceable to the partnership enterprise.

Where a partner incurs any debt irrelevant to the partnership enterprise, the relevant creditor shall not offset its credit against the debt it owes to the partnership enterprise, nor may it exercise the said partner's rights in the partnership enterprise by subrogating this partner. If the partner's own properties are insufficient to pay off the debt, this partner may use the proceeds acquired from the partnership enterprise, to pay for the debt. The creditor may also plead the court to enforce the repayment of the debt by the said partner's property share in the partnership enterprise according to the law. When the court so enforces, a notice shall be sent to all partners. The other partners have the preemptive right to the property share of the said partner. If the other partners do not purchase it, nor consent to assign it to others, a withdrawal settlement shall be made for the said partner by the court, or a settlement shall be made to decrease the property share of him correspondingly.

4.2.5　Dissolution of a General Partnership Enterprise 普通合伙企业的解散

A general partnership enterprise may be dissolved by the agreement of the partners, or by law. The partners may agree on the dissolution of the partnership enterprise in advance in the partnership contract to establish the enterprise, by specifying the expiry time of the partnership or other causes for dissolution. If there is no such agreement made in advance in the partnership contract, the partners may also reach such agreement after some particular events happened.

In general, a partnership enterprise may be required by law to disband in any of the following cases:

(1) Any of the partners dies or withdraws from the partnership unless otherwise agreed upon by the partners;

(2) The partnership enterprise or any of the partners goes into bankruptcy;

(3) An event which makes it unlawful for the business of the partnership enterprise to be carried on happens;

(4) When a partner is found to be of permanently unsound mind, or permanently incapable of performing his part of the partnership contract, or guilty of any conduct being bad to the nature of the business; or when the business of the partnership can only be carried on at a loss, any of the partners may apply to the court for dissolution of the partnership enterprise.

When a partnership enterprise is dissolved, it shall be liquidated by liquidators. All partners may act as liquidators. Alternatively, the partners may designate or entrust one or several partners or third persons to act as liquidators. The liquidators shall handle the following affairs during the process of liquidation:

(1) To sort out the properties of the partnership enterprise;

(2) To handle the pending affairs of the partnership enterprise;

(3) To settle credits and debts;

(4) To distribute the remaining properties after the partnership enterprise repays its debts.

4.2.6   Limited Partnership Enterprise   有限合伙企业

A limited partnership is formed by general partners who bear unlimited liabilities for the partnership's debts and limited partners who bear limited liabilities to the extent of their capital contributions. In the continental law jurisdictions, limited partnership had another name of dormant partnership[12] and later evolved into a special company acquiring the legal status of juridical person.

In 1807, France first made legal provisions on limited partnership. Later, most western countries, such as the UK, the US, acknowledged the limited partnership to be one of the types of partnership that is without the status of juridical person.

In a limited partnership, the general partners have the similar rights and liabilities to those in a general partnership. As for limited partners, the main rights and liabilities of them are as follows:

(1) The limited partners may not take part in the management of the partnership enterprise and their conducts are not enforceable to the partnership;

(2) The name of any limited partner is not to be contained in the name of the partnership or else he shall assume the unlimited liabilities for the partnership's debts;

(3) The death or bankruptcy, or withdrawal of any limited partner may not affect the existence of the partnership;

(4) The limited partners may not notify to dissolve the partnership enterprise;

(5) The limited partners have the right to consult the account books of the partnership.

Compared with a general partnership, the establishment of a limited partnership is more complicated. Most countries require a limited partnership enterprise to register with the relevant authoritative agency, and submit the partnership contract. A contract to form a limited partnership shall have all the essential elements of general partnership contract and particularly indicate that it is a limited partnership and show the names of the limited partners.

Reading Material

Forms of Business Organizations in Common Law Countries

The law of business organizations originally derived from the common law of England, but has evolved significantly in the 20th Century.

In common law countries today, the most commonly addressed forms are sole proprietorships, partnerships (sometimes called "general partnerships"), limited partnerships (LP), limited liability partnerships (LLP), Corporations (Inc., Co., Corp.), limited liability company (LLC), not-for-profit corporations.

The organization most often referenced by the word "corporation" is a public or publicly traded company whose shares are traded on a public stock exchange. Most of the largest businesses in the world are publicly traded companies. However, the majority of corporations are said to be closely held, privately held or close corporations, meaning that no ready market exists for the trading of shares. Many such corporations are owned and managed by a small group of businesspeople or companies, although the size of such a corporation can be as vast as the largest public corporations.

There are other less commonly addressed business forms in common law counties, including the limited liability limited partnership (LLLP), the Series LLC, and the limited company (LC). Other types of business organizations, such as cooperatives, credit unions and publicly owned enterprises, can be established with purposes that parallel, supersede, or even replace the profit maximization mandate of business corporations.

4.3　Company Law
公司法

4.3.1　An Overview of Company　公司概述

1. Definition and features of company

A company (corporation)[13] is a separate legal entity established in accordance with the legal procedures and for the purpose of conducting a business for profit.

A company has the following legal features.

1) Aiming to make profit

The primary aim of a company is to make profit by conducting its business and increase the assets of it. This important feature makes a company distinct from those nonprofit legal entities, such as administrative departments and public welfare organizations[14].

2) Separate juridical person

A company is a separate juridical person. It enjoys most of the rights and responsibilities that a natural person possesses; that is, a company has the right to enter into contracts, loan and borrow money, sue and be sued, hire employees, own assets and pay taxes. A company's property and operation is separate from its owners and the death or bankruptcy of its owners will not affect its continuity of existence.

3) Relatively complicated procedures for incorporation

Most countries make strict legal requirements on the formation of a company. Normally complicated procedures need to be fulfilled for the incorporation of a company and most countries require companies to be registered with the administrative authority.

2. Types of companies

There are various types of companies that can be formed in different jurisdictions and each country may have its own categories of companies. Typically, at present, the limited liability company and the stock limited company[15] are the two major types of companies in most countries.

1) Limited liability company

A limited liability company is a company formed for the purpose of conducting a business for profit by natural or legal persons who shall make a capital contribution and who shall be liable for the debts or obligations of the company to the extent of their respective capital contributions.

Most countries make limitation on the maximal number of the shareholders of a limited liability company and interdict such a company issuing shares or bonds publicly. Moreover, the shareholders of a limited liability company may not transfer their shares without the consent of statutory quorum of shareholders and other shareholders have the preemptive right of purchase.

Since there are different categories of companies in different jurisdictions, some countries have companies with similar features to but different names from the limited liability company. For example, the private company in the UK and the closely held company in the US.

2) Stock limited company

A stock limited company is a company formed for the purpose of conducting a business for profit by natural or legal persons who assume limited liabilities for the debts or obligations of the company and the capital of the company shall be evenly divided into shares of equal value.

Most counties make limitation on the minimal number of the shareholders of a stock limited company and allow it to issue shares publicly. All the shareholders take limited liabilities for the debts or obligations of the company to the extent of their respective shareholdings. The shareholders may transfer their shares at will in accordance with the law.

In normal cases, a stock limited company shall have a board of directors[16] and a general manager appointed by the board. The board shall annually make financial reports and statements to the administrative authority, the shareholders and even the public.

A stock limited company may be called a listed company[17] when its shares are traded on at least one stock exchange.

4.3.2 Stock Limited Company 股份有限公司

1. Formation of a stock limited company

Every country may have different requirements on formation of a stock limited company. Typically, there shall be some promoters[18] who establish the corporate constitution[19] and subscribe for capital stocks. Then the establishment meeting shall be held and the initial members of management shall be elected at the meeting. Thus the stock limited company may be legally formed after registration with and approval by the relevant administrative authority.

1) Promoter

The promoters, also called sponsors, refer to some persons or entities who take active steps in the formation, organization, or financing of a stock limited company. Most countries may fix the minimal number of the promoters.

The Company Law of the PRC provides that there shall be at least 2 but no more than 200 promoters to establish a stock limited company and half of whom shall be domiciled in China.

2) Corporate constitution

In almost every jurisdiction in the world, a company is required to have a corporate constitution, which defines the existence of the company and regulates the structure and control of the company.

By convention, most common law jurisdictions divide the corporate constitution into two separate documents: the Memorandum of Association and the Articles of Association[20]. The Memorandum of Association is the primary document, and will generally regulate the company's activities with the outside world, such as the company's objects and powers and specify the authorized share capital of the company. The Articles of Association is the secondary document, and will generally regulate the company's internal affairs and management, such as procedures for board meetings, dividend entitlements, etc.

In continental law jurisdictions, the company's constitution is normally consolidated into a single document, often called the company charter.

3) Establishment

A stock limited company may be established either by sponsorship or public share offer[21].

Establishment by sponsorship means establishment of the company through subscription by the sponsors (promoters) for all the shares to be issued by the company.

Establishment by public share offer means establishment of the company through subscription by sponsors for part of the shares to be issued by the company, and public or targeted placement of the remaining shares. The proportion of the shares subscribed for by the sponsors to the total shares of the company is definitely prescribed in most jurisdictions. In China, the proportion is required by the company law to be no less than 35%.

At present, in western countries, the most popular way to establish a stock limited company is by sponsorship because of its relatively simple procedures. A few countries, such as Germany, even provide to establish a stock limited company only by sponsorship. The Chinese company law allows establishment of a stock limited company either by sponsorship or public share offer.

4) Minimum amount of capital

The total number of issued shares in a stock limited company is said to represent its capital. Many jurisdictions regulate the minimum amount of capital which a stock limited company may have, although some countries only prescribe minimum amounts of capital for companies engaging in certain types of business (e. g. banking, insurance). Generally speaking, the continental law countries make stricter regulations on minimum amounts of capital than the common law countries.

According to the article 81 of the Company Law of the PRC, the minimum amount of the registered capital of a stock limited company in China shall be RMB 5,000,000.

5) Initial registration

Most jurisdictions require stock limited companies to register with the company registration authority. Typically, the board of directors elected at the establishment meeting shall apply for initial registration by submitting to the registration authority certain documents required by law. After approving such an application, the registration authority may issue the registration certificate to the company and at the same date the company is formally established and acquires the status of a legal person.

2. Corporate capital of a stock limited company

1) Share capital[22]

Corporate capital, also known as a company's equity, refers to the total capital distributed by the shareholders on formation according to the corporate constitution. The corporate capital of a stock limited company is raised by issuing shares and usually called share capital.

Many jurisdictions fix the minimum amount of capital which a company may have, and also regulate the maintenance of capital, and prevent companies returning funds to shareholders by way of distribution because this might leave the company financially exposed.

As for particular provisions on share capital, there are two different systems in the present world: authorized capital system and statutory capital system[23].

● Authorized capital system

Many common law countries adopt authorized capital systems. Under such systems, there are two types of share capital of a stock limited company: authorized capital and issued capital[24].

The authorized capital is the maximum amount of share capital that the company is authorized by its corporate constitution to issue to shareholders. Part of the authorized capital can remain unissued on formation. So the authorized capital is also called nominal capital.

The part of the authorized capital which has been issued to shareholders is referred to as the issued capital of the company.

The authorized capital system facilitates the formation of a stock limited company and is popular in most western countries.

● Statutory capital system

Some continental law countries strictly require the amount of share capital of a stock limited company authorized in its corporate constitution to be totally subscribed by shareholders before its formation.

Since such strict requirements may slow down the formation of a stock limited company, in recent decades, more and more continental law countries amend their company laws and make new provisions similar to those under authorized capital system.

2）Shares

The capital of a stock limited company shall be evenly divided into shares of equal value and every one share represents a unit of capital and a share of ownership in the company. Normally, shares of a company are represented by share certificates that are issued by the company certifying the share held by a shareholder. A share certificate typically contains the following major items: the name of the company, the date of registration and formation, the par value per share, the class and number of shares represented, the serial number of the share certificate.

Reading Material

Share & Stock

In financial markets, a share is a unit of account for various financial instruments including stocks, mutual funds and etc.

In British English, use of the word "shares" in the plural to refer to stock is so common that it almost replaces the word "stock" itself. In American English, the plural "stocks" is widely used instead of "shares" to refer to the stock (or perhaps originally stock certificates) of a company.

A share is one of a finite number of equal portions in the capital of a company, entitling the shareholder to a proportion of distributed, non-reinvested profits known as dividends, and to a portion of the value of the company in case of liquidation. Shares can be voting or non-voting, meaning they either do or do not carry the right to vote on the board of directors and corporate policy. Whether this right exists often affects the value of the share.

By different criteria, shares (or stocks) of a stock limited company may be divided into different categories as follows.

- Common stock & preferred stock[25]

Common stock typically carries voting rights that can be exercised in corporate decisions. Preferred stock differs from common stock in that it typically does not carry voting rights but has a fixed rate that entitles the shareholders to receive a certain proportion of dividend payments before any dividends can be distributed to other shareholders. In case of liquidation, the preferred stock holders get reimbursement prior to the common stock holders.

Preferred stocks may convertible. A convertible preferred stock is a preferred stock that includes an option for the holder to convert the preferred shares into a fixed number of common shares, usually anytime after a predetermined date.

Although there is a great deal of commonality between the stocks of different companies, each new issue of stocks may have legal clauses attached to it that make it dynamically different from general cases. For instance, some common stocks may be issued without the typical voting rights being included, or some shares may have special rights unique to them and issued only to certain parties.

- Par value stock & non par value stock[26]

Most stocks of a company are par value stocks that have par value specified in the stock certificates.

The issuing price per share of such stocks may be at par value, or above par value, but may not be below par value.

By contrast, non par value stocks refer to those stocks without par value per share defined in the stock certificates. At present, only a few countries, such as the US, Japan and Luxemburg, allow the issuance of non par value stocks under strict control and regulation. The Chinese company law interdicts the issuance of non par value stocks.

- Registered stock & bearer stock[27]

Registered stocks refer to the stocks with the names of the shareholders on the stock certificates while bearer stocks are those stocks without the names of the shareholders on the certificates.

Transfer of registered stocks shall be effected by the shareholder's endorsement on the share certificates. Bearer stocks may be transferred just by delivering the stock certificates to the transferee.

According to the Chinese company law, stocks issued by the company to its sponsors or legal persons shall be registered stocks with the names of such sponsors or legal persons on the stock certificates.

3) Corporate bond

A corporate bond is a debt security issued by a company, through which the company borrows money from the public. Many countries make strict legal provision on the issuer and the issuance of corporate bonds. According to the Chinese company law, the issue of corporate bonds shall be applied to the relevant department authorized by the State Council and meet the requirements set forth by the Chinese securities law.

There are two major types of corporate bond: secured corporate bonds and unsecured corporate bonds[28]. A secured corporate bond is a corporate bond whose issuing company pledges some or all his assets as collateral for the principal and interest payments. On the contrary, an unsecured corporate bond is not collateralized by any specified assets but by the credit of the company.

Like stocks, corporate bonds may be registered or bearer bonds and respectively transferred by endorsement or delivery. In addition, some companies may issue convertible corporate bonds[29] that can be exchanged, at the option of the holder, for a specific number of shares of the company's stock.

Stocks and corporate bonds are the two major instruments for companies to raise money. However, there are important differences between the two instruments.

(1) Stock holders may take part in the management of the company; corporate bonds holders are creditors of the company and not entitled to participate in the management of the company.

(2) Stock is a perpetual investment and the money subscribed for stocks can not be repaid; corporate bonds are debts and the principal shall be repaid on the expiry date.

(3) Most stocks (common stocks) have no fixed rates and the amount of dividends depend upon the profit of the company; corporate bonds have fixed interest rate and the fixed interest shall be paid to holders no matter whether the company makes a profit or not.

(4) Corporate bond holders shall get reimbursement prior to stock holders when the company is dissolved and liquidated.

3. Organizational structure of a stock limited company

In modern economy, a stock limited company has three major organs: general meeting of shareholders[30], board of directors and board of supervisors[31].

1) General meeting of shareholders

The general meeting of shareholders composed of all shareholders is the company's organ of supreme authority. The general meeting of shareholders regularly holds an annual meeting each year but an interim general meeting of shareholders[32] may be held irregularly under particular circumstances.

The shareholders meeting shall exercise the following functions and powers:

(1) To decide on the business policy and investment plan of the company;

(2) To elect and recall directors and supervisors;

(3) To examine and approve reports of the boards of directors and supervisors;

(4) To examine and approve the annual financial budget plan and final accounts plan of the company;

(5) To examine and approve plans for dividends distribution of the company;

(6) To adopt resolutions on the increase or reduction of the registered capital of the company;

(7) To adopt resolutions on the issuance of company bonds;

(8) To adopt resolutions on matters such as the merger, division, transformation, dissolution and liquidation of the company;

(9) To amend the corporate constitution of the company;

(10) Other functions and powers provided for in the corporate constitution.

In most jurisdictions, when a shareholder attends the general meeting of shareholders, each share he holds is entitled to one vote. A resolution adopted by the general meeting of shareholders requires affirmative votes by a majority of the votes held by shareholders attending the meeting. However the resolution with regards to amendment to the corporate constitution, increase or decrease of registered capital, merger, division or dissolution of the company or change of the form of the company requires affirmative votes by at least two-thirds of the votes held by shareholders attending the meeting.

2) Board of directors

A stock limited company must have a board of directors elected by the general meeting of shareholders. In China, the number of directors is required by law to be 5 to 19.

The board of directors is accountable to the general meeting of shareholders and shall exercise the following functions:

(1) Being responsible for convening shareholders meetings and presenting reports thereto;

(2) Implementing resolutions adopted by the shareholders meeting;

(3) Determining the company's operational plans and investment programs;

(4) Preparing annual financial budget plans and final accounting plans of the company;

(5) Preparing profit distribution plans and plans to cover company losses;

(6) Preparing plans for increasing or reducing registered capital of the company or issuing company bonds;

(7) Drafting plans for merger, division, change of corporate form or dissolution of the company;

(8) Determining the organizational structure of the company's internal management;

(9) Appointing or removing the general manager of the company, appointing or removing, upon the general manager's recommendation, deputy managers of the company and the officer in charge of finance, and determining the remuneration for those managers and officers;

(10) Formulating the basic management system of the company;

（11）Other functions stipulated by the corporate constitution.

3) Board of supervisors

In a stock limited company, the board of directors has many powers and these powers may be misused. In order to supervise and restrict the acts of the board of directors, some countries (such as Germany) require the stock limited company to set up a board of supervisors. In other countries, such as the US and the UK, a stock limited company need not have a board of supervisors; whereas in France a stock limited company may set up a board of supervisors in accordance with the corporate constitution.

Generally, the board of supervisors may have the following authorities:

（1）Reviewing the financial affairs of the company;

（2）Monitoring the acts of the directors or the senior officers of the company in the course of performance of their duties;

（3）Requiring the directors or the senior officers to make rectification when any act thereof causes harm to the interests of the company;

（4）Proposing for interim general meetings of shareholders;

（5）Attending as a nonvoting delegate in meetings of the board of directors.

Chinese company law provides that a stock limited company shall have a board of supervisors, which shall be composed of not fewer than 3 members and any director or senior officer of the company may not serve concurrently as a supervisor.

4. Dividends and accumulation fund[33]

Dividends are payments made by a company to its shareholders. By law, dividends must be paid from profits and may not be paid from a company's capital. For a stock limited company, a dividend is allocated as a fixed amount per share and a shareholder receives a dividend in proportion to their shareholding, unless otherwise stipulated in the corporate constitution.

Most stock limited companies pay the remainder of the profit to the shareholders as dividends, after having covered its losses and made allocation to the accumulation fund. The accumulation fund is an account set aside by the company in accordance with law and the corporate constitution to meet any unexpected costs that may arise in the future as well as the future costs of upkeep.

Typically, there are two major types of accumulation fund: statutory accumulation fund and discretionary accumulation fund[34]. Statutory accumulation fund is the accumulation fund set aside by law while the latter is set aside according to the corporate constitution or the resolution of the general meeting of the shareholders.

In light of the article 167 of the Chinese company law, a stock limited company shall allocate 10% of its current year aftertax profit to its statutory accumulation fund and such an allocation may be waived once the total amount of the fund therein exceeds 50% of the company's registered capital. However, in some western countries, such as Germany and France, the above two proportions provided for by law are much lower and respectively 5% and 10%.

5. Merger and dissolution

1) Merger

Merger refers to the combination of two or more companies. Mergers may be classified into merger by absorption and merger by consolidation[35]. One company absorbing another company is merger by absorption, and the company being absorbed shall be dissolved. Merger of two or more companies through establishment of a new company is a consolidation, and all the companies being consolidated shall be dissolved.

The merger of companies shall be resolved by the general meeting of shareholders and the companies shall implement a merger agreement reached by them. The companies shall notify their creditors the merger resolutions and the creditors are entitled to claim full payment of the debts of the companies or require the provision of appropriate assurances.

Once the companies are merged, the creditor's rights and debtor's liabilities of the merged companies shall be assumed by the surviving company or the newly formed company after merger.

2) Dissolution

In general, a company may be dissolved for any one of the following reasons:

(1) The term of operation prescribed in the corporate constitution has expired, or any other cause for dissolution prescribed in the corporate constitution has occurred;

(2) The general meeting of shareholders has adopted a resolution for dissolution;

(3) Dissolution is required due to merger or division of the company;

(4) The business license of the company is revoked by law, or the company is ordered by the court or the relevant authority to terminate or cancelled.

The assets of the company shall be liquidated after the company is dissolved. The liquidator may be the directors of the company, or be appointed by the general meeting of shareholders or the court. In most jurisdictions, a liquidator's powers are defined by law.

Chinese company law defines the powers of a liquidator as follows:

(1) Identifying the company's assets, and preparing a balance sheet and a listing of assets respectively;

(2) Notifying creditors through notice or public announcement;

(3) Handling the company's ongoing businesses which are related to liquidation;

(4) Making full payment of taxes owed and the taxes incurred during liquidation;

(5) Identifying the company's creditor's rights and debtor's liabilities;

(6) Disposing of the remaining assets after full payment of the company's debts;

(7) Participating in civil actions on behalf of the company.

Upon completion of a company's liquidation, the liquidator shall prepare a liquidating report, which shall be submitted to the general meeting of shareholders or the relevant authority for ratification. After the liquidating report being ratified, the liquidator shall submit the report to the company registration authority to strike off the register of the company, and make a public announcement of the company's termination.

Group Discussion ▶▶▶

1. Which form of business organization do you think is most important?
2. Talk about a partnership enterprise known to you.
3. Discuss the advantages and disadvantages of a partnership.

4. State the important features of a company.
5. Say something about the stock limited companies in China.
6. Compare stocks and corporate bonds.

NOTES ▶▶▶

1　Attorney General　（美国）州检察长

2　individual proprietorship　个人企业，个人独资企业，独资经营企业（亦用 sole proprietorship）

3　unlimited liability　无限责任

4　civil partnership　民事合伙；commercial partnership　商业合伙，商事合伙

5　Partnership Act 1890　（英国）《1890 年合伙法》

6　Uniform Partnership Act　（美国）《统一合伙法》（常缩写为 UPA）

7　general partnership　普通合伙；limited partnership　有限合伙

8　joint and several liability　连带责任，共同责任

9　special general partnership　特殊的普通合伙

10　limited liability partnership（LLP）　有限责任合伙

11　bona fide　善意的

12　dormant partnership　隐名合伙（在大陆法国家，"有限合伙"被称为"隐名合伙"，后来发展成为大陆法系所特有的"两合公司"，因此"有限合伙"与"两合公司"的英文均为 limited partnership）

13　company（corporation）　公司（英国英语多用 company，美国英语多用 corporation，corporation 还有"法人"的意思；"公司法"英国英语多用 company law；美国英语多用 corporate law，有时也用 corporation law）

14　public welfare organization　公益组织

15　limited liability company　有限责任公司；stock limited company　股份有限公司

16　board of directors　董事会

17　listed company　上市公司

18　promoter　发起人（有时也用 founder 或 sponsor）

19　corporate constitution　公司章程（亦用 company charter）

20　Memorandum of Association　（英国英语）公司组织大纲（美国英语用 Articles of Incorporation）；Articles of Association　（英国英语）公司内部细则（美国英语用 Bylaws）

21　establishment by sponsorship　发起设立；establishment by public share offer　募集设立

22　share capital　（英国英语）股份资本，股本（即：股份有限公司的公司资本，美国英语多用 capital stock；"股份"一词在英国英语里多用 shares，在美国英语里多用 stocks）

23　authorized capital system　授权资本制；statutory capital system　法定资本制

24　authorized capital　授权资本；issued capital　发行资本

25　common stock　普通股；preferred stock　优先股

26　par value stock　有票面金额股；non par value stock　无票面金额股

27　registered stock　记名股；bearer stock　无记名股

28　secured corporate bond　担保公司债；unsecured corporate bond　无担保公司债

29　convertible corporate bond　可转换公司债

30 general meeting of shareholders 股东大会

31 board of supervisors 监事会

32 interim general meeting of shareholders 临时股东大会

33 accumulation fund 公积金（亦用 reserve fund）

34 statutory accumulation fund 法定公积金；discretionary accumulation fund 任意公积金

35 merger by absorption 吸收合并；merger by consolidation 新设合并

Dodge v. Ford Motor Company
道奇诉福特公司案

Dodge v. Ford Motor Company (*1919*), was a famous case in which the Michigan Supreme Court held that Henry Ford owed a duty to the shareholders of the Ford Motor Company to operate his business for profitable purposes as opposed to charitable purposes.

By 1916, the Ford Motor Company had accumulated a capital surplus of $60 million. The price of the Model T, Ford's mainstay product, had been successively cut over the years while the cost of the workers had dramatically, and quite publicly, increased. The company's president and majority stockholder, Henry Ford, sought to end special dividends for shareholders in favor of massive investments in new plants that would enable Ford to dramatically grow the output of production, and numbers of people employed at his plants, while continuing to cut the costs and prices of his cars. In public defense of this strategy, Ford declared: "My ambition is to employ still more men, to spread the benefits of this industrial system to the greatest possible number, to help them build up their lives and their homes. To do this we are putting the greatest share of our profits back in the business." While Ford may have believed that such a strategy might be in the long-term benefit of the company, he told his fellow shareholders that the value of this strategy to them was not a primary consideration in his plans. The minority shareholders objected to this strategy, demanding that Ford stop reducing his prices when they could barely fill orders for cars and to continue to pay out special dividends from the capital surplus in lieu of his proposed plant investments. Two brothers, John Francis Dodge and Horace Elgin Dodge, who owned 10% of the company, among the largest shareholders next to Ford, brought suit to compel the directors to declare a special dividend of not less than 75% of the accumulated cash surplus. The court ordered the declaration of a dividend of $19 million. Defendants appealed.

The Michigan Supreme Court held that a business corporation is organized primarily for the profit of the stockholders, as opposed to the community or its employees. The discretion of the directors is to be exercised in the choice of means to attain that end, and does not extend to the reduction of profits or the nondistribution of profits among stockholders in order to benefit the public, making the profits of the stockholders incidental thereto. Because this company was in business for profit, Ford could not turn it into a charity. This was compared to a spoliation of the company's assets. The Court therefore upheld the order of the trial court requiring that directors declare an extra dividend of $19 million.

Piercing the Corporate Veil
揭开公司面纱

The corporate law concept of piercing (lifting) the corporate veil describes a legal decision where a shareholder or director of a corporation is held liable for the debts or liabilities of the corporation despite the general principle that shareholders are immune from suits in contract or tort that otherwise would hold only the corporation liable. Sometimes, in practice, it may be extended to such an extent that the shareholders may be considered to have the same rights and obligations with his corporation.

This doctrine is also known as "Lifting the veil of incorporation" and plays an important role in the common law jurisdictions.

The following judicial precedents at common law are examples of piercing the corporate veil.

In *Gilford Motor Company Ltd v. Horne* (1933), Mr. Horne, a former employee who was bound by a covenant not to solicit customers from his former employers set up a company to do so. He argued that while he was bound by the covenant the company was not. The court found that the company was merely a front for Mr. Horne and issued an injunction against him.

In *Jones v. Lipman* (1962), Mr. Lipman had entered into a contract with Mr. Jones for the sale of land. Mr. Lipman then changed his mind and did not want to complete the sale. He formed a company in order to avoid the transaction and conveyed the land to it instead. He then claimed he no longer owned the land and could not comply with the contract. The judge found the company was but a front for Mr. Lipman and granted an order for specific performance.

In *Catamaran Cruises Ltd.* (*abbreviated as CCL*) *v. Williams* (1994), Williams was employed by CCL. Williams set up a company and CCL then subcontracted with this company, paying the company Williams's wages gross of tax. Williams worked and had the same benefits as all other employees of CCL. CCL ended their contract with Williams's company, but the courts held that this was the same as dismissing Williams directly, and Williams was able to sue for unfair dismissal (however, Williams lost this case, since the dismissal was held to be fair).

The Case Not Applied to the Rule of Piercing the Corporate Veil
没有应用揭开公司面纱原则的案例

Carlton owned and ran a cab company in which he set up ten separate corporations, each holding the minimum amount of liability insurance of $10,000, in which he was the primary stockholder. Though the companies were separate legal entities, they were run by Carlton in unison. Each corporation just owned one or two cabs. When one of his cabs negligently injured a pedestrian, Walkovszky, the plaintiff could only sue one of the subsidiary companies that contained a very limited amount of assets.

The issue before the Court was whether Carlton could be personally liable for the injury to a pedestrian on account of attempting to "defraud the members of the general public".

Finally, New York Court of Appeals held that Carlton was not personally liable. If the corporation was run purely for personal ends and not for the benefit of the corporation then there would be a basis for making the shareholder liable, however, this is not the case here. A corporation with a minimum amount of assets is a valid one and cannot be ignored.

However, Justice Keating, in dissent, said that Carlton should be liable. The corporation was intentionally undercapitalized in order to avoid liability, which is a clear abuse of the corporate entity. The interests of the state in protection of victims of negligence is a sufficient basis to pierce the corporate veil. He held that "a participating shareholder of a corporation vested with a public interest, organized with capital insufficient to meet liabilities which are certain to arise in the ordinary course of the corporation's business, may be held personally responsible for such liabilities." This "insufficient capitalization" rationale has not been widely persuasive with courts, perhaps due to a fear that it would chill entrepreneurial activity.

Not long after the decision, the state increased the minimum amount of liability insurance required by a corporation.

Negotiable Instrument Law
票据法

Learning Objectives

☑ To learn the definition and legal principles of negotiable instruments
☑ To know about the important international conventions on negotiable instruments
☑ To understand the important legal provisions on the acts of bill of exchange
☑ To learn the important provisions on promissory note and check

 Opening Vignette

The Meaning of Negotiable Instruments

In modern business, transactions involving huge sums of money take place everyday. It is quite inconvenient as well as risky for either party to make and receive payments in cash. Therefore, it is a common practice for businessmen to make use of certain documents as means of making payment. Some of these documents are called negotiable instruments[1].

To understand the meaning of negotiable instruments, let us take a few examples of day-to-day business transactions.

Suppose A, a shoes manufacturer has sold shoes to B for $10,000 on three months credit. To be sure that B will pay the money after three months, A may write an order addressed to B that he is to pay after three months, for value of goods received by him ($10,000). Then A or anyone holding the order may present it to B for payment. This written document has to be signed by B to show his acceptance of the order. Now, A can hold the document with him for three months and on the due date can collect the money from B. He can also use it for meeting different business transactions. For instance, after a month, if required, he can borrow money from C for a period of two months and pass on this document to C. He has to write on the back of the document an instruction to B to pay money to C, and sign it. Now C becomes the owner of this document and he can claim money from B on the due date. C, if required, can further pass on the document to D after instructing and signing on the back of the document. This passing on process may continue further till the final payment is made.

In the above example, B who has bought shoes worth $10,000 can also give an undertaking stating that after three month he will pay the amount to A. Now A can retain that document with himself till the end of three months or pass it on to others for meeting certain business obligation (like with C, as discussed above) before the expiry of that three months time period.

You must have heard about a cheque. What is it? It is a document issued to a bank that entitles the person whose name it bears to claim the amount mentioned in the cheque. If he wants, he can transfer it in favor of another person. For example, if A issues a cheque worth $5,000 in favor of B, then B can claim $5,000 from the bank, or he can transfer it to C to meet any business obligation, like paying back a loan that he might have taken from C. Once he does it, C gets a right to $5,000 and he can transfer it to D, if required. Such transfers may continue till the payment is finally made to somebody.

In the above examples, we find that there are certain documents used for payment in business transactions and are transferred freely from one person to another. Such documents are called negotiable instruments. Thus, we can say a negotiable instrument is a transferable document, where negotiable means transferable and instrument means document.

In a word, negotiable instruments are documents meant for making payments, the ownership of which can be transferred from one person to another many times before the final payment is made. The document mentioned in the first example is a bill of exchange and that in the second is a promissory note, and a cheque[2], apparently, is described in the third example. They are the three classifications of negotiable instruments most commonly used in international business.

 Warm-up Questions

1. Please give your own definition of negotiable instruments.
2. Why are negotiable instruments popular in business?
3. Try to define the bill of exchange, promissory note and cheque.

5.1　An Intruduction to Negotiable Instrument
票据概述

5.1.1　Definition of Negotiable Instrument　票据的概念

A negotiable instrument, is a written promise or order signed by the maker to pay a specified sum of money on demand or at a fixed future time to the person named on the instrument or to the bearer. At law, a negotiable instrument is a document representing a particular civil right of property and this right will be transferred simultaneously when the instrument is negotiated.

In today's international business, negotiable instruments are widely used in noncash settlement. In some developed countries, the domestic trade also tends to gradually replace the paper currency with negotiable instruments for settlement. For example, in the US, about 85% of the commercial transactions use negotiable instruments instead of money to make payment. It is undoubted that negotiable instruments play an increasingly important role in modern business.

5.1.2   Legal Principles of Negotiable Instrument   票据的法理

In most jurisdictions, the following legal principles of negotiable instrument are recognized.

1. An instrument shall be negotiated promptly and easily

Generally, civil rights of property may be transferred on condition that the debtor has been informed of such a transfer. But the transfer of rights under an instrument is different in this regard. The negotiation of a negotiable instrument, may be effected by, without the prior notice to the debtor, delivery alone or endorsement and delivery. A negotiable instrument may be negotiated many times before the holder claims payment from the debtor to the instrument and the debtor shall not refuse to pay by arguing that he has not got the notice.

This legal principle is established for the purpose of promoting the currency of negotiable instruments.

2. An instrument shall be separated from its underlying relationships

Instrument relationships[3] refer to the relationships between the parties to a negotiable instrument arising out of the acts of the instrument. The underlying relationships of a negotiable instrument are those legal relationships established before the instrument is issued and also known as noninstrument relationships[4].

The underlying relationships of an instrument mainly include the causing relationship of instrument and the funding relationship of instrument[5]. Causing relationship refers to the reasons for the parties to issue or transfer the instrument. For example, the parties may be seller and buyer, or borrower and lender. Funding relationship means how the money represented by the instrument is to be funded and reimburse between the payer and the issuer.

The negotiable instrument itself is separated from the underlying relationships. In other words, the effect of the instrument will not be affected by the underlying relationships. The creditor to an instrument shall claim payment only by holding it, no matter whether its underlying relationships exist or not.

3. An instrument shall emphasize on protecting the bona fide third parties

In most countries, the negotiable instrument laws place much emphasis on protecting the bona fide third parties. A bona fide transferee of a negotiable instrument who exchanged something of value may hold better title than the prior holder[6] and his title is not subject to the prior holder's defective title[7]. This is a significant distinction from the assignment of obligatory rights in civil law.

For example, if A obtained an instrument from B lawfully but he does not know that B stole this instrument from C, A may be entitled all the rights derived from the instrument and C can not ask A to return it.

4. A negotiable instrument is a formal security[8]

A negotiable instrument is a formal document and shall meet legal requirements on the form. The negotiable instrument laws of most countries make detailed provisions on the form of a negotiable instrument and an instrument may be considered to be invalid if it does not conform to such requirements strictly.

Being legally formal helps to make clear the rights and debts of the parties and facilitates the use and negotiation of negotiable instruments.

5.1.3 Types of Negotiable Instrument 票据的种类

There are three types of negotiable instruments: bill of exchange, promissory note and cheque.

A bill of exchange and a cheque are negotiable instruments signed by the drawer, committing the drawee to pay a sum of money at due time unconditionally. So they are all instruments on commission. But a cheque differs from a bill of exchange in that the drawee of a cheque must be a bank.

A promissory note, as its name indicates, is an instrument on promise, and signed by the drawer to promise to pay a sum of money at due time unconditionally by himself.

However, the three types of negotiable instruments are not recognized unanimously in all countries. In Germany and France, negotiable instruments include only bills of exchange and promissory notes, and cheques are governed by separate regulation. In the UK and the US, the cheques are classified under the bill of exchange and regarded as a special type of bill of exchange.

5.1.4 Functions of Negotiable Instrument 票据的作用

1. As a means of payment

In the beginning of international trade, payments were usually made in cash (gold or silver) and it is very inconvenient, expensive and risky for the merchants to ship great deals of gold or silver across national boundaries. From the13[th] century A. D. , bills of exchange were created, gradually taking the place of cash as a means of international payments. Later, promissory notes and cheques were also emerged, together with the bills of exchange, commonly used for international or domestic payments.

2. As a credit instrument

A bill of exchange in its origin was a device to avoid the transmission of cash from place to place to settle trade debts. A seller may agree to accept deferred payment against the creditworthiness of the buyer by drawing a time bill of exchange[9] on the buyer. Moreover, through the negotiation of an instrument from one party to another, the creditor's right is transferred and the debts between the parties may be set off.

A negotiable instrument may also be used to get loans from the bank or to discount it for money at money market. Time bills and notes may be discounted or rediscounted by a bank or other financial institution. However, it should be stressed that a cheque may not be used as a credit instrument because cheques are all payable at sight.

Reading Material

A Negotiable Instrument Differs from a Contract

A negotiable instrument is not a contract, as contract formation requires an offer and acceptance, and consideration or cause, none of which is an element of a negotiable instrument. Normally, a negotiable instrument is a formal document while a contract is not.

Unlike ordinary contract, the right to the performance of a negotiable instrument is linked to the possession of the document itself (with certain exceptions such as loss or theft). The rights of the payee (or the lawful holder) are better than those provided by ordinary contracts as follows:

- The rights to payment are not subject to set-off, and do not rely on the validity of the underlying contract giving rise to the debt (for example if a cheque was drawn for payment for goods delivered but defective, the drawer is still liable on the cheque);
- No notice needs to be given to any prior party liable on the instrument for transfer of the rights under the instrument by negotiation;
- Transfer free of equities — the lawful holder in due course can hold better title than the party he obtains it from.

5.1.5 The International Conventions on Negotiable Instrument
关于票据的国际公约

Most countries have their own laws governing negotiable instruments. In order to overcome the disparities and uncertainties in negotiable instrument laws among nations, some international conventions were entered into.

1. Geneva Conventions

In the years of 1930 and 1931, more than 30 countries signed 6 conventions on negotiable instruments in Geneva. They are the Convention Providing a Uniform Law for Bills of Exchange and Promissory Notes[10], the Convention on the Settlement of Certain Conflicts of Laws in Connection with Bills of Exchange and Promissory Notes[11], the Convention Providing a Uniform Law for Cheques[12], the Convention on the Settlement of Certain Conflicts of Laws in Connection with Cheques[13], the Convention on the Stamp Laws in Connection with Bills of Exchange and Promissory Notes[14], the Convention on the Stamp Laws in Connection with Cheques[15]. The 6 conventions together are customarily referred to as the Geneva Conventions or Geneva uniform laws on negotiable instruments.

However, most common law countries refused to enter into the Geneva Conventions, because they considered that these conventions were primarily based on continental law.

2. Convention on International Bills of Exchange and International Promissory Notes[16]

In 1988, the Convention on International Bills of Exchange and International Promissory Notes is adopted by the UNCITRAL[17] for the purpose of eliminating the differences between continental law and common law.

According to the provisions of this convention, it shall come into force after 10 countries have ratified or accessed it. Although this convention has not become effective up to now, it does have considerable influence on the negotiable instrument laws of many countries.

5.2 Bill of Exchange
汇票

5.2.1 Basic Points 基本要点

1. Definition of a bill of exchange

As defined in the Negotiable Instruments Law of the PRC, a bill of exchange is a bill signed by the drawer, requiring the drawee to make unconditional payment in the fixed amount at sight of the bill or at a fixed date to the payee or the holder.

2. Parties to a bill of exchange

Besides the three basic parties specified on the bill (drawer, drawee and payee), there are other parties who may participate in transactions of a bill of exchange, such as endorser, endorsee, holder and guarantor[18].

1) Drawer

The drawer, may be also referred to as an issuer, is the party who draws and signs a bill of exchange on the drawee and delivers it to the payee. He is a debtor to the bill and bears liability to the payee or holder of it. In the event that the drawee dishonors the bill by nonacceptance or nonpayment, the drawer must redeem and pay the bill. However, when the bill is accepted, his liability becomes secondary.

2) Drawee

The drawee, or the payer of the bill of exchange, is the party on whom the bill is drawn and to effect payment to the payee.

However, when the bills is presented to him, the drawee can make a choice whether to honor or dishonor it because he can not prevent any party to whom he owes no debt from drawing a draft on him. Before the drawee agrees to honor the draft, he is not yet a debtor to the bill; and if he assents to do so, he must make acceptance or payment upon presentation.

For a time bill of exchange, if the drawee assents to honor the bill, he shall accept it by writing words indicating his assent and signing his name on the face of the bill upon presentation. Then he will become the acceptor who is primarily liable on the bill.

3) Payee

The payee refers to the person shown in the bill of exchange to whom the money is payable. He is the first creditor to the bill and the first legal owner of it. He can either demand payment against the bill or transfer the bill to another party. If he transfers the bill, he will become a transferor or endorser who bears debtor's liability to the transferee or endorsee to whom he transfers the bill.

4) Endorser

An endorser is the payee or the holder who signs his name on the back of a draft for the purpose of negotiation. Because the payee is the first holder, he shall be the first endorser if the draft is negotiated. When the payee becomes an endorser, he transforms himself from a creditor to a debtor who bears liability on the draft to the subsequent holders[19] (include the endorsee to whom he transferred the draft). In the process of negotiation of a bill of exchange, there may be the first endorser, the second, the third, the fourth and so on.

5) Endorsee

An endorsee is the party to whom the bill of exchange is transferred. He becomes the new holder of the bill and a creditor to it. An endorsee can also become an endorser if he wishes to transfer the instrument to another party by signing his name on its back. And by doing so, he transforms himself into a debtor. If, as mentioned in the above paragraph, the process of negotiation creates a sequence of endorsers, correspondingly, it will also bring about a series of endorsees.

6) Holder

A holder refers to the party who is in possession of a bill of exchange. A lawful holder (or a holder in due course[20]) is entitled all the rights arising out of the bill and may be the payee or the endorsee. A holder is liable to present the bill for acceptance or for payment within the expiry period of time and is entitled to claim payment against the endorser or the drawer if the bill is dishonored.

7) Guarantor

A guarantor is a third party who guarantees a debtor to the bill of exchange to perform his obligations. Such a debtor may be the drawer, endorser, or acceptor. The liabilities of the guarantor may be the same as those of the debtor guaranteed by him.

3. Contents of a bill of exchange

Although the bills of exchange used in international business are different in contents and forms, most countries require by law that a bill of exchange shall bear certain essential items, such as words denoting "draft", "exchange" or "bill of exchange", commission on unconditional payment, the amount of money fixed, time for payment, name of the payer, name of the payee, date of draft and signature of the drawer. A draft lacking one of the essential items listed above may be deemed invalid.

An example of bill of exchange is illustrated as the Figure 5 – 1. In this example, the bill is drawn on the day of March 1, 2008 by the A Company, Shanghai (the drawer) on Bank of China, Singapore (the drawee), payable to the order of Bank of China, Shanghai (the payee). The bill is payable 60 days after the drawee's sight of it and the amount payable is 100,000 US dollars.

EXCHANGE FOR USD100,000.00   SHANGHAI, CHINA, MARCH 1, 2008

AT 60 DAYS SIGHT PAY TO THE ORDER OF BANK OF CHINA, SHANGHAI THE SUM OF US DOLLARS ONE HUNDRED
THOUSAND ONLY.

TO: BANK OF CHINA,
    SINGAPORE   FOR A COMPANY, SHANGHAI
                                                          (Signature)

Figure 5 – 1   An example of a bill of exchange

5.2.2 Drawing 出票

Drawing of a bill of exchange refers to the act of the drawer to sign a draft and deliver it to the payee. The drawer shall have real authorized payment relations with the payee and have reliable sources of fund to pay the draft amount. By drawing a draft the drawer commits himself to ensure that the draft is to be honored by all means.

When drawing a bill of exchange, the drawer shall put down the essential items on the bill according to the law by which the bill of exchange is governed. According to article 22 of the Negotiable Instruments Law of the PRC, a draft shall bear the following items: Chinese characters denoting "draft"; commission on unconditional payment; the amount of money fixed; name of the payer; name of the payee; date of draft; signature of the drawer.

However, legal provisions on the essential items of a bill of exchange may vary by country.

1. Words denoting "draft", "exchange" or "bill of exchange"

Most continental law countries require a bill of exchange to bear the words denoting "draft", "exchange", or "bill of exchange" in order to distinguish a draft from other types of instrument such as promissory notes or cheques. But the common law countries do not so required.

2. A commission on unconditional payment

The payment of a bill of exchange must be made unconditional at the time of drawing. If the payment instruction is subject to any condition, it is not a bill of exchange. For example, if the payment instruction on the bill is expressed as "Pay to A company or order the sum of five thousand pounds providing the goods they supply are in compliance with the terms of contract", it is an invalid bill.

3. A sum certain in money

The draft amount must be stated explicitly and definitely.

As provided in the Bills of Exchange Act 1882[21] of the UK, the sum payable by a bill is a sum certain, although it was required to be paid with interest, by stated instalments, by stated instalments with a provision that upon default in payment of any instalment the whole shall become due, or according to an indicated rate of exchange or according to a rate of exchange to be ascertained as directed by the bill. Where a bill is expressed to be payable with interest, unless the instrument otherwise provides, interest runs from the date of the bill, and if the bill is undated from the issue thereof. Where the sum payable is expressed in words and also in figures, and there is a discrepancy between the two, the sum denoted by the words is the amount payable.

In light of article 8 of the Negotiable Instruments Law of the PRC, the amount of a negotiable instrument shall be written in both Chinese characters and in numerals and the two shall tally; if the two amounts do not tally the instrument shall be invalid. Additionally, it is a common practice in some countries that whichever amount smaller is to be considered as the amount payable.

As to the draft amount payable by instalments, it is not allowed by the Geneva Conventions and the Chinese bill law.

4. Name of the payer and place of payment

Most countries require the name of the drawee to be stated in a draft clearly. The drawer may draw a draft either on another person or on himself. A draft drawn on the drawer himself may be regarded as a draft or a promissory note in different jurisdictions. Under common law, the holder of such a draft may deem it as a draft or a promissory note at his option.

Typically the drawee shall be one person. But more than one drawees are also allowable. In such cases, any of the drawees shall take the complete liability for payment and the others will be discharged the liability after one of the drawees effects payment.

The place of payment is not an essential item of a draft in most countries. Nevertheless, if the place of payment is specified in the draft, the payment shall be effected in this place. In the UK, the holder may present the draft to the payer for payment in any place wherever he finds him. However, the Geneva Conventions require the place of payment to be stated in a draft and if not, the address shown beside the name of the payer on the draft is considered as the place of payment.

Chinese bill law provides that if a draft does not bear the place of payment, the place of payment shall be the place of business or the residence of the payer or the place where the payer often lives.

5. Name of the payee

According to whom the draft amount is payable to, the drafts may be categorized into two types: bearer draft and order draft[22]. A bearer draft may be a draft expressing that it is payable to bearer or to the order of bearer or otherwise indicating that the person in possession of it is entitled to payment, or stating that it is not payable to an identified person, or even not mentioning anything about the payee. An order draft is a draft expressing that it is payable to an identified person or to the order of an identified person. The bearer drafts can be transferred by delivery alone while the order drafts shall be negotiated by endorsement and delivery.

It should be noted that the Geneva Conventions require the name of the payee to be specified on a draft and do not recognize the bearer drafts in principle. The Chinese bill law also provides that the name of the payee is to be shown on a draft or else it shall be invalid.

Unless a bill of exchange is payable to bearer, the payee must be named with reasonable certainty. A bill may be made payable to two or more payees jointly, or to either of the two payees, or to one or some of several payees alternatively. A bill may also be made payable to the drawer himself. If the payee is a fictitious or nonexisting one, the bill may be treated as payable to bearer.

In practice, there may be a special draft which identifies an exclusive payee. For example: the clause of payee is expressed as: "Pay to David Harrison only" or "Pay to David Harrison not transferable". Such drafts are nonnegotiable and may not be classified into the category of negotiable instruments.

6. Date and place of draft

The date and place of draft respectively refer to the date when and the place where a bill of exchange is formally issued.

The date of a bill of exchange is an item of great significance. It is used to ascertain the reasonable time for presenting the bill for acceptance or payment, and compute the date of payment if the bill is payable after a fixed time from the date. The Geneva Conventions and the Chinese bill law all provide the issuing date as an essential item of a bill of exchange and a bill issued undated shall be deemed to be invalid. In contrast, the common law countries do not consider the date of draft as an essential item, and if a draft is issued undated, any holder may fill therein the true date of issue that he believes in and the draft shall be paid accordingly.

The place of a bill of exchange is necessary to determine the applicable law of international bills. By convention, the law of the place of draft is applied to an international draft. The Geneva Conventions provide that a draft shall bear the place of draft, and if not, the address shown beside the name of the drawer is deemed as the place of draft. Under common law, the place of draft is not essential, and the place of business, residence or the place where the drawer often lives may be considered as the place of draft if a draft does not bear such a place. In this regard, the Chinese bill law has similar provisions to those of common law.

7. Signature of the drawer

A bill of exchange must be signed by the drawer or a person authorized by the drawer. No bill is valid without the signature of the drawer. Forged or unauthorized signature of the drawer makes the bill invalid. After signing the draft, the drawer shall bear the liability for ensuring the acceptance and payment of the draft. If the holder fails to get acceptance or payment, the drawer shall be liable to pay the holder the draft amount and other relevant expenses provided for by law.

In the UK and the US, a drawer may draw a draft without recourse by writing words of such meaning on the draft to relieve himself from the liability for payment to the holder. But under the Geneva Conventions and the Chinese bill law, the drawer shall not be exempted from the liability for payment.

If the draft is drawn by a company, an authorized natural person may sign his name on the behalf of the company. The words "For", "On behalf of", "For and on behalf of" or "Per pro" shall be prefixed to the name of the company and the authorized person's rank in the company may be followed. Here is an example of a signature of a draft drawn by a company:

For ABC Co. , London

(Signature)

John Smith, Manager

8. Maturity

Maturity of a bill of exchange means the date of payment. It is not an essential item and if a draft bears no date of payment it may be deemed as a sight draft. Typically, a sight draft may have a clause of maturity expressed as: "at sight", "on demand", or "upon presentation".

As for a time draft, the maturity shall be stated clearly on the draft in one of the following ways:

(1) Payable at a fixed date, for example: "On Jan. 15, 2010";

(2) Payable at certain time after sight, for example: "At 30 days after sight";

(3) Payable at certain time after the date of draft, for example: "At 2 months after date".

Normally, if a draft is payable at certain time after sight or date of draft, the maturity is counted from the next day after sight or date. For example, a draft payable at 30 days sight, if accepted on May 1, is payable on May 31. If the certain time is specified in month, it means the calendar month, and If no same date exists, the last date of a month will be applied. For example, a draft payable at 2 months after date, if issued on July 31, is payable on Sept. 30. If the maturity date is a nonbusiness day, it may be extended to the succeeding business day.

In addition, the English bill law also allows a draft to be payable at certain time after a specified event. For example: "At 90 days after the date of bill of lading". However this is neither allowed under the Geneva Conventions nor in China.

5.2.3　Endorsement　背书

1. Definition of endorsement

Endorsement of a bill of exchange refers to the act of a holder to sign a draft on the back and deliver it to the endorsee. An endorsement may be made in blank or special, or contain terms making it restrictive. The order drafts shall be transferred by endorsement and delivery. The endorser is the transferor and the endorsee is the transferee.

By endorsement, the endorser transfers the right derived from the draft to the endorsee and takes the liability to the subsequent holders for the acceptance and payment of the draft. If the draft is dishonored, the holder has the right of recourse to claim payment against any endorser who signed his name on the draft as well as the drawer.

2. Types of endorsement

1) Special endorsement and blank endorsement[23]

According to whether the endorsee's name is specified, the endorsement can be divided into special endorsement and blank endorsement.

A special endorsement means that the endorser also specifies the name of the endorsee to whom or to whose order the draft is to be negotiated, in addition to signing his own name on the back of the draft. For example, the endorser wrote "Pay to John Smiths" or "Pay to the order of John Smiths" above his signature.

In contrast with the special endorsement, a blank endorsement (also called general endorsement) means that the endorser only signs his own name. A draft, whether has been endorsed before, becomes payable to bearer when endorsed in blank. On the other hand, a holder may change a blank endorsement into a special endorsement by writing his name above the endorser's signature to make the draft nonpayable to bearer.

Under the Chinese bill law, the bearer draft is not acknowledged and consequently the blank endorsement is not allowed.

2) **Restrictive endorsement**[24]

A restrictive endorsement is an endorsement prohibiting further negotiation of the draft. For example, "Pay to John Smith only" or "Not negotiable" is written above the endorser's signature.

The English bill law interdicts a draft with restrictive endorsement from being negotiated further whereas in the US a restrictive endorsement may not prevent the further negotiation of the draft. The Geneva Conventions and the Chinese bill law allow such a draft to be negotiated further but the endorser who made the restrictive endorsement only bears liability to the endorsee to whom he transferred the draft.

3) **Qualified endorsement**[25]

If the endorser writes "without recourse" or other words of the similar meaning when making an endorsement, it is a qualified endorsement. Such an endorsement is allowed in some countries, such as the US, and the endorser is exempted the liability for payment.

4) **Conditional endorsement**[26]

A conditional endorsement is an endorsement stating a condition to the right of the endorsee to receive payment. In most jurisdictions, such an endorsement is considered to be ineffective and may not affect the right of the endorsee to enforce the draft. The payer may disregard the condition, and payment to the endorsee is valid whether the condition has been fulfilled or not.

5) **Endorsement not for negotiation**

In practice, some endorsements are not made for negotiation, such as endorsement for collection and endorsement of pledge[27].

An endorsement for collection means that the endorser makes the endorsement not to transfer the draft but to request the endorsee collect the draft money for him. Such an endorsement usually shows the words "For collection" or "By procuration". An endorsee of the endorsement for collection may be regarded as the agent of the endorser.

An endorsement of pledge is an endorsement made for the purpose of pledge and usually contains the words "Value in pledge" or "Value in security". The endorser of such an endorsement is a pledger who holds the rights under the draft in pledge and the endorsee is the pledgee who may exercise the rights under the draft in accordance with law.

5.2.4 Presentment 提示

Presentment of a draft refers to the act of the holder to present the draft to the payer and demand for payment or acceptance by the payer. Accordingly, there are two types of presentment: presentment for payment and presentment for acceptance[28].

When a draft is payable after sight, presentment for acceptance is necessary in order to fix the maturity of the draft and it shall be presented for acceptance within a reasonable time. In no other cases the presentment for acceptance is necessary unless otherwise stipulated in the draft or by law. When a draft is payable at sight, it shall be presented for payment within a reasonable time and when not, it shall be presented for payment on the day it falls due. If a holder has failed to make necessary presentation in due time, he loses the right of recourse against the prior endorsers and the drawer, but still retains the right to claim payment from the acceptor.

Under the Geneva Conventions, a draft payable after sight shall be presented for acceptance within 1 year starting from the date of draft and a draft payable at sight shall be presented for payment within 1 year starting from the date of draft. In contrast, the English and American laws do not provided for the particular time limits for presentments but just require a draft to be presented within a reasonable time.

The Chinese bill law provides that a draft payable at a fixed date or at fixed date set after the date of draft shall be presented for acceptance to the payer before the due date of draft. For a draft payable at a fixed time after sight shall be presented for acceptance to the payer within 1 month starting from the date of draft and if the holder has failed to make such presentation within the prescribed time limit, he may lose the right of recourse against the prior holders. Presentation for payment shall be made to the payer within 1 month starting from the date of draft for a draft payable at sight and to the acceptor within 10 days starting from the due date for a draft payable at a future time; if the holder has failed to make such presentation within the time limit, the acceptor or payer may continue to undertake the liability of payment to the holder after he made explanations.

5.2.5 Acceptance 承兑

1. Definition of acceptance

The acceptance of a bill of exchange is the signification by the drawee of his assent to the order of the drawer. An acceptance is invalid unless it is written on the face of the bill and signed by the drawee. In some countries, such as the UK and the US, the mere signature of the drawee without additional words is sufficient. However, the Geneva Conventions and the Chinese bill law require the words "Accepted" or other words of the same meaning to be written on the bill. The bills payable at sight do not need to be accepted.

It is not required by law that all bills nonpayable at sight must be accepted before being presented for payment. Nevertheless, in practice, most holders are readily to present a bill for acceptance unless it bears a clause of "Not for acceptance".

By acceptance the drawee becomes an acceptor who is primarily liable on the bill. The acceptor has a duty to pay for the bill at maturity and if he does not do so after the bill is presented for payment, the holder (or even the drawer) has the right to bring an action against him, and the exercising of such a right may not prejudice the holder's right of recourse against the drawer and the prior holders.

2. Types of acceptance

Acceptance is generally divided into the two types of general acceptance and qualified acceptance[29].

1) General acceptance

A general acceptance is an acceptance by which the acceptor assents without qualification to the order of the drawer. In most cases, an acceptance of a draft is a general acceptance that only contains the signature of the acceptor and, if any, the words "Accepted" or other words of similar meaning.

2) Qualified acceptance

A qualified acceptance is an acceptance with certain qualifications in expressed terms.

In particular, an acceptance is qualified which is:

(1) Conditional — which makes payment by the acceptor dependent on the fulfillment of a condition

therein stated (for example, containing a clause of "Payable on the delivery of the bill of lading");

(2) Partial — an acceptance to pay only part of the amount for which the bill is drawn;

(3) Local — an acceptance to pay only at a particular specified place;

(4) Qualified as to time (for example, containing a clause of "The acceptance is valid for 60 days");

(5) The acceptance of some one or more of the drawees, but not of all (in the case of a draft drawn on more than one drawees).

According to the English bill law, the holder may reject a qualified acceptance and consider it as a refusal to accept; if the holder, without the assents of the prior endorsers and the drawer, choose to take a draft accepted with qualification, the prior endorsers and the drawer may be released from their liabilities on the draft. The Geneva Conventions require an acceptance to be unqualified but allow the partial acceptance. The Chinese bill law provides that there shall be no conditions attached in accepting a draft, or else it shall be regarded as a non-acceptance.

3. Acceptance by intervention[30]

As prescribed in the Bill of Exchange Act 1882 of the UK and the Geneva Conventions, where a bill of exchange has been dishonored by nonacceptance or by other reasons (such as the death or bankruptcy of the drawee) and is not overdue, any person other than the debtor to the bill may, with the consent of the holder, intervene and accept the bill for the purpose of saving the honor of the drawer or an endorser of the bill. This act is known as acceptance by intervention, or acceptance for honor, which shall be written on the bill, and indicate that it is an acceptance for honor and be signed by the acceptor for honor[31]. Where an acceptance for honor does not expressly state for whose honor it is made, it is deemed to be an acceptance for the honor of the drawer.

The acceptor for honor of a bill by accepting it engages that he will, upon due presentment, pay the bill according to the tenor of his acceptance, if it is not paid by the drawee. He is liable to all parties to the bill subsequent to the party for whose honor he has accepted. However, unlike the acceptor, the acceptor for honor is not primarily liable on the bill and he may refuse to pay finally. If he pays the bill on the due date, he may exercise the right of recourse against the party for whose honor he has accepted and all the prior parties liable to that party.

It should be noted that if a bill payable after sight is accepted for honor, its maturity is calculated from the date of the noting for nonacceptance, and not from the date of the acceptance for honor. If a holder consents to an acceptance for honor, he shall not exercise the right of recourse before the maturity date against the party for whose honor the bill has been accepted and the holders subsequent to that party.

5.2.6 Guarantee 保证

Guarantee of a bill of exchange means that a third party other than the debtor to the draft undertakes the liabilities of guaranty for the debt under the draft. Typically, the guarantor shall write the word "Guaranteed" and specify the name of the debtor guaranteed and sign his own name on the bill or allonge. The drawer may be deemed as the debtor guaranteed if there is no name of debtor specified.

The guarantor may make guarantee for a debtor to the draft such as the drawer, endorser or acceptor and his duty on the draft are the same as that of the debtor guaranteed. The holder may firstly make presentation for payment to or exercise the right of recourse against the guarantor. The guarantor bears the liability on the draft to a lawful holder even if the principal debt of the draft becomes invalid, unless the invalidation is resulted from a lack of formality in the draft. After performing his duty, the guarantor transforms himself into a holder of the draft and may exercise the right of recourse against the debtor guaranteed and the parties prior to the said debtor.

The Geneva Conventions and the Chinese bill law make detailed provisions on guarantee of a draft; whereas in most common law countries, guarantee of a draft is mentioned in rare cases.

5.2.7 Payment 付款

1. Definition of payment

Payment of a bill of exchange refers to the act of making payment by the drawee on the due time. Generally, after being paid, the holder is required to sign for payment and write the words "Paid" or other words of similar meaning on the bill and deliver it to the payer. A bill and the debt arising out of it shall be discharged by payment.

2. Time for payment

Normally, a draft payable at sight shall be paid on the day it is presented and a draft payable at a future time shall be paid on the day it falls due. If the day is a nonbusiness day, the payment time shall be extended to the next business day.

The English bill law allow three days of grace to calculate the maturity of drafts payable at a future time. In contrast, no days of grace is permitted under the Geneva Conventions.

3. Payment by intervention[32]

As prescribed in the Bill of Exchange Act 1882 of the UK and the Geneva Conventions, where a bill of exchange has been dishonored for nonpayment, any person other than the debtor to the bill may intervene and pay it for the honor of any party liable thereon. This is an act referred to as payment by intervention, or payment for honor. The drawer may be regarded as the party for whose honor the bill is paid, if the payer for honor[33] has not specified such a party.

If a bill has been paid for honor, all parties subsequent to the party for whose honor it is paid are discharged from liabilities on the bill, but the payer for honor may exercise the right of recourse against the party for whose honor the bill has been paid and all the prior parties liable to that party. If the holder of a bill refuses to receive payment for honor, he may lose his right of recourse against any party who would have been discharged by such payment.

5.2.8 Dishonor and Recourse 拒付与追索

Dishonor of a bill of exchange refers to nonpayment or nonacceptance of the bill. It may results from expressed refusal of the drawee, or the death, bankruptcy or evasion of the drawee.

When a draft is dishonored, the holder may exercise the right of recourse against the endorser, drawer or other debtors to the draft no matter whether it matures or not.

The term recourse is used to signify the right of the holder of a bill of exchange to compel the prior endorsers and the drawer to perform their legal obligations by effecting the payment, if the bill is dishonored by the drawee.

In most jurisdictions, after a draft has been dishonored, unless it contains the clause of "without protest", the holder shall obtain a protest for dishonor[34] made by a notary public or another authorized organ, and also give the notice of dishonor[35] to the drawer and the prior endorsers within a reasonable time. If either of the two acts is not done, all prior parties except the acceptor (if the draft has been accepted) will cease to be liable to the holder. In other words, the holder may not exercise the right of recourse against the prior parties (include the drawer) who do not receive the notice of dishonor.

5.2.9   Forged Signature   伪造签名

A forged or unauthorized signature on a bill of exchange, as a general rule, is a nullity.

According to the English bill law, if the signature of drawer on a bill is forged, such a bill is invalid; however, if it is endorsed or accepted, the endorser or acceptor is liable to the holder. If an endorsement is forged, such an endorsement is invalid and the bill is not considered being negotiated; therefore any party subsequent to the holder whose name was forged has not the right of the bill and shall return the bill to the holder whose name was forged; the payer may not be discharged from liability on the bill if he has paid to a holder subsequent to the holder whose name was forged, unless the drawee is a bank which has paid a bill payable at sight.

The Geneva Conventions differs very much from the English bill law in this regard. The Geneva Conventions provide that a forged signature on a draft is neither valid for the one whose name was forged nor for the one who forged it but it shall not affect the validity of any genuine signature on the draft; Any person who loses the draft is not entitled to require the holder to whom the draft is endorsed to return it, unless the holder is in bad faith or seriously default in obtaining it; any payer who pays the draft on maturity shall be discharged from the liability on the draft unless he is in bad faith or seriously default in performing his obligation and the payer is liable for checking the continuity of the endorsement but not for authenticity of them.

It may be concluded from the above paragraphs that the English bill law tends to protect the real owner of the bill whereas the Geneva Conventions intend to protect the bona fide holder.

In light of article 14 of the Chinese bill law, matters recorded on the negotiable instruments shall be true to the facts, forging or alteration is not allowed. Those who forge or alter the signatures or seals or other items recorded on the negotiable instruments shall be prosecuted legal liabilities. The forged or altered signatures or seals do not affect the validity of the true signatures or seals on the same negotiable instrument.

5.3   Promissory Note and Cheque
本票与支票

5.3.1   Promissory Note   本票

1. Definition of a promissory note

A promissory note is an unconditional promise in writing, made by one person (the maker[36]) to another (the payee or the holder), signed by the maker, engaging to pay on demand or at a fixed or determinable future time a sum certain in money, to or to the order of the another person. The maker may be a natural person or juristic person.

The Chinese bill law defines a promissory note as an instrument written and issued by a maker, promising to pay unconditionally a fixed amount of money to a payee or holder at the sight of the instrument and only recognizes the promissory note issued by a bank.

A promissory note is also a negotiable instrument and has much in common with a bill of exchange. Most legal provisions on bills of exchange are also applicable to promissory notes. Therefore in most countries the negotiable instrument law makes detailed provisions on bills of exchange most of which also apply to promissory notes.

2. Contents of a promissory note

Typically a promissory note shall bear the following items: the words indicating "promissory note", unconditional promise to pay, amount of money fixed, name of the payee, date of issue, signature of the maker. A promissory note may be deemed to be invalid if one of the above items is missing. An example of a promissory note is shown in Figure 5 – 2.

PROMISSORY NOTE FOR USD5,000.00	LONDON, JULY 8, 2008
AT 60 DAYS AFTER DATE	
WE PROMISE TO PAY A COMPANY, LONDON OR ORDER	
THE SUM OF SAY US DOLLARS FIVE THOUSAND ONLY	
	FOR BANK OF EUROPE, LONDON
	(signature)

Figure 5 – 2　An example of a promissory note

3. Distinction between a promissory note and a bill of exchange

As compared with a bill of exchange in Table 5 – 1, a promissory note does have some distinctive features, although the two instruments are governed by similar legal rules.

Table 5 – 1　Distinction between a promissory note and a bill of exchange

A promissory note	A bill of exchange
1. It contains an unconditional promise.	1. It contains an unconditional order.
2. There are two basic parties — the maker and the payee.	2. There are three basic parties — the drawer, drawee, and the payee.
3. The liability of the maker is primary and absolute.	3. The liability of the drawer is secondary and conditional upon nonpayment by the drawee.
4. Acceptance is not required to hold the maker to be primarily liable on a note payable at a future time.	4. Acceptance is required to hold the drawee to be primarily liable on a bill payable at a future time.

5.3.2　Cheque　支票

1. Definition of a cheque

As defined in the Chinese bill law, a cheque is an negotiable instrument issued by a drawer, at the sight of which the cheque deposit bank or other financial institution unconditionally pay the fixed amount to the payee or holder. Like a bill of exchange, a cheque also has three basic parties specified on it: the drawer, drawee, payee. But the drawee of a cheque must be a bank or other financial institution.

According to the English bill law, a cheque is a bill of exchange drawn on a banker payable on demand. Therefore, in the UK most legal provisions applicable to a bill of exchange payable on demand also apply to a cheque.

2. Contents of a cheque

Typically, a check shall records the following essential items: the word "cheque" or "check", an unconditional commission to pay, drawer's name and signature, date and place of issue, a fixed amount of money, the name of payee. An example of a cheque is shown as Figure 5 – 3.

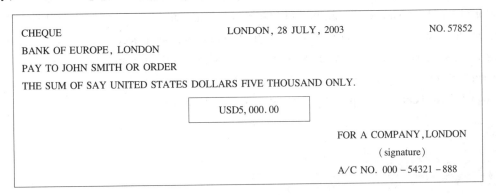

Figure 5 – 3   An example of a cheque

3. Bad cheque[37]

The drawer of a cheque is a depositor of the drawee bank and the bank will pay the cheque because it can debit the amount to the drawer's account. The amount of a cheque shall not exceed the actual amount deposited in the drawee bank by the drawer at the time of payment, or else the cheque is a bad cheque that will be dishonored. In modern societies, the drawers who draw bad cheques deliberately will be given strict penalties and even criminal sanctions.

On the other hand, if a bank finds that a cheque is a bad one after it has effected the payment, it has no right to require the payee refund the money.

4. Stop payment and certification

In some jurisdictions, the drawer, after drawing a cheque, is allowed to countermand the payment or notify the drawee bank to stop payment. In such cases, the holder may not claim the payment on the drawee bank but to exercise the right of recourse against the drawer and the prior holders.

The payee may request the drawee bank to certify the cheque in order to prevent the payment from being countermanded or stopped. If a cheque is certified by the drawee bank, the bank becomes the exclusive debtor to the cheque and all other parties (include the drawer) are discharged from liabilities on the cheque.

5. Crossed Cheque[38]

A crossed cheque refers to a cheque marked on its face with two parallel transverse lines. Such a cheque can not be cashed and the amount of payment shall be transferred though banks. A cheque may be crossed either "generally" or "specially" and consequently there are two types of crossed cheques: general crossed cheque and special crossed cheque[39].

A general crossed cheque is a crossed cheque that bears the words "company" or any abbreviation thereof between two parallel transverse lines or two parallel transverse lines simply; while a special crossed cheque bears the name of a bank between the two parallel transverse lines. For a general crossed cheque, the amount of payment can be transferred to the bank nominated by the holder whereas for a special crossed cheque, the amount can only be transferred to the bank named between the two parallel transverse lines on the cheque.

In western countries, cheques are crossed for the purpose of preventing from being cashed by impostors but the negotiability of a cheque may be restricted after being crossed. The crossed cheque is not mentioned but the cash cheque and the transfer cheque[40] are stated in the Chinese bill law. In light of article 83 of this law, a cheque can be cashed or transferred into other accounts; for account transfer, a clear indication shall be made across the face of the cheque; if cheques are made specially for account transfer, such cheques are transfer cheques and can only be used for account transfer; similarly, the cash cheques which have been made specially for cash can only be cashed.

Group Discussion ▶▶▶

1. Discuss the legal principles of negotiable instrument.
2. Describe the definition and contents of a bill of exchange.
3. Talk about the debtors to a bill of exchange and compare one debtor with another.
4. Explain the right of recourse.
5. Differentiate bills of exchange, promissory notes, and cheques.
6. Try to compare the major provisions of the Negotiable Instruments Law of the PRC on bills of exchange with the English bill law, and the Geneva Conventions.

NOTES ▶▶▶

1　negotiable instrument　票据（有时也用 bill 或 instrument）
2　bill of exchange　汇票（亦用 draft）；promissory note 本票；cheque（英国英语）支票（美国多用 check）
3　instrument relationship　票据关系（亦用 bill relationship）
4　non-instrument relationship　非票据关系
5　causing relationship of instrument　票据的原因关系；funding relationship of instrument　票据的资金关系
6　prior holder　前手
7　defective title　权利瑕疵
8　formal security　要式证券

9   time bill of exchange   远期汇票，定期汇票

10   Convention Providing a Uniform Law for Bills of Exchange and Promissory Notes   《统一汇票本票法公约》

11   Convention on the Settlement of Certain Conflicts of Laws in Connection with Bills of Exchange and Promissory Notes   《解决汇票本票法律冲突的公约》

12   Convention Providing a Uniform Law for Cheques   《统一支票法公约》

13   Convention on the Settlement of Certain Conflicts of Laws in Connection with Cheques   《解决支票法律冲突的公约》

14   Convention on the Stamp Laws in Connection with Bills of Exchange and Promissory Notes   《汇票本票印花税法公约》

15   Convention on the Stamp Laws in Connection with Cheques   《支票印花税法公约》

16   Convention on International Bills of Exchange and International Promissory Notes   (联合国)《国际汇票本票公约》

17   UNCITRAL   联合国国际贸易法委员会

18   drawer   (汇票或支票)出票人；drawee   受票人，付款人；payee   收款人；endorser   背书人；endorsee   被背书人；holder   持票人；guarantor   保证人

19   subsequent holder   后手

20   holder in due course   正当持票人

21   Bills of Exchange Act 1882   (英国)《1882 年汇票法》

22   bearer draft   无记名汇票；order draft   记名汇票

23   special endorsement   特别背书，记名背书，完全背书(亦用 full endorsement)；blank endorsement   空白背书，无记名背书(亦用 endorsement in blank, open endorsement, general endorsement)

24   restrictive endorsement   限制转让背书

25   qualified endorsement   无追索权背书

26   conditional endorsement   附条件背书

27   endorsement for collection   委托取款背书；endorsement of pledge   质权背书，设质背书

28   presentment for payment   付款提示；presentment for acceptance   承兑提示

29   general acceptance   普通承兑，单纯承兑，无条件承兑(亦用 absolute acceptance, clean acceptance, clear acceptance)；qualified acceptance   附有限制条件的承兑，非单纯承兑

30   acceptance by intervention   参加承兑(亦用 acceptance for honor)

31   acceptor for honor   参加承兑人

32   payment by intervention   参加付款(亦用 payment for honor)

33   payer for honor   参加付款人

34   protest for dishonor   (汇票)拒付证书

35   notice of dishonor   拒付通知

36   maker   (本票)出票人(有时也用 promisor 或 promiser)

37   bad cheque   空头支票(亦用 rubber cheque 或 kiting cheque)

38   crossed cheque   划线支票

39   general crossed cheque   普通划线支票；special crossed cheque   记名划线支票

40   cash cheque   现金支票；transfer cheque   转账支票

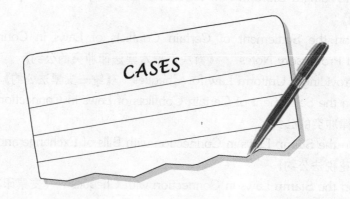

Whether the Document is a Bill of Exchange?
这样的单据是否是汇票?

A document held by the Korea Exchange Bank (plaintiff) contained the words: "Bill of exchange ... At 90 days D/A sight ... ". The plaintiff and defendant (a company in the UK) disagreed as to the balance of payment under the document. The plaintiff claimed the document to be a "bill of exchange" and the defendant contended that the parties' rights and obligations would vary depending on whether the document was a "bill of exchange". The trial judge held that the document appeared to be a bill of exchange. The defendant appealed. The Court of Appeals in the UK held that the document was not a "bill of exchange" within the meaning of article 3 of the Bills of Exchange Act 1882 (UK). The decision was reached on the basis that the abbreviation "D/A" did not suggest a fixed or determinable time for the maturity of the "bill" and therefore this instrument falls short of the necessary clarity.

However, the outcome of this case would have been absolutely different if it had been heard in Hong Kong. In a Hong Kong case, *NCNB National bank v. Gonara (HK) Ltd* (1984), which involved similar facts as the above case, the document in question stated that the bill was to be "payable at 120 days D/A sight". The High Court of Hong Kong held that the expression D/A (Document against Acceptance) was not part of the drawer's order to the drawee, and should thus be eliminated from the wording, leaving the words "payable at 120 days sight". In this way, the meaning of the instrument was clear and the bill of exchange was enforceable.

The Promisor's Duty to Indemnify the Guarantor of the Dishonored Promissory Notes
本票被拒付后出票人对保证人的赔偿责任

Export Credits Guarantee Department (ECGD) (plaintiff) was the guarantor for Universal Oil Co, Procon and Procon (Great Britain) Ltd. (defendants) which issued a number of promissory notes in favor of certain banks for repaying a loan advanced by the banks. The defendants designed and erected an oil refinery in Newfoundland in 1970 and took a large loan from a group of banks. The loan was to be repaid by a number of promissory notes drawn in the banks' favor at different maturity dates. ECGD was asked to provide a guarantee to the banks. A premium agreement was entered into between ECGD and the defendants, under which the defendants undertook to indemnify ECGD. The defendant went into liquidation in 1973 and left a large sum of money represented by the promissory notes unpaid. The banks called the guarantee. ECGD sought indemnity from the defendants after having paid the banks under the guarantee. The defendants intended to avoid liability on the ground that the indemnity clause in the premium agreement amounted to a penalty clause, which was prohibited by law. The trial court and appellate court gave judgment in favor of ECGD. The defendants further appealed to the House of Lords.

The House of Lords affirmed the judgement and held that the defendants were obliged to indemnify ECGD and the clause in question was not a penalty clause.

Payee Owed No Special Duty to Drawer of Forged Check
收款人对被伪造签名的支票出票人不承担特殊责任

For three years a secretary and a bookkeeper conspired to defraud their employer, Simmons, a lawyer, of funds he kept in various account. His signature was forged on numerous checks drawn without his knowledge. One check, for $13,000, was payable to Lennon, who sold a vehicle to the secretary and received the forged check in payment for the vehicle. This check was written and cashed more than a year before Simmons discovered the fraud. According to Simmons, Lennon should have known that the check was forged when he accepted it, and sued to recover the $13,000. Lennon had once been romantically involved with the secretary, who had cheated him out of money, so he should have been on notice of her behavior and suspected the fraud. The trial judge granted judgment in favor of payee Lennon. Simmons appealed. Decision of the first instance was affirmed.

The appellate court held that a payee of a check that contained the forged signature of the drawer, was an innocent recipient of the forged instrument and does not have to repay the funds to the drawer. The drawer, Simmons, was not entitled to recover against the payee. Under article 3-419 of the Uniform Commercial Codes (UCC) of the US, the drawer may not sue the payee for conversion of the check paid on the drawer's forged signature. Similarly, under common law, the drawer could not successfully sue the payee for conversion of the check. The payee owed no duty to warn the drawer of his employee's history of forgery; there was no contractual privity between the parties. Lennon accepted the check in good faith and properly endorsed it to cash it.

The UCC was redrafted after this incident occurred and article 3-420 was added concerning conversion, but it would not change the outcome of the case.

Checks Paid by Bank on Which Stop Payment Orders Had Been Placed
已经发出止付指令却被银行支付的支票

Seigel, a Maryland resident, gambled in Atlantic City, New Jersey at various casinos. He wrote checks to the casinos to get gambling chips. The checks were written against his cash management account at Merrill Lynch. When he returned home, after losing a substantial sum, he told his broker that he did not want the checks to be paid. On advice of his broker, he placed stop payment orders on the checks and liquidated the account. While Merrill Lynch did not pay many of the checks, it accidentally paid checks totaling $143,000. Seigel sued Merrill Lynch for breach of contract, negligence, and breach of trust, demanding a return of $143,000. The trial court decided in favor of Merrill Lynch, the drawee, and Seigel, the drawer, appealed. Decision Affirmed.

The appellate court held that under the Uniform Commercial Codes (UCC) of the US, the drawer did not suffer an actual loss from the drawee's mistakenly paying checks upon which stop payment orders were placed. Since the debts were valid and owed to the casinos (the payee of the checks) by the drawer, and the drawer was liable to the payee of the checks, there was no actual loss for which the drawee — Merrill Lynch, could be held liable.

Chapter 6

Product Liability Law
产品责任法

Learning Objectives

☑ To know the definition of product liability
☑ To understand the principles and development of product liability law in the US
☑ To know about the product liability law in the EU
☑ To learn about the important provisions of the Product Quality Law of the PRC

 Opening Vignette

Making a Product Liability Claim in the US

If you've been injured by a product — anything from matches to a car — you may bring a product liability claim against the product's manufacturers and distributors. Whether your case is worth pursuing depends on how you were injured, whether you contributed to that injury and the laws in your state.

1. The Basics

In the US, there are generally three types of product liability cases: negligence, breach of warranty and strict liability[1]. Like most laws, these vary by state and not all provisions apply in every state, so you need to consult a lawyer to figure out what's most appropriate for your situation.

2. Negligence

As the name suggests, negligence cases require showing that carelessness caused your injury. First, you have to prove there was a duty to sell a safe product. That part's not too difficult, since all individuals and companies that make and distribute consumer products are obliged to prevent injuries resulting from their products. If they sold you something, then they probably have this duty. Next, you need to show that the defendant somehow breached that duty. You also need to show that you've been damaged. You can't bring a claim without an injury. Merely pointing out the defect in a product you bought and saying it might hurt someone is not enough. Finally, you have to prove that the defect, and not some unrelated illness or accident, is what caused your damage.

3. Breach of Warranty

When you're suing for breach of warranty, you have to prove that the manufacturer or distributor broke a written or implied promise that the goods are free from defects. Then, of course, you need to show that breach caused your injury. There are three basic types of defects: manufacturing defect, design defect, insufficient instructions or warnings.

4. Strict Product Liability

If you can prove that a product is "unreasonably dangerous" — that it has a design or manufacturing defect — then you may be able to establish that the defendant is "strictly liable." Unlike negligence cases, you may not have to prove the manufacturer knew about the danger, because even if they didn't, they should have. (One of the main purposes of this provision is to hold manufacturers accountable for developing safe products). You still, however, have to prove that the product caused your damages.

5. Damages

When you pursue a product liability case, there are many types of damages you can recover. Compensation varies from state to state, but generally you can be compensated for the cost of medical care (present and future), lost wages, physical pain and suffering, and mental suffering. In some states you can also pursue punitive damages, which punish the defendant and prevent similar deeds from occurring.

6. Preserving Evidence

People who are involved in litigation are responsible for ensuring that relevant evidence (including a vehicle or its component) is protected from loss or destruction. This duty exists before the lawsuit is filed, and it arises once litigation is reasonably anticipated. Courts may impose sanctions, that is, penalties, for the destruction of the actual accident vehicle or actual accident component.

7. Getting Help

Pursuing a product liability case is complex and expensive. Lawyers in this field often specialize in certain areas, such as prescription drug liability cases, automobile cases or toxic torts (injuries resulting from toxins, such as asbestos or diesel fuel). If you can find someone you like who specializes in your type of case, you'll obviously benefit.

Most product liability lawyers will take these cases on a contingency fee, meaning they get no legal fee until the case settles or a verdict is reached. This fee depends on the complexity of the case and where you're located, among other things. Some lawyers require a retainer up front to pay for costs associated with the case.

It may be difficult for you to find a lawyer if your case is unusual. Be prepared to meet with or talk with several lawyers about your case.

 Warm-up Questions

1. What do you think about product liability?
2. Is it easy to make a product liability claim in the US?
3. What do you know about the product liability law in China?

6.1　An Overview of Product Liability Law
产品责任法概述

6.1.1　Definition of Product Liability　产品责任的定义

In simple words, product liability means that businesses making or selling products are responsible for ensuring that those products are safe and do not pose a hazard to the public.

Product liability law is the area of law in which manufacturers, distributors, suppliers, retailers, and others who make products available to the public are held responsible for the injuries those products cause.

The purpose of product liability law is to protect consumers against damage caused to health or property by products they bought.

6.1.2　Development of Product Liability Laws　产品责任法的发展

In comparison with other industrialized countries, the US took the first step in the development of product liability law.

Product liability began to have meaning in the mid-1800s, when the American courts increasingly found that suppliers of goods had a duty to use reasonable care in the production of those goods. Suppliers were held liable to third parties for negligence in the manufacture or sale of goods inherently dangerous (the danger of injury arises from the product itself, rather than from a defect in the product) to human safety, ranging from food and beverages to drugs, and explosives.

In the early 1960s, tort principles were first applied to product liability. During this time, the concept of inherently dangerous goods was still held to be significant, but there was a shift to negligence principles that held that producers of goods were required to apply "due care" in the marketing of goods to consumers.

Since that time, businesses have operated under an understanding that because they knowingly market products which affect the interests of consumers, they owe a legal duty of caution and prudence to consumers. Since manufacturers may foresee potentially harmful product effects, they are responsible for attempting to minimize harm. Establishing this legal duty between the manufacturer and the consumer made it possible for plaintiffs to argue the negligent breach of that duty.

These principles are now accepted throughout the country and followed by all American courts. Eventually, the concept of inherently dangerous products fell into disuse and the concept of negligence was expanded beyond production to include labeling, installation, inspection, and design.

6.2 Product Liability Law in the US
美国的产品责任法

In the US, product liability law is normally governed by state law and varies from one state to another. On the whole, there are three types of theories or counts upon which an injured party can bring an action in product liability law. The plaintiff may include a count for each theory, or may choose to sue on only one. The theories are negligence, breach of warranty and strict liability.

These theories overlap to a great extent and are milestones in evolution of product liability law, with strict liability being the newest.

6.2.1 Theories of Product Liability　产品责任的法学理论

1. Negligence

In common law jurisdictions, negligence is a tort[2]. It refers to the absence of, or failure to exercise, proper or ordinary care. It means that an individual who had a legal obligation either omitted to do what should have been done or did something that should not have been done.

The duty to guard against negligence and supply a safe product applies to everyone in the chain of production, distribution and retail, including a manufacturer who carelessly makes a defective product, the company that uses the product to assemble something else without discovering an obvious defect, and the vendor who should exercise greater care in offering products for sale. These individuals owe a duty of reasonable care to anyone who is likely to be injured by such a product if it is defective, no matter whether there is privity of contract[3] between them, including the initial buyer, that person's family members, any bystanders, and persons who lease the item or hold it for the purchaser.

Reading Material

Famous Cases in the Evolution of Product Liability Law

The case of *MacPherson v. Buick Motor Co.* (1916) is the famous New York Court of Appeals opinion by Judge Benjamin N. Cardozo, which removed privity of contract from duty in negligence actions.

The plaintiff, Donald C. MacPherson, was injured when one of the wooden wheels of his automobile crumbled. The defendant Buick Motor Company had manufactured the vehicle, but not the wheel, which had been manufactured by another party and installed by the defendant. It was conceded that the defective wheel could have been discovered upon inspection. The defendant denied liability because the plaintiff had purchased the automobile from a dealer, not directly from the defendant.

The Judge Benjamin N. Cardozo holds that the defendant manufacturer owed a duty of reasonable care to the ultimate purchaser despite the absence of privity of contract.

In the earlier precedent, duty was imposed on defendants by voluntary contract via privity as in the famous English case of *Winterbottom v. Wright* (denying injured man's suit against manufacturer because the judge found no privity of contract between the defendant carriage maker and the injured plaintiff). This case brought products injuries into the modern tort law theory of a duty that all citizens owe each other by virtue of a defendant's relationship to the plaintiff. This is the precursor rule for products liability.

Additionally, the duty to exercise due care involves all phases of getting a product to the consumers or users. The product must be designed in such a way that it is safe for its intended use. It must be inspected and tested at different stages, made from the appropriate materials, and assembled carefully. The product's container or packaging must be adequate. The manufacturer must also furnish adequate warnings and directions for use with the product. The seller shall be proscribed from misrepresenting the safety or character of the product and must disclose all defects.

Any person or entity that does not provide reasonable care when it has the legal responsibility to do so can be found guilty of negligence. This includes inaction as well as careless and malicious action. An example of negligence is when a furniture manufacturer haphazardly assembles a piece of furniture that breaks, injuring someone. Another example is that if a customer falls on a wet floor in a store and if posting a warning sign could have prevented the accident from occurring, the storeowner will likely be found liable for the personal injury incurred.

In a negligence claim a plaintiff must prove that a manufacturer, seller, wholesaler or other party involved in the distributive chain or group had a duty to exercise reasonable care in the process of manufacturing or selling a product and failed to fulfill that duty, resulting in injury to the plaintiff. Negligence consists of doing something that a person of ordinary prudence would not do under the same or similar circumstances or failing to do something that a person of ordinary prudence would do under the same or similar circumstances. The plaintiff shall also prove that such negligence directly causes the injury to him.

2. Breach of warranty

Breach of warranty refers to the failure of a manufacturer or seller to fulfill the terms of a promise, claim, or representation made concerning the quality or type of the product. The law assumes that a manufacturer or seller gives certain warranties concerning goods that are produced or sold and that he or she must stand behind these assertions.

Breach of warranty is most often associated with a failure to warn consumers about the inherent dangers of a product or use of the product. Breach of warranty is considered by some authors to be a more specifically defined form of negligence.

Warranties are certain kinds of express or implied representations of fact that the law will enforce against the warrantor. Product liability law is concerned with three types of warranties involving the product's quality or fitness for use: express warranty, implied warranty of merchantability, and implied warranty of fitness for a particular purpose. These and other warranties are codified in the Uniform Commercial Code (UCC), which every state has adopted, at least in part.

An express warranty can be created in one of three ways: through an affirmation of fact made by the vendor of the goods to the purchaser relating to the goods, which becomes part of the bargain; by way of a description of the goods, which is made part of the basis of the bargain; and through a sample or model, which is made part of the basis of the bargain. An express warranty can be words spoken during negotiations or written into a sales contract, a sample, an earlier purchase of the same kind of product, or claims made in publicity or on tags attached to the product. An express warranty is created when a salesperson states that the product is guaranteed to be free from defects for one year from the date of the purchase.

Implied warranties are those created and imposed by law, and accompany the transfer of title to goods unless expressly and clearly limited or excluded by the contract. However, with respect to damages for personal injury, the UCC states that any such contractual limitations or exclusions are "prima facie unconscionable" and cannot be enforced. The implied warranty of merchantability requires that the product and its container meet certain minimum standards of quality, chiefly that the product be fit for the ordinary purposes for which such goods are sold. This requirement includes a standard of reasonable safety.

The implied warranty of fitness for a particular purpose imposes a similar requirement in cases in which the seller knows or has reason to know of a particular purpose for which the goods are required and in which the buyer is relying on the seller to select or furnish suitable goods. The seller then warrants that the goods are fit for that particular purpose. For example, assume that the buyer tells the seller, a computer supplier, that he needs a high-speed computer to manage inventory and payroll functions for his business. Once the seller recommends a particular computer to handle these requirements, the seller is making an implied warranty of fitness. If the computer cannot adequately process the inventory and payroll, the buyer may file a suit.

The action for breach of one of these warranties has aspects of both tort and contract law. Its greatest value to the injured product user lies in the fact that liability for breach is strict. No negligence or other fault need be shown. The plaintiff just need show the warranty he relies on made by the defendant and breach of the warranty resulting in injury to him.

3. Strict liability

Strict liability, sometimes called absolute liability, is the legal responsibility for damages, or injury, even if the person found strictly liable was not at fault or negligent. Strict liability has been applied to certain activities in tort, such as holding an employer absolutely liable for the torts of her employees, but today it is most commonly associated with defectively manufactured products.

In product liability cases involving injuries caused by manufactured goods, strict liability has had a major impact on litigation since the 1960s. In 1963, in the famous case of *Greenman v. Yuba Power Products*, the California Supreme Court became the first court to adopt strict tort liability for defective products.

In the above-mentioned case, the plaintiff's wife purchased at retail a "shop-smith combination of power saw and drill" manufactured by the defendant company and give it to him as a present. The plaintiff incurred serious head injuries when a piece of wood flew out of the machine while he was using it. The court conceded that the plaintiff's action might fail if based on warranty alone, because notice of the warranty breach had not been given. Yet the court held the manufacturer "strictly liable in tort" and spelled out this theory as follows: "A manufacturer is strictly liable in tort when an article he places on the market, knowing that it is to be used without inspection for defects, proves to have a defect that causes injury to a human being. Recognized first in the case of unwholesome food products, such liability has now been extended to a variety of other products that create as great or greater hazards if defective." The court then cited 14 cases where similar results were reached involving such defective products as automobiles, bottles, vaccines, and automobile tires.

As the most recent evolution in tort law, strict liability, has transformed the very nature of product liability because it eliminates the entire question of negligence. Strict liability only requires a plaintiff to demonstrate that a product caused an injury because it was defective; the reason for the defect is irrelevant. The product itself, not the defendant, is under investigation.

Under strict liability, the manufacturer is held liable for allowing a defective product to enter the marketplace. The issue is a matter of public policy, not the manufacturer's unreasonable or negligent conduct. The introduction of a defective product into the marketplace brings each member of the product's distribution channel into liability for negligence. The theory of strict liability holds that manufacturers have the greatest control over the quality of their products; can distribute their costs by raising prices; and have special responsibilities in their role as sellers.

With strict liability it does not matter if the manufacturer exercised great care in creating the product. What matters is that the product itself has been deemed defective and has caused injury. Negligence is not claimed in strict liability cases. In strict liability cases it is assumed that the manufacturer of the product is the expert over the product and should know whether the product is dangerous or not. The consumer is not considered an expert in most cases and assumes less responsibility to know the dangers of products.

In a strict liability case, an injured party must show that the item was defective, that the defect proximately caused the injury, and that the defect rendered the product unreasonably dangerous. The plaintiff has to prove the product caused the harm but do not have to prove exactly how the manufacturer was careless. A plaintiff may recover damages even if the seller has exercised all possible care in the preparation and sale of the product. Purchasers of the product, as well as injured guests, bystanders, and others with no direct relationship with the product, may sue for damages caused by the product.

6.2.2 Defences 被告的抗辩

In product liability cases, the defendants may present some defences in order to avoid or limit liability. The followings are those defences most commonly presented.

1. Disclaimer or limitation of warranty[4]

If the plaintiff sues for breach of warranty, it may be a defence if such a warranty has been disclaimed or limited by the defendant when selling the product. Such a defence can not be presented to defend claims for negligence or strict liability.

2. Contributory negligence and comparative negligence[5]

Contributory negligence is a common law defence to a claim based on negligence. It applies to cases where plaintiffs have, through their own negligence, contributed to cause the damages they incurred when using the product. The defence of contributory negligence would prevent the plaintiff from recovering any damages at all.

Most jurisdictions in the US have modified the doctrine, either by court decision or by legislation and have accordingly changed the name to comparative negligence wherein, rather than awarding no damages at all, the jury reduces the compensation to be awarded by a percentage reflecting the degree to which the plaintiff's negligence contributed to cause the damages.

3. Assumption of the risk[6]

Assumption of risk is a defence in a product liability case based on negligence, breach of warranty or strict liability. The defendant may be relieved or exempted from liability, if he can demonstrate that the plaintiff was fully aware that the product was defective or dangerous and voluntarily and knowingly assumed the risks associated with the product and was injured as a result of his assumption of the risks.

4. Abnormal use, misuse or abuse of the product[7]

In a product liability case, it may be a defence if the defendant can prove that the plaintiff use the product abnormally, misuse or abuse the product. However, if such abnormal use, misuse or abuse of the product is reasonably foreseeable, the defendant may not be exempted from liability unless he took some reasonable precautionary measures.

5. Subsequent alteration[8]

It may also be a defence in product liability cases if the defendant can demonstrate that the plaintiff made subsequent alteration on the product or some parts of the product and such alteration resulted in the injury to himself.

6. Product with unavoidable dangerous feature[9]

Certain special products have some unavoidable dangerous features inherently while they are necessary and beneficial to public, such as drugs. This may be a defence in a product liability case, even a strict liability case.

6.2.3 Damages 损害赔偿

1. Damages for personal injury or death

In product liability cases, the plaintiff may claim for damages for personal injury or death. In the US, such compensatory damages may cover all financial expenses and all ailments associated with personal injury, including pain and suffering, loss of wages, emotional distress, permanent disability, mental suffering, medical bills, earning capacity impairment, loss of profits and etc.

2. Damages for loss of property

Damages for loss of property normally are compensatory damages for repair or replacement of the property that damaged by the product at issue.

3. Commercial damages

Commercial damages refer to compensation for the loss associated with the product itself if the product itself was damaged or destructed at the same time when the plaintiff used it and was injured. Such commercial damages may cover repair or replacement of the product, value impairment, loss of operating profits and etc.

4. Punitive damages

The purpose of punitive damages is a public one — to punish wrongdoing and deter future misconduct by either the defendant or other potential wrongdoers. In order to sustain an award for punitive damages, proof of malice does not require an actual intent to harm. Conscious disregard for safety of another or other public policies, may be sufficient where the defendant is aware of the probable dangerous consequences of his conduct, and he willfully fails to avoid those consequences.

6.2.4 Impact of Product Liability Law on American Foreign Trade
产品责任法对美国对外贸易的影响

American product liability laws are typically domestic laws, whereas some product liability cases may be involved with foreign trade. Under certain conditions, Americans may make product liability claims against imported products, or foreign consumers may claim against products made in the US.

1. Jurisdiction

Since American product liability laws are state laws and historically, a state could exercise jurisdiction only within its territorial boundaries; therefore, a nonresident defendant could be brought into court only when service of process was effected while that defendant was within the boundaries of the state. The US Supreme Court upheld this principle, and raised it to a constitutional level.

The requirement of physical presence within the state's boundaries was expanded in *International Shoe Co. v. State of Washington*. In this case, the Supreme Court held that due process required that the defendant have "certain minimum contacts[10]" with the forum in order for a state to assert jurisdiction. Such minimum contacts include transacting business within the forum, advertising within the forum, or accepting insurance payments from persons within the forum and etc.

Since then, the Supreme Court has set forth several criteria to be used in analyzing whether jurisdiction over a nonresident is proper. These criteria require:

(1) That the defendant has purposefully availed himself of the benefits of the state so as to reasonably foresee being haled into court in that state;

(2) That the forum state has sufficient interest in the dispute;

(3) That haling the defendant into court does not offend "notions of fair play and substantial justice".

Since 1963 all states and the District of Columbia have enacted "long-arm" statutes setting forth their requirements for personal jurisdiction[11] over nonresidents which enable American courts to exercise "long-arm" jurisdictions over foreign manufacturers who are liable for personal injury or damage to property in the US.

2. Choice of law

American laws may be applicable to product liability cases where foreign plaintiff was injured or incurred losses by using American products. However, the court must determine which state's legal rules should control.

The doctrine of most significant contact[12] is one of the possible choice of law rules applied to product liability cases. The court shall evaluate the contacts between the states and each party to the case, and determines which state has the most significant contacts with the litigation as a whole. The contacts to be evaluated include the place where the injury was incurred, the place where the action resulting in the injury took place, the domicile or business place of each party, and etc.

6.3   Product Liability Law in the EU
欧盟的产品责任法

One of the most significant single events in the history of product liability law in Europe occurred on 25 July 1985 with the promulgation of the "Council Directive on the Approximation of the Laws, Regulations, and Administrative Provisions of the Member States concerning Liability for Defective Products[13]" (also known as "Product Liability Directive"). This Directive came into force in 1988 and was amended in 1999.

The Directive requires all European Union Member States to issue conforming "strict product liability" laws and covers any defective product manufactured or imported into the European Union that causes damages to individuals or private property.

The EU Product Liability Directive calls upon the Member States to impose strict liability on producers of defective products that cause personal injury or property damage. However, the Directive does not provide for a cause of action. Cause of action is left to Member States. Product liability cases are tried in national courts under national laws.

The main contents of the Directive are briefed as follows.

6.3.1   Liability without Fault   无过失责任原则

The EU Directive introduces the concept of strict liability without fault on the part of the producer in favor of the victim. It places the burden of proof on the injured party insofar as the damage, the defect, and the causal relationship between the two is concerned. In other words, the injured party is not required to prove that the producer was at fault.

Moreover, it establishes joint and several liability of all operators in the production chain in favor of the injured party, so as to provide a financial guarantee for compensation of the damage.

6.3.2   Definition of Producer   生产者的定义

The Directive defines the producer not only as the manufacturer of a finished product, but also as: a) the maker of any raw material or the manufacturer of a component part; b) any person who, by putting his/her name, trademark or other distinguishing feature on the product, presents himself/herself as the producer; c) any person supplying a product if the producer cannot be identified; d) importers placing products on the European Union market.

Reading Material

Purpose of the EU Product Liability Directive

The purpose of the EU Product Liability Directive is to ensure consumer protection against damage caused to health or property by a defective product and to reduce the disparities between national laws.

It is said in the preface of the Directive that "Whereas approximation of the laws of the Member States concerning the liability of the producer for damage caused by the defectiveness of his products is necessary because the existing divergences may distort competition and affect the movement of goods within the common market and entail a differing degree of protection of the consumer against damage caused by a defective product to his health or property; Whereas liability without fault on the part of the producer is the sole means of adequately solving the problem, peculiar to our age of increasing technicality, of a fair apportionment of the risks inherent in modern technological production . . . "

6.3.3   Definition of Product   产品的定义

According to the Directive, a product means physical property and goods, as opposed to land or rights in or to real property. A product could include a whole product, part of another product, or part of a fixture attached to real property.

The new revision of the Directive amended in 1999 redefined "product" as all movables even if incorporated into another movable or into an immovable. In the original Directive, primary agricultural products and game were excluded. However, the new Directive extended the scope of the Directive so that it now includes primary agricultural products (such as meat, cereals, fruit and vegetables) and game. The Member States were directed to apply the rules of the new Directive as of December 4, 2000.

6.3.4   Definition of Defective Product   有缺陷产品的定义

The Directive applies only to defective products; that is, products not providing the safety to which a consumer is entitled. Factors to be taken into account include: a) the presentation of the product (including any instructions or warnings, packaging, and advertising); b) whether the product is being put to reasonable use; and c) the time the product was put into circulation. However, the fact that a better product is manufactured afterwards does not automatically render older models defective.

6.3.5   Producer's Defences   生产者的抗辩

In light of article 7 of the Directive, a producer will not be liable if he can prove that:

(1) The producer was not responsible for placing the product on the market;

(2) The defect which caused the damage did not exist at the time the product was placed on the market by the producer, or that this defect came into being afterwards;

（3）The product was neither manufactured by the producer for sale or any form of distribution for economic purpose, nor manufactured, or distributed by the producer in the course of business;

（4）The defect is due to compliance of the product with mandatory regulations issued by public authorities;

（5）The state of scientific and technical knowledge at the time the producer placed the product on the market was not such as to enable the defect to be discovered;

（6）Where the producer is a subcontractor, the defect is attributable to either the design of the finished product in which the component has been fitted, or to defective instructions given to subcontractor by the producer of the finished product.

6.3.6　Damages　损害赔偿

The Directive outlines two types of damage that may be the subject of a claim: damage caused by death or personal injury, and property damage.

Property damage must satisfy the following criteria:

（1）It must be intended for private use;

（2）It must be used by the person who has suffered the loss mainly for his own private use or consumption;

（3）The total damages claimed by a person in respect of loss of property must exceed 500 ECU[14].

6.4　Product Quality Law in China
中国的产品质量法

The Product Quality Law of the PRC was promulgated in 1993 and amended in 2000. The main contents of it are to be briefed as follows.

6.4.1　Responsibilities and Obligations of the Producers for the Quality of Their Products　生产者的产品质量责任与义务

The Product Quality Law of PRC provides that producers shall be responsible for the quality of products they produce. In detail, quality of products shall meet the following requirements.

（1）Products shall be free from any irrational dangers threatening the safety of people and property. If there are national standards or industry standards for securing health and safety of people and property, the products shall conform to such standards.

（2）Products shall have the value for use and/or performance characteristic that they are due to have, except cases in which there are explanations about the defects of the performance of the products.

（3）Products shall be in accordance with the standards prescribed or specified on their packages and with the quality specified in the instructions for use or shown in the providing samples.

The descriptions and marks on the packages of products shall conform to the following requirements.

（1）There shall be certificates for quality inspection.

（2）There shall be the names of products and the names and addresses of producers in Chinese.

（3）If, according to the characteristics and requirements for use, the specification, grades or the names and contents of major elements are required to be specified, they shall be specified clearly on the package.

(4) Products which have a time limit for use, the date of production, or the period for safe use or date of losing effect shall be specified.

(5) Products which may cause harm to human body or likely to threaten the safety of people and property if improperly used shall have warning marks or warnings words in Chinese.

Products which are highly toxic, dangerous, easy to break or cannot be handled upside down in the process of storage or transportation or have other special handling requirements shall have particular packages meeting the corresponding requirements, and warning marks or warnings words in Chinese specifying the points for attention in handling.

Producers are forbidden to produce the products which have been eliminated according to laws or decrees, or to fake the place of origin and quality marks, or use the names and addresses of other producers. Producers shall not adulterate their products, or sell the false product as genuine, the defective products as best, or sell the products that are not up to standard as those up to.

6.4.2   Responsibilities and Obligations of the Sellers 销售者的责任与义务

Sellers shall implement the system of check before acceptance for goods procured, verifying the product quality certificates and other marks.

Sellers shall take measures to maintain the quality of products for sale. Sellers are not allowed to sell products which have been eliminated according to laws or decrees or have lost effect or deteriorated.

The responsibilities of the descriptions and marks on the packages of products taken by the sellers are the same as the producers, which have been mentioned previously.

Sellers are forbidden to fake the place of origin and quality marks, the names and addresses of producers, or adulterate the products for sale, or sell the false product as genuine, the defective products as best, or sell the products that are not up to standard as those up to.

6.4.3   Liabilities and Time Limitation   责任与时效

If products produced or sold are not in accordance with the provisions of this law, the producers or sellers are liable to repair or replace the products, or refund to the purchaser.

If damages are incurred to persons or property due to defect of products, the victims may claim for damages either against the producers or the sellers. Sellers shall be held labile for damages if they cannot identify the producers or suppliers of the defective products. Additionally, sellers shall be held liable if such damages are caused by the defects resulting from fault on the part of sellers.

For personal injury caused by defect of products, producers or sellers shall pay the medical fees, loss of wages and incomes, living allowances for handicapped cases. If defect of products caused death, the funeral fees, pensions and the living expenses for dependents supported by the dead shall be paid.

For damages to property caused by defect of products, producers or sellers shall be responsible for restitution or compensation.

The time limitation for claiming for damages caused by defect of products is 2 years, starting from the date when the parties concerned is notified or should have known the matter. The victim may lose the right of claiming for damages after 10 years from when the product at issue was first delivered to consumers. However, there are exceptional cases where the specified period of the product for safe use has not expired.

According to the penalty provisions of this law, if the case is serious enough to constitute a crime, producers or sellers may be prosecuted for criminal liabilities.

Group Discussion

1. What do you think about product liability?
2. Discuss the three theories of product liability in the US.
3. Try to compare product liability laws in the US with those in the EU.
4. Talk about the Chinese product quality law.

NOTES

1   negligence   疏忽；breach of warranty   违反担保；strict liability   严格责任
2   tort   民事侵权行为
3   privity of contract   合同关系
4   disclaimer or limitation of warranty   担保的排除或限制
5   contributory negligence   承担疏忽；comparative negligence   相对疏忽
6   assumption of the risk   自担风险
7   abnormal use, misuse or abuse of the product   非正常使用、误用或滥用产品
8   subsequent alteration   擅自改动产品
9   product with unavoidable dangerous feature   产品带有不可避免的不安全性
10 minimum contact   最低限度的接触
11 personal jurisdiction   对人的管辖权
12 doctrine of most significant contact   最密切联系原则
13 Council Directive on the Approximation of the Laws, Regulations, and Administrative Provisions of the Member States concerning Liability for Defective Products   《理事会关于使各成员国有关对有缺陷产品的责任的法律法规及行政规章互相接近的指令》（简称《产品责任指令》）
14 ECU (European Currency Unit)   欧洲货币单位

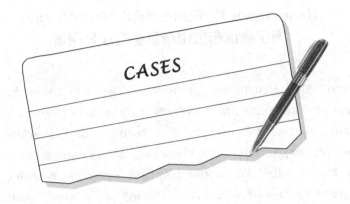

Escola v. Coca Cola Bottling Company of Fresno
艾丝克拉诉可口可乐弗雷斯诺瓶装公司案

Plaintiff, Escola, a waitress in a restaurant located in California, was injured when a bottle of Coca Cola broke in her hand. She alleged that defendant company, which had bottled and delivered the alleged defective bottle to her employer, was negligent in selling "bottles containing said beverage which on account of excessive pressure of gas or by reason of some defect in the bottle was dangerous ... and likely to explode."

Defendant's driver delivered several cases of Coca Cola to the restaurant, placing them on the floor, one on top of the other, under and behind the counter, where they remained at least thirty-six hours. Immediately before the accident, plaintiff picked up the top case and set it upon a nearby ice cream cabinet in front of and about three feet from the refrigerator. She then proceeded to take the bottles from the case with her right hand, one at a time, and put them into the refrigerator. Plaintiff testified that after she had placed three bottles in the refrigerator and had moved the fourth bottle about 18 inches from the case "it exploded in my hand." The trial jury made a verdict in favor of plaintiff. Defendant appealed.

The appellate court held that it is true that defendant presented evidence tending to show that it exercised considerable precaution by carefully regulating and checking the pressure in the bottles and by making visual inspections for defects in the glass at several stages during the bottling process. It is well settled, however, that when a defendant produces evidence to rebut the inference of negligence which arises upon application of the doctrine of *res ipsa loquitur* (the thing itself speaks), it is ordinarily a question of fact for the jury to determine whether the inference has been dispelled. Therefore the judgment is affirmed.

Many authorities state that the happening of the accident does not speak for itself where it took place some time after defendant had relinquished control of the instrumentality causing the injury. Under the more logical view, however, the doctrine may be applied upon the theory that defendant had control at the time of the alleged negligent act, although not at the time of the accident, provided plaintiff first proves that the condition of the instrumentality had not been changed after it left the defendant's possession.

Henningsen V. Bloomfield Motors, Inc.
海宁森诉布鲁姆费尔德汽车公司案

Husband of plaintiff Mrs. Henningsen purchased a Plymouth automobile, manufactured by defendant Chrysler Corporation, from defendant Bloomfield Motors, Inc. On May 7, 1955, Mr. and Mrs. Henningsen visited the place of business of Bloomfield Motors, Inc., an authorized Plymouth dealer, to look at a Plymouth. Mr. Henningsen intended the car as a Mother's Day gift to his wife. When the purchase order or contract was prepared and presented, the husband executed it alone. His wife did not join as a party. On May 19, Mrs. Henningsen drove to Asbury Park. The highway was paved and smooth, and contained two lanes for northbound travel. She was riding in the right-hand lane on Route 36 in Highlands, New Jersey, at 20 – 22 miles per hour. On the way down and in returning the car performed in normal fashion until an accident occurred. Suddenly she heard a loud noise from the bottom, by the hood. It "felt as if something cracked." The steering wheel spun in her hands; the car veered sharply to the right and crashed into a highway sign and a brick wall. A bus operator driving in the left-hand lane testified that he observed plaintiffs' car approaching in normal fashion in the opposite direction; "all of a sudden (it) veered at 90 degrees ... and right into this wall." As a result of the impact, the front of the car was so badly damaged that it was impossible to determine if any of the parts of the steering wheel mechanism or workmanship or assembly were defective or improper prior to the accident. The condition was such that the collision insurance carrier, after inspection, declared the vehicle a total loss. It had 468 miles on the speedometer at the time. The insurance carrier's inspector and appraiser of damaged cars, with 11 years of experience, advanced the opinion, based on the history and his examination, that something definitely went "wrong from the steering wheel down to the front wheels" and that the untoward happening must have been due to mechanical defect or failure; "something down there had to drop off or break loose" to cause the car to act in the manner described.

Mrs. Henningsen instituted the suit against both defendants to recover damages on account of her injuries. The complaint was predicated upon breach of express and implied warranties and upon negligence. At the trial the negligence counts were dismissed by the court and the cause was submitted to the jury for determination solely on the issues of implied warranty of merchantability. Verdicts were returned against both defendants and in favor of the plaintiff. Defendants appealed. The matter was certified by this court prior to consideration in the appellate court.

Both defendants contend that since there was no privity of contract between them and Mrs. Henningsen, she cannot recover for breach of any warranty made by either of them. On the facts, she was not a party to the purchase agreement. Her right to maintain the action, therefore, depends upon whether she occupies such legal status thereunder as to permit her to take advantage of a breach of defendants' implied warranties. For the most part the cases that have been considered dealt with the right of the buyer or consumer to maintain an action against the manufacturer where the contract of sale was with a dealer and the buyer had no contractual relationship with the manufacturer. In the present matter, the basic contractual relationship is between Mr. Henningsen, Chrysler, and Bloomfield Motors, Inc. The precise issue presented is whether Mrs. Henningsen, who is not a party to their respective warranties, may claim under them. In the judgment of the appellate court, the principles of those similar cases and the supporting texts are just as proximately applicable to her situation. The judges are convinced that the cause of justice in this area of the law can be served only by recognizing that she is such a person who, in the reasonable contemplation of the parties to the warranty, might be expected to become a user of the automobile. Accordingly, her lack of privity does not stand in the way of prosecution of the injury suit against the defendants. Therefore the judgement of the first trial was upheld.

Chapter 7

Law of Agency
代理法

Learning Objectives

- ☑ To learn the definition and creation of agency
- ☑ To understand the respective duties of principal and agent
- ☑ To know the relations between principal, agent and third parties
- ☑ To know about the important legal provisions on agency in China

 ## Opening Vignette

Principal and Agent

In law, an agent[1] is a person authorized to do some act or acts in the name of another, who is called his principal[2]. Either agent or principal may be a natural person or a fictitious person.

The law regulating the relations of principal and agent has its origin in the law of mandate among the Romans, and in England the spirit of that system of jurisprudence pervades this branch of the law. The law of agency is thus almost alike throughout the whole British Empire, and a branch of the British commercial code, in which it is of great importance that different nations should understand each other's system, differs only slightly from the law of the rest of Europe.

In a general view of the law of agency it is necessary to have regard to the rights and duties of the principal, the agent, and the third parties. The agent should not do what he has no authority for; yet if he is seen to have authority, those with whom he deals should not be injured by secret and unusual conditions. The principal is bound by what his agent does in his name, but the third parties are not entitled to take advantage of obligations which are known to be unauthorized and unusual. The agent is entitled to demand performance by the principal of the obligations undertaken by him within the bounds of his commission, but he is not entitled to pledge him with a recklessness which he would certainly avoid in the management of his own affairs. It is in the regulation of these powers and corresponding checks in such a manner that the legal principle shall apply to daily practice, that the niceties of this branch of the law consist.

Agents are of different kinds, according to their stipulated or consuetudinary powers. The main restraint in the possible powers of an agent is in the old maxim, *delegatus non potest delegare*[3], designed to check the complexity that might be created by inquiries into repeatedly-deputed responsibility. The agent cannot delegate his commission or put another in his place; but in practice this principle is sometimes modified, for it so may arise from the nature of his office that he is to employ other persons for the accomplishment of certain objects. Thus, there is nothing to prevent a commercial agent from sending a portion of the goods entrusted by him to his own agent for disposal.

In general, agency is created by the acceptance of the mandate or authority to act for the principal, and the evidence of this may be either verbal or in writing. However, it is a general rule that those obligations which can only be undertaken by solemn formalities cannot be entered on by a delegate who has not received his authority in writing. But it is often constituted, at the same time that its extent is defined, by mere appointment to some known and recognized function — as where one is appointed agent for a banking establishment, factor for a merchant, broker, supercargo, or attorney. In these cases, usages and practices define the powers granted to the agent; and the principal will not readily be subjected to duties going beyond the usual functions of the agency; nor will the third parties dealing with the agent be bound by private instructions inconsistent with its usual character.

 Warm-up Questions

1. **What do you think about the relation between principal and agent?**
2. **Try to define agency with your own words.**

7.1　An Overview of the Law of Agency
代理法概述

7.1.1　Definition of Agency　代理的定义

Agency refers to such circumstances where the agent, by the authorization of the principal, to act on the behalf of the principal to conclude a contract with a third party or perform other juristic acts, as a result the rights and/or the obligations caused by the agent's actions falling within the scope of the authority will bind the principal.

The law of agency is based on the Latin maxim: *Qui facit per alium*, *facit per se*, which means "he who acts through another is deemed in law to do it himself". Agency, in its legal sense, nearly always relates to commercial or contractual dealings and is generally evidenced by an agency contract or agreement entered into by the principal and the agent.

Agency involves a tripartite set of relationships among the principal, the agent and the third party. The relationship between the principal and the agent is referred to as the internal relationship of agency while the relationship between the principal or the agent and the third party is the external relationship of agency.

7.1.2 Creation of the Authority of Agent 代理权的产生

1. Under the Continental Law System

In the continental law jurisdictions, there are two methods to create the authority of agent — voluntary agency and statutory agency[4].

1) Voluntary agency

As to voluntary agency, the authority of agent is created by the expression of intention of the principal. The principal may express such an intention orally or in writing, may express to the agent or the third party with whom the agent is dealing.

2) Statutory agency

In most continental law counties, all agencies created other than by expression of intention of the principal are referred to as statutory agencies, and the agent of such an agency is called statutory agent[5]. The authority of a statutory agent may be created: a) by law, for example, the parents have the authority of agent to their underage children; b) by the appointment of the court, such as the liquidator appointed by the court; c) by the appointment of private individuals, such as the guardian of an orphan appointed by the orphan's relatives.

As a fictitious person[6], a company must have agents to act on the behalf of it. Normally, the directors are the primary agents of a company, and their authorities may be created by corporate constitution or by law.

2. Under the Common Law System

At common law, authority of agent may be created by the following causes.

1) Express appointment[7]

Express appointment is that the principal expressed explicitly to appoint someone as the agent. The principal may make such an appointment orally or in writing. A formal power of attorney[8] is required when making the appointment, if the principal authorizes the agent to conclude a deed contract under seal with a third party.

2) Implied authority[9]

Implied authority means that the principal's words or conduct caused the agent to be authorized to conclude contracts on the behalf of the principal, and thereby the principal is bound by the contracts just like he appointed the agent expressly. For example, A usually requests B to order goods on his behalf from C, and makes payments to C on time; then such an order shall still be binding on A if B continues to order from C on his behalf, unless otherwise notice made by A to B as well as C. This may be also called agency by estoppel[10] at common law.

3) Agency of necessity[11]

Agency of necessity arises where the entrusted person must have the authority of agent in order to preserve certain property when he is entrusted with the property by another person.

The doctrine of agency of necessity which prescribes that in a situation of emergency the agent is automatically authorized to act on the behalf of the principal is one of the oldest means of creating an agency. The origin of this agency is found in the authority of shipmaster to act in emergencies as agent of the shipowner in order to preserve the ship and the cargo on it.

However, in practice, the courts are very cautious to recognize an agency of necessity.

4) Agency by ratification[12]

If an agent concluded a contract on the behalf of the principal without or exceeding the authority, the principal will not be bound by this contract. However, the principal may ratify such a contract afterwards and then an agency by ratification arises. The agency by ratification makes such a contract the same as one concluded by authorization and binding on the principal upon conclusion.

7.1.3 Unauthorized Agency 无权代理

Unauthorized agency refers to the act of agency performed by an agent without authority. Strictly speaking, unauthorized agency is illegal. In practice, unauthorized agency may be caused by any of the following reasons:

(1) Agency without implied authority;

(2) Agency by noneffective authority;

(3) Agency exceeding the scope of authority;

(4) Agency after the termination of authority.

Any unauthorized agency, without ratification by the principal, shall not be binding on the principal. In an unauthorized agency, the agent shall be held liable for the losses resulted from such an agency, incurred by a bona fide third party who is unaware of the fact of unauthorized agency. However, there are some different provisions on unauthorized agency in different jurisdictions.

1. Under the Continental Law System

Most continental law countries allow the third party to exhort the principal to ratify an unauthorized agency, or revoke the contract entered into with the unauthorized agent.

In principle, the unauthorized agent shall be liable for the third party who does not know whether he has the authority. French law and Swiss law provide that an unauthorized agent shall compensate the damages to the third party. But in Germany, the third party may choose to claim for damages, or require the unauthorized agent to perform the contract.

2. Under the Common Law System

At common law, unauthorized agency is referred to as breach of implied warranty of authority[13]. It is considered by common law that the agent gives an implied warranty of authority to the third party when he concludes a contract with the third party on the behalf of the alleged principal. Therefore, if the agent concludes a contract with a third party without or exceeding the authority, the third party may sue him for breach of implied warranty of authority.

A lawsuit for breach of implied warranty of authority shall be lodged by the third party and, provided that the third party does not know that the agent has no authority, the unauthorized agent shall be held liable no matter whether he performed this act of unauthorized agency fraudulently or innocently, even if his authority has been terminated, without his awareness, by death or mental disorder of the principal. Nevertheless, if an unauthorized agency is caused by the ambiguous instructions given by the principal and the agent performed the instructions reasonably and with the best of intentions, he will not be held liable.

7.1.4　Termination of Agency　代理的终止

1. Termination of agency

Agency may be terminated by certain act of the parties to the agency, or by operation of law.

1) By certain act of the parties

If the principal and the agent have fixed the term of agency in the agency contract, the agency will expire at the fixed time. The agency may be also terminated by the mutual agreement of the parties, if there is no term of agency fixed in the agency contract.

In principle, most countries allow the principal to revoke the authority of the agent unilaterally at any time. However, such a revocation shall be informed to the agent in advance reasonably, and the principal shall compensate the damages for the loss of the agent, including the loss of commission and other remunerations, if such a revocation is not in conformity with the terms of the agency contract.

In some jurisdictions, the power of the principal to revoke the authority of the agent may be limited in two directions.

(1) If a principal has allowed the agent to assume authority, a revocation of the authority will only be effective as against the third parties whom are informed of the revocation of the authority.

(2) If the principal has given the agent an authority coupled with an interest, the authority is irrevocable. For example, A borrowed some money from B and appointed B as his agent to collect the rents of his estate to repay the debt he owes B. In such a case, A can not revoke the authority given to B before the debt is paid off.

2) By operation of law

In most jurisdictions, an agency may be terminated by operation of law under any of the following circumstances:

(1) Death, bankruptcy or loss of capacity of the principal;

(2) Death, bankruptcy or loss of capacity of the agent.

2. Effect of termination of agency

1) Between the principal and the agent

After the termination of agency, the agent loses his authority and it will be an unauthorized agency if he continues to perform the act of agency.

In some continental law countries, such as Germany, in order to protect the interest of the agent, the agent is entitled to claim damages against the principal after the termination of agency if he has established good will for the principal in the course of his agency. Such damages may be determined upon:

(1) The principal gains substantial benefits from third parties introduced by the agent;

(2) The agent should have gained commissions if the agency is not terminated;

(3) Paying the damages to the agent is fair and reasonable.

2) To the third parties

Whether the termination of agency is effective to a third party, depends on the knowledge of the third party of the termination of agency. The termination of agency shall only be effective to third parties after they have been informed of such a termination. If a third party, without his knowledge of the termination of agency, concludes a contract with the agent after such a termination, then this contract shall be binding on the principal.

7.2 Internal Relationship of Agency 代理的内部关系

Internal relationship of agency refers to the relationship between the principal and the agent. Typically, the rights and duties of both parties are prescribed in the agency contract entered into between the principal and the agent.

In most countries, the following basic duties are required to be performed respectively by the agent and the principal.

7.2.1 Duties of the Agent 代理人的义务

1. To exercise due diligence in the performance of acts of agency

An agent shall exercise due diligence, care and reasonable skill in acting on the behalf of principal, or else he may be held liable for the loss incurred by the principal resulting from his failure to exercise so.

2. To be in good faith and loyal to the principal

An agent shall make known all the information he has acquired about the third parties to the principal, which may be taken into consideration by the principal to make decisions.

An agent shall not conclude contracts on the behalf of the principal with himself without the consent of the principal. For example, the principal authorized the agent to sell some goods in great demand, the agent can not enter into a contract with the principal to purchase the goods, unless the principal has consented to this in advance. Without specific consent of his principal, an agent shall not act on the behalf of any third party to conclude contracts with the principal and gain commissions from both sides.

An agent shall not take bribes or make secret profits, or collude with any third party to impair the interest of the principal. If an agent does make a secret profit, or takes a bribe from the third party with whom he contracted on the behalf of the principal, the principal may be entitled the following rights:

(1) Recover the amount of the secret profit from the agent;

(2) Refuse to pay the commission or other remuneration to the agent;

(3) Dismiss the agent without notice;

(4) Avoid the contract concluded by the agent and this third party;

(5) Claim damages against the agent and this third party. According to the Prevention of Corruption Act 1906[14] of the UK, both the agent taking the bribe and the third party paying the bribe may be prosecuted for their criminal liabilities.

3. Not to disclose confidential information entrusted to him by the principal

The agent, within the term of agency or after the termination of agency, shall not disclose the confidential information he acquired in the course of agency to the third parties, or use the information to compete with the principal unfairly.

Nevertheless, after the termination of agency, the principal may not immoderately limit the agent's use of technology or experience acquired in the course of agency, except for those reasonable limitations on trade.

4. To render an account to the principal

The agent is responsible to keep an accurate account of all transactions he does on the behalf of the principal, and render the account to the principal as required by him or in the agency contract. In principle, all the proceeds the agent obtained for the principal shall hand in to the principal. However, if the principal fails to pay the agent due commission or other remuneration on time, the agent may has a lien on the principal's goods, or draw money from the proceeds obtained for the principal to set off such commission or other remuneration.

5. Not to delegate his authority to others

Normally, an agent shall not delegate his authority to others, unless the principal consents or it is a usual practice in trade, or there is an external need to do so.

7.2.2 Duties of the Principal 本人的义务

1. To pay the commission to the agent

In most countries, there is no detailed provision of law on commission of agency. Therefore, the amount of the commission and the terms under which it is payable depend entirely on the terms of the agency contract.

2. To indemnify the agent for special expenses caused by performing his duties

Generally, the principal need not pay the normal expenses the agent incurred in the execution of his authority. However, if the agent incurs expenses or losses because he performs some acts according to instruction of the principal, the principal shall indemnify such expenses or losses. For example, as instructed by the principal, the agent brings an action against a third party in breach with whom the agent entered into a contract on the behalf of the principal and incurs some expenses, and then the principal shall indemnify such expenses to the agent.

3. To allow the agent check the relevant accounts

Some continental law countries entitle the agent to consult the relevant accounts of the principal in order to calculate and check the commissions.

7.3 External Relationship of Agency 代理的外部关系

The external relationship includes the relationship between the principal and the third party, and the relationship between the agent and the third party.

7.3.1 Under the Continental Law System 大陆法系

At continental law, the agency is divided into two types: direct agency and indirect agency[15]. A direct agency is such an agency where the agent, within the scope of the authority, acts as a representative of the principal and contracts with a third party in the name of the principal, and the parties to this contract are the principal and the third party.

On the contrary, an agency where the agent, within the scope of the authority, concludes a contract with a third party on the account of the principal but in his own name, is an indirect agency. To such a contract, the parties are the agent and the third party. The principal may claim the contractual rights against the third party only after the agent transfers these contractual rights to the principal by concluding another contract with the principal.

In some continental law countries, such as Germany and Japan, indirect agency is limited in the trade of movable properties and securities; whereas there is no such a limitation in France.

7.3.2 Under the Common Law System 普通法系

At common law, external relationship of agency may be created in the following three cases.

1. Agent for a named principal

If an agent makes it clear to the third party that he acts on the behalf of a named principal when entering into a contract with the third party, the agent incurs neither rights nor liabilities under the contract and will drop out of the contract after the conclusion of contract.

However, there are some exceptions:

(1) The agent shall be liable for the contract if he signed his own name on a deed contract under seal;

(2) The agent shall be liable for the bill of exchange if he signed his own name on a bill of exchange;

(3) The agent shall be liable when a common usage in practice makes him liable.

2. Agent for a unnamed principal

If an agent expressly contracts with a third party as an agent but does not indicate the name of the principal, he will not be liable for the contract. However, if the agent does not, on the face of the contract, explicitly show that he is merely an agent (for example, only referring to himself as "Manager" or "Broker"), he may incur personal liability.

3. Agent for an undisclosed principal

Sometimes, the agent discloses neither the existence nor the name of the principal to the third party when contracting with the third party. In fact, he contracts as if he were the principal.

In such a case, the undisclosed principal has the right to intervene in the contract and claim the contractual rights against, or if necessary, sue the third party directly. If he exercises this right, he renders himself personally liable to the third party. However, the undisclosed principal can not exercise this right if the exercise of the right will contravene the express or implied terms of the contract conclude between the agent and the third party, or if the third party concludes the contract with the agent relying on his skill or solvency.

The third party, after having discovered the principal, has an option to elect to claim the contractual rights on the principal or the agent. If the third party unequivocally elects to claim against either the principal or the agent, he may not change his mind afterwards and sue the other. Commencement of litigation against either is prima facie evidence[16] of such election, the third party may sue the other subsequently if this evidence is rebutted. However, judgement of the court against either is conclusive evidence[17] of such election, so the third party, even if unsatisfied, may not sue the other.

7.4 Agents Assuming Special Liabilities
承担特别责任的代理人

In general, the agent will drop out of the contract after concluding a contract with the third party on the behalf of the principal. He assumes neither contractual liability to the third party, nor to the principal if the third party fails to perform the contract.

However, in practice, there are some agents assuming special liabilities to the principal or the third party.

7.4.1 Agents Assuming Special Liabilities to the Principal
对本人承担特别责任的代理人

A del credere agent[18] assumes special liability to the principal. Such an agent sells goods on the behalf of the principal and guarantees that the buyer (the third party) is absolute solvent. He will be liable for damages incurred by the principal resulting from the nonpayment of the buyer whom he introduced.

Typically, a del credere agent shall conclude a del credere contract with the principal in addition to the agency contract, or an agency contract containing a del credere clause.

7.4.2 Agents Assuming Special Liabilities to the Third Parties
对第三人承担特别责任的代理人

1. Confirming agent[19]

A confirming agent is an agent who places an order to the domestic supplier (the third party) on the behalf of the foreign buyer (the principal) and confirms the order to be paid. If the foreign buyer fails to pay the price, he will be liable for the payment to the domestic supplier. In the UK, a confirm agent is also known as confirming house or export house[20].

In international trade, there is another confirming agent who assumes special liability to the third party, that is, the confirming bank[21] under a letter of credit. A confirming bank is a bank which engages to honor a letter of credit issued by another bank. To the confirming bank, the issuing bank is the principal and the beneficiary of the credit is the third party. The confirming bank shall be liable to pay the amount of the credit to the beneficiary against the complying presentation of documents if the issuing bank fails to pay.

2. Forwarding agent[22]

An agent for the exporter in moving cargo to an overseas destination is called forwarding agent, or freight forwarder. These agents are familiar with the import rules and regulations of foreign countries, the methods of shipping, and the documents related to foreign trade.

Reading Material

Freight Forwarder: Agent or Principal Contractor?

Whether the freight forwarder is an agent or a principal contractor depends on the facts of each case and on the law in the particular jurisdiction in question. One must look at all the circumstances of the arrangements between the freight forwarder and the shipper, including but not limited to: contract, telephone calls, correspondence, tariff, bill of lading issued (if any), previous dealings, etc. between the freight forwarder and carriers, as well as the correspondence between the freight forwarder and the shipper.

Merely because a freight forwarder issues a document entitled "bill of lading" may not necessarily mean that the freight forwarder is a carrier. The forwarder might have issued a bill of lading and the ocean carrier issued an ocean bill of lading as well; the contract between the shipper and freight forwarder, however, might have explicitly provided that the latter acted only as agent. Furthermore, the forwarder might have been paid a commission from the shipper or a brokerage from the carrier rather than making a profit from a difference in the freight rates.

By customary rule in some countries, a forwarding agent who books ship space from a carrier (the third party) for the exporter (the principal) incurs liability to the carrier. He shall pay dead freight[23] to the carrier if the exporter does not load the cargo to the ship booked, and then he may claim damages against the exporter.

3. Insurance broker[24]

In international trade, it is a usual practice that the buyer or the seller purchases the cargo insurance through an insurance broker. An insurance broker concludes the insurance contract with the insurer (the third party) on the behalf of the insured (the principal) and is liable for the insurance premium to the insurer. If the insured fails to pay the premium, the insurance broker shall pay to the insurer directly.

It should be noted that, by convention, the commission (or brokerage) to the insurance broker is paid by the insurer.

7.5　Provisions and Regulations Relating to Agency in China
中国与代理有关的法律法规

7.5.1　Provisions of the General Principles of the Civil Law of the PRC
《中华人民共和国民法通则》中的规定

The section 2 of the chapter 4 of the General Principles of the Civil Law of the PRC makes particular provisions on agency.

The article 63 states that citizens and legal persons may perform civil juristic acts through agents. An agent shall perform civil juristic acts in the name of the principal within the scope of the authority. The principal shall bear civil liability for the agent's acts of agency.

The article 64 divides agency into entrusted agency, statutory agency and appointed agency[25]. The entrusted agency means that the agent is appointed by the principal himself, which is similar to the voluntary agency at continental law. A statutory agent is authorized by law and an appointed agent is designated by a people's court or other legal individual or organization. The statutory agency, together with the appointed agency, prescribed in the Chinese civil law is similar to the statutory agency at continental law.

According to the article 65, a civil juristic act may be entrusted to an agent in writing or orally. It shall be in writing if so required by law.

The article 66 provides that the principal shall be liable for an act performed by an actor without authority or exceeding the scope of his authority or after termination of agency, only if he ratifies the agency retroactively. If a principal is aware that an act is being executed in his name but fails to repudiate it, his consent shall be deemed to have been given. An agent shall be held liable if he fails to perform his duties and causes damage to the principal. If an agent and a third party in collusion do harm to the principal's interests, the agent and the third party shall bear the joint and several liabilities. If a third party is aware that an actor has no authority or is exceeding the authority of agency, or his authority of agency has expired and yet joins him in a civil act and thus brings damage to other people, the third party and the actor shall take the joint and several liabilities.

The article 67 says that if an agent is aware that the matter entrusted is illegal but still carries it out, or if a principal is aware that his agent's act is illegal but does not express to oppose it, the principal and the agent shall take the joint and several liabilities.

7.5.2　Provisions of the Contract Law of the PRC
《中华人民共和国合同法》中的规定

The chapters 21, 22 and 23 of the Contract Law of the PRC make provisions on three types of contracts relating to agency: contracts for commission, contracts for brokerage and contracts for intermediation[26].

This law defines a contract for commission as a contract whereby the principal and the agent agree that the agent shall handle the matters of the principal. According to the provisions of the chapter 21, the agent, within the scope of the authority, concludes a contract with a third party in his own name, and the third party knows the proxy relationship between the agent and principal at the time of concluding the contract, the contract shall directly bind the principal and the third party, unless there are conclusive evidences to prove that the said contract only binds the agent and the third party. On the contrary, if the third party does not know the proxy relationship between the agent and principal and if the agent does not perform the obligation in respect of the principal due to causes on the part of the third party, the agent shall disclose the third party to the principal. The principal hence may exercise the contractual rights against the third party, except that the third party will not conclude the contract with the agent if he knows the principal at the time of concluding the contract. If the agent does not perform the obligations in respect of the third party due to causes on the part of the principal, the agent shall disclose the principal to the third party. The third party hence may choose to claim the contractual rights against the agent or the principal, but the third party may not change his mind after he made the choice.

Under the Chinese contract law, a contract for brokerage refers to a contract whereby the broker is, in his own name, engaged in trade activities for the benefit of the principal, and the principal pays his the remuneration. The expenses which the broker incurred in handling the entrusted matters shall be borne by the broker unless otherwise agreed upon by the parties. Where a contract is concluded between a broker and a third party, the contract is directly binding on the broker. If the third party fails in performing the obligations and causes losses to the principal, the broker shall be liable for damages to the principal unless otherwise agreed upon by the parties. The principal shall pay to the broker corresponding remuneration when the broker has finished the whole or part of the entrusted matters. Where the principal fails to pay the remuneration in due time, the broker shall have a lien on the entrusted articles unless otherwise agreed upon by the parties.

A contract for intermediation, according to the Chinese contract law, is a contract whereby the intermediator reports to the principal the opportunity for concluding a contract or provides intermediate service for concluding a contract, and the principal pays him the remuneration. The principal shall pay the intermediator remuneration in accordance with the terms of the intermediation contract if the intermediator has facilitated the conclusion of the contract, but the expenses for the intermediate service shall be borne by the intermediator himself. Contrarily, if the intermediator fails in facilitating the conclusion of a contract, he may not request for the payment of remuneration, but may request the principal to pay the necessary expenses for the intermediate service.

Group Discussion ▶▶▶

1. Compare the major provisions on agency under the two major law systems.
2. Tell your own opinions about unauthorized agency.
3. Talk about some agents assuming special liabilities in international business.
4. Discuss the important legal provisions relating to agency in China.

NOTES ►►►

1　agent　代理人

2　principal　本人，委托人

3　delegatus non potest delegare　受权之人不能授权于人（拉丁谚语，相当于英语中的 a delegate can not delegate）

4　voluntary agency　意定代理；statutory agency　法定代理

5　statutory agent　法定代理人

6　fictitious person　法人

7　express appointment　明示的指定

8　power of attorney　委任书，授权书

9　implied authority　默示的授权

10　agency by estoppel　不容否认的代理

11　agency of necessity　客观必需的代理

12　agency by ratification　追认的代理

13　breach of implied warranty of authority　违反有代理权的默示担保

14　Prevention of Corruption Act 1906　（英国）《1906 年反贪污法》

15　direct agency　直接代理；indirect agency　间接代理

16　prima facie evidence　初步证据

17　conclusive evidence　确证，决定性证据

18　del credere agent　信用担保代理人

19　confirming agent　保付代理人

20　confirming house　保付商行；export house　出口商行

21　confirming bank　（信用证）保兑行

22　forwarding agent　运输代理人（亦用 freight forwarder）

23　dead freight　空舱费

24　insurance broker　保险经纪人

25　entrusted agency　委托代理；statutory agency　法定代理；appointed agency　指定代理

26　contract for commission　委托合同；contract for brokerage　行纪合同；contract for intermediation　居间合同

Restraining Agent from Misusing Confidential Information
限制代理人滥用机密信息

Take Ltd. , the claimant, is an English company specialized in the importation, wholesale and design of high and medium quality furniture. The second defendant was the sole director of the first defendant, BSM Marketing Ltd. In the year 2000, the second defendant was working as agent for the claimant. In November 2000, the second defendant agreed to carry out consultancy work for the claimant through the first defendant, for which he was to be paid on an agreed formula largely based on the net sales of the claimant. The second defendant's agency agreement was renegotiated in subsequent years. The last signed agreement covered the period from 1 April 2004 to 31 March 2005. The second defendant continued to perform services for the claimant·after that date until a date in October or November 2005. In October 2005, the claimant requested an interim injunction against the defendants, which was continued on the basis of undertakings by the defendants not to use or disclose any confidential information acquired directly or indirectly by the defendants in respect of certain named customers and suppliers.

The claimant issued proceedings based on two grounds. First, that the second defendant had acted in breach of his duty of loyalty to the claimant during the time that he was the claimant's agent. Secondly, that the second defendant acted in breach of his duty not to misuse information which he obtained in confidence either during his agency or afterwards. Whilst giving evidence, the second defendant conceded that he had been disloyal to the claimant in the last months of his agency. The claimant alleged that the second defendant's breach of loyalty caused a substantial loss of business from two existing customers, and was responsible for its failure to obtain substantial orders from another potential customer. The second defendant denied that he had caused the claimant any damage in that regard. Moreover, the claimant claimed that the second defendant had been in receipt of, and misused, four categories of confidential information: (a) a list of 32 customers serviced by the second defendant; (b) the claimant's pricing structure setting out the prices at which the claimant's products were sold to its customers; (c) production costs paid by the claimant to its suppliers; and (d) information concerning the preferences of the claimant's customers such as terms of style, size and design of the products. It was said that such information had been divulged by the second defendant in circumstances which breached his duty of confidence and that he would continue to divulge such confidential information unless restrained from doing so by permanent injunction.

The court held that in the circumstances of the case, the second defendant had, in relation to one customer, acted in breach of his fiduciary duty of loyalty to the claimant. He had played an active part in the formation of a group which had acted in competition with the claimant, and which had been responsible for that customer ceasing to order goods from the claimant. In respect of the other customer, although the second defendant had acted in conflict with his duty of loyalty, it had not been shown that he was responsible for the loss of margins which the claimant alleged to have suffered. The second defendant's disloyal actions had also caused the claimant to lose orders which it would otherwise have received from a potential customer. In respect of the confidential information, it would be appropriate to protect the claimant in respect of the prices at which it sold to individual customers and its manufacturing costs from individual suppliers. The undertakings as injunctions would, to that limited extent, be continued. The defendants would also be restrained from disclosing any of the claimant's documents to third parties, and would be required to return all relevant documents howsoever stored.

Duty of Care Owed by Agent
代理人应尽的谨慎义务

Plaintiff, Henderson, was a Lloyd's name (individual member) who was among the members of syndicates managed by the defendant underwriting agents, Merrett Syndicates. The relationship between the names, members' agents and managing agents was regulated by the terms of agency and subagency agreements which gave the agent 'absolute discretion' in respect of underwriting business conducted on behalf of the name but it was accepted that it was an implied term of the agreements that the agents would exercise due care and skill in the exercise of their functions as managing agents. Clause 2(a) of such agency agreements provided that "the agent shall act as the underwriting agent for the name for the purpose of underwriting at Lloyd's for the account of the name such classes and descriptions of insurance business ... as may be transacted by the Syndicate".

The plaintiffs brought proceedings against the defendants alleging that the defendants had been negligent in the conduct and management of the plaintiffs' syndicates, and wished, for limitation purposes, to establish a duty of care in tort in addition to any contractual duty that might be owed by the defendants. The judge decided in favor of the plaintiffs. The defendants appealed to the Court of Appeals, which dismissed the appeal. The defendants further appealed to the House of Lords.

The appeal was dismissed by the House of Lords for the following reasons.

(1) Where a person assumed responsibility to perform professional or quasi-professional services for another who relied on those services, the relationship between the parties was itself sufficient, without more, to give rise to a duty on the part of the person providing the services to exercise reasonable skill and care in doing so. Accordingly, managing agents at Lloyd's owed a duty of care to names who were members of syndicates under the agents' management, since the agents by holding themselves out as possessing a special expertise to advise the names on the suitability of risks to be underwritten and on the circumstances in which, and the extent to which, reinsurance should be taken out and claims should be settled, plainly assumed responsibility towards the names in their syndicates. ... The fact that the agency and subagency agreements gave the agent " absolute discretion " in respect of underwriting business conducted on behalf of the name did not have the effect of excluding a duty of care, contractual or otherwise. The discretion given to agents merely defined the scope of the agents' authority, not the standard of skill and care required of agents in carrying on underwriting business on behalf of names.

(2) An assumption of responsibility by a person rendering professional or quasi-professional services coupled with a concomitant reliance by the person for whom the services were rendered could give rise to a tortious duty of care irrespective of whether there was a contractual relationship between the parties. In consequence, unless the contract between the parties precluded him from doing so, a plaintiff who had available to him concurrent remedies in contract and tort was entitled to choose that remedy which appeared to him to be the most advantageous ...

(3) Clause 2 (a) of the agency agreement contained an express undertaking by the underwriting agent to act as the underwriting agent of the name, whether the agent was acting as a members' agent or was a combined agent acting as managing agent in respect of a syndicate of which the name was a member, the only difference being that in the former case the members' agent carried out the underwriting through the agency of a managing agent under the terms of the prescribed form of subagency agreement, whereas in the latter case the agent carried out the underwriting itself. It followed that members' agents were responsible to the names for any failure to exercise reasonable skill and care on the part of managing agents to whom underwriting was delegated by the members' agents.

Chapter 8

Anti-dumping Law and Anti-subsidy Law
反倾销法与反补贴法

Learning Objectives

- ☑ To understand the definition of dumping and subsidy in international trade
- ☑ To learn the basic rules of anti-dumping law and anti-subsidy law
- ☑ To know about the Chinese anti-dumping law and anti-subsidy law

 Opening Vignette

Anti-dumping and Countervailing Duty Investigations in the US

Both anti-dumping and anti-subsidy are non-trade-means of each country carrying out to protect their trade under the international trade regulations. These two succor measures are most adopted when the domestic industry of the importing country is damaged by the improper behavior of competition. As an act of trade protection permitted by WTO, anti-dumping and anti-subsidy have been included into the core of foreign-trade policies and laws all over the world.

In the US, the International Trade Commission (ITC) and the Department of Commerce are responsible for conducting anti-dumping (AD) and countervailing duty (CVD) (anti-subsidy) investigations and five-year (sunset) reviews under Title VII of the Tariff Act of 1930. Under this law, US industries may petition the ITC and the Department of Commerce for relief from unfairly priced (dumped) and subsidized imports.

Dumping occurs when a foreign producer sells a product in the US at a price that is below that producer's sales price in its home market, or at a price that is lower than its cost of production. Subsidizing occurs when a foreign government provides financial assistance to benefit the production, manufacture, or exportation of a good. If the Department of Commerce finds that an imported product is dumped or subsidized and the ITC finds that a US industry producing a like product[1] is materially injured or threatened with material injury, an anti-dumping duty order or countervailing duty order will be imposed to offset the dumping or subsidies.

When an anti-dumping or countervailing duty order is imposed, the Department of Commerce instructs the Bureau of Customs and Border Protection (Customs) to assess anti-dumping or countervailing duties on imports of the product into the US to offset the unfair trade practice. Under the Continued Dumping and Subsidy Offset Act of 2000 (CDSOA or Byrd Amendment), anti-dumping and countervailing duties collected are distributed annually to affected domestic producers for qualifying expenditures incurred. Following imposition of an AD or CVD order, the ITC provides Customs with a list of affected domestic producers (those producers who publicly expressed support for the petition during the investigation); those producers can then submit certifications to Customs of qualifying expenditures in order to receive a pro rata share of the annual distribution of duties collected.

The Department of Commerce and the ITC review each outstanding anti-dumping and countervailing duty order every five years to determine whether revocation of the order would be likely to lead to continuation or recurrence of dumping or subsidies and of material injury within a reasonably foreseeable time. If both agencies make affirmative determinations, the order is continued for another five years; if not, the order is revoked.

Warm-up Questions

1. What is the meaning of dumping?
2. What is the meaning of subsidizing?
3. Summarize the anti-dumping and anti-subsidy investigation procedures in the US.

8.1　Anti-dumping Law
反倾销法

8.1.1　Dumping and International Anti-dumping Legislation
倾销及国际反倾销立法

1. Dumping

Dumping occurs when foreign producers sell their products to an importer in the domestic market at prices lower than in their own national markets, or at prices below cost of production, the sale or importation of which injures or threatens to injure a domestic industry producing like or comparable products or retards the establishment of a potential industry. It is a form of price differentiation between two national markets and is not a prohibited practice under international trade agreements. However, remedial action may be taken where dumping causes (or threatens to cause) material injury to an import country industry.

According to the article 2 of the Agreement on Implementation of Article VI of GATT 1994[2], a product is to be considered as being dumped, i. e., introduced into the commerce of another country at less than its normal value, if the export price of the product exported from one country to another is less than the comparable price, in the ordinary course of trade, for the like product when destined for consumption in the exporting country.

2. International anti-dumping legislation

Dumping could be backdated to the mercantilism age, when Adam Smith was in. With the beginning of the industrial revolution and the development of the world economic trade, the contradiction between dumping and anti-dumping became a "kink" of international economic relationship. Today, it has become an important international trade issue which the whole world pays attention to. The legislature of every nation pointed out that the aim of anti-dumping law was to restrict unfair trade practices and anti-dumping law is primarily a measure of trade protection.

With the restrictions on use of the non-tariff trade barriers and tariff concessions, anti-dumping becomes a kind of important non-tariff trade defense measures of every nation to prevent or stop the behaviors of dumping, and to protect domestic industry gradually. For this reason, the countries all over the world revised and perfected the anti-dumping legislation one after another, and the developing countries also joined in the ranks of the anti-dumping legislation and the practice of fair trade.

Canada, for the first time, stipulated the measures of anti-dumping in the Customs Tariff Act[3] in 1904. The Anti-dumping law of United States was derived from the US Tariff Act of 1930. Along with further development of world economic integration and globalization, most countries adopt anti-dumping measures, as a prevailing and important legal means to combat unfair competition and protect domestic industry.

In order to solve a series of important problems in international anti-dumping rules, the original members of GATT reached Art VI of the GATT 1947 to regulate the anti-dumping measures of its members. The Art VI of the GATT 1947 is very brief and states little about the procedural and substantive issues that arise in anti-dumping cases.

Negotiations in the Kennedy Round[4] have resulted in a revision Agreement in 1967, that is, Agreement on Implementation of Article VI of GATT[5] (also called the Anti-dumping Code). The Anti-dumping Code provides for the rights of contracting members to apply anti-dumping measures. This Code is the first international treaty on anti-dumping. Moreover, this code specified minimal procedural standards for anti-dumping cases. This code was revised by the Tokyo Round[6] negotiations in 1979 and came into effect in 1980. At the last round of negotiations under GATT, the Uruguay Round[7], the Agreement on Implementation of Article VI of GATT 1994 (also called the Anti-dumping Agreement) was reached through complicated and difficult negotiations and became effective at the same time as the WTO was established on Jan. 1st, 1995. The new Agreement provides with greater clarity and more details for the rules in relation to the methods of determining that a product is dumped, the criteria to be taken into account in a determination that dumped imports cause injury to a domestic industry, the procedures to be followed in initiating and conducting anti-dumping investigations, and the implementation and duration of anti-dumping measures. In addition, the new Agreement clarifies the role of dispute settlement panels in disputes relating to anti-dumping actions taken by domestic authorities. Therefore, the anti-dumping law of GATT in 1994 is a typical example of the anti-dumping legislation for various countries. It is binding on all the WTO members and is the main sign of the internationalization of anti-dumping legislation.

8.1.2 Major Principles of the Anti-dumping Agreement
反倾销协议的主要原则

If a company exports a product at a price lower than the price it normally charges on its own home market, it is said to be dumping the product. Whether an anti-dumping measure is legitimate or not depends on the method and result of injury determination. In light of the Anti-dumping Agreement, dumping shall be determined if three factors occurred simultaneously and the three factors are dumping (price difference), injury, causal link between dumping and injury.

1. Determination of dumping

The price difference is the first factor in determination of dumping. Price difference means the amount by which the normal value (the price prevailing in the exporting country) exceeds the export price (selling price to an importer).

1) Determination of normal value

Normal value refers to the price of product in domestic market of the exporting country. Usually when an export price below its normal value, it may be said that dumping exists. When there are no sales of the like product in the ordinary course of trade in domestic market of the exporting country or when, because of the particular market situation or the low volume of the sales in the domestic market of the exporting country, such sales do not permit a proper comparison, the margin of dumping shall be determined by comparison with a comparable price of the like product when exported to an appropriate third country, provided that this price is representative, or with the cost of production in the country of origin plus a reasonable amount for administrative, selling and general costs and for profits.

2) Determination of export price

After determination of a normal price, export price shall be determined in order to determinate whether the imported products are dumped or not. The export price of the imported products shall be determined in either of the following ways according to different circumstances:

(1) In case the imported products have an actual payment price or a payable price, such price shall be the export price;

(2) In cases where there is no export price or where it appears that the export price is unreliable because of association or a compensatory arrangement between the exporter and the importer or a third party, the export price may be constructed on the basis of the price at which the imported products are first resold to an independent buyer, or if the products are not resold to an independent buyer, or not resold in the condition as imported, on such reasonable basis as the authorities may determine.

In case where products are not imported directly from the country of origin but are exported to the importing country from an intermediate country, the price at which the products are sold from the country of export to the importing country shall normally be compared with the comparable price in the country of export. However, comparison may be made with the price in the country of origin, for example, if the products are merely transshipped through the country of export, or such products are not produced in the country of export, or there is no comparable price for them in the country of export.

A fair comparison shall be made between the export price and the normal value. This comparison shall be made at the same level of trade, normally at the ex-factory level, and in respect of sales made at as nearly as possible the same time. Due allowance shall be made in each case, on its merits, for differences which affect price comparability, including differences in conditions and terms of sale, taxation, levels of trade, quantities, physical characteristics, and any other differences which are also demonstrated to affect price comparability.

Apparently, it is most easy to determine dumping in case a product is exported at a price even lower than its cost of production.

2. Determination of injury

Injury refers to material injury to a domestic industry, threat of material injury or material retardation of the establishment of a domestic industry in the importing country.

1) Definition of domestic industry

First, in order to determine the domestic industry, the like product shall be interpreted. The term like product refers to a product which is identical, i.e., alike in all respects to the product under consideration, or in the absence of such a product, another product which, although not alike in all respects, has characteristics closely resembling those of the product under consideration.

Second, the term domestic industry shall be defined as the domestic producers as a whole of the like products or to those of them whose collective output of the products constitutes a major proportion of the total domestic production of those products, except that: a) when producers are related to the exporters or importers or are themselves importers of the allegedly dumped product, the term domestic industry may be interpreted as referring to the rest of the producers; b) in exceptional circumstances the territory of a country may, for the production in question, be divided into two or more competitive markets and the producers within each market may be regarded as a separate industry if the producers within such market sell all or almost all of their production of the product in question in that market, and the demand in that market is not to any substantial degree supplied by producers of the product in question located elsewhere in the territory. In such circumstances, injury may be found to exist even where a major portion of the total domestic industry is not injured, provided there is a concentration of dumped imports into such an isolated market and provided further that the dumped imports are causing injury to the producers of all or almost all of the production within such market.

2) Determination of injury

The determination of injury may be classified as causing a material injury, or constituting a threat of material injury to an already established domestic industry, or causing a material retardation to the establishment of a domestic industry.

A determination of a material injury shall be based on positive evidence and involve an objective examination of both the volume of the dumped imports and the effect of the dumped imports on prices in the domestic market for like products, and the consequent impact of these imports on domestic producers of such products. With regard to the volume of the dumped imports, the investigating authorities shall consider whether there has been a significant increase in dumped imports, either in absolute terms or relative to production or consumption in the importing country. With regard to the effect of the dumped imports on prices, it shall be taken into account that whether there has been a significant price undercutting by the dumped imports as compared with the price of a like product of the importing country, or whether the effect of such imports is otherwise to depress prices to a significant degree or prevent price increases, which otherwise would have occurred, to a significant degree. The examination of the impact of the dumped imports on the domestic industry concerned shall include an evaluation of all relevant economic factors and indices having a bearing on the state of the industry, including actual and potential decline in sales, profits, output, market share, productivity, return on investments, or utilization of capacity; factors affecting domestic prices; the magnitude of the margin of dumping[8]; actual and potential negative effects on cash flow, inventories, employment, wages, growth, ability to raise capital or investments, etc.

A determination of a threat of material injury shall not be based on allegation, conjecture or remote possibility merely but on facts. The change in circumstances which would create a situation in which the dumping would cause injury must be clearly foreseen and imminent. In making a determination regarding the existence of a threat of material injury, the authorities should consider, among other things, such factors as: a) a significant rate of increase of dumped imports into the domestic market indicating the likelihood of substantially increased importation; b) sufficient freely disposable, or an imminent, substantial increase in, capacity of the exporter indicating the likelihood of substantially increased dumped exports to the importing country's market, taking into account the availability of other export markets to absorb any additional exports; c) whether imports are entering at prices that will have a significant depressing or suppressing effect on domestic prices, and would likely increase demand for further imports; and d) inventories of the product being investigated are huge.

Generally, no one of these factors by itself can necessarily give decisive guidance but the totality of the factors considered must lead to the conclusion that further dumped exports are imminent and that, unless protective action is taken, material injury would occur.

3. Causal link between dumping and injury

The causal link between dumping and injury refers to a finding that the material injury suffered by the domestic industry is the direct result of the importation of the dumped product. It must be clearly demonstrated that the injury suffered is directly attributable to the alleged dumping.

Usually, the demonstration of a causal link between the dumped imports and the injury to the domestic industry shall be based on an examination of all relevant evidence before the authorities. In addition, the authorities shall also examine any known factors other than the dumped imports which at the same time are injuring the domestic industry, and the injuries caused by these other factors must not be attributed to the dumped imports. Factors which may be relevant in this respect include, among other things, the volume and prices of imports not sold at dumping prices, contraction in demand or changes in the patterns of consumption, trade restrictive practices of and competition between the foreign and domestic producers, developments in technology and the export performance and productivity of the domestic industry.

4. The procedure of anti-dumping investigation

Differing from the ecumenical commercial dispute case, the procedure of an anti-dumping investigation has its own features in practice. Typically, each country (or region) has a competent authority which is in charge of its foreign trade. In light of the Anti-dumping Agreement, the procedure of the anti-dumping investigation involves the following steps.

1) Application

The application is the first step of an anti-dumping investigation. An investigation to determine the existence, degree and effect of any alleged dumping shall be initiated upon a written application by or on behalf of the domestic industry.

An application shall include evidence of dumping, injury, and a causal link between the dumped imports and the alleged injury. Simple assertion, unsubstantiated by relevant evidence, cannot be considered sufficient.

2) Initiating an investigation

After received a written application, the authorities shall examine the accuracy and adequacy of the evidence provided in the application to determine whether there is sufficient evidence to justify the initiation of an investigation.

Before proceeding to initiate an investigation the authorities shall notify the government of the country of export or origin about the impending dumping investigation. From the initiation of the investigation, the authorities notifies all known interested parties about the initiation of the investigation and sends a proforma respondent's questionnaire to all the interested parties.

Unless a decision has been made to initiate an investigation, the authorities shall avoid any publicizing of the application for the initiation of an investigation. However, after receipt of a properly documented application and before proceeding to initiate an investigation, the authorities shall notify the government of the exporting country concerned.

If, under special circumstances, the authorities concerned decide to initiate an investigation without having received a written application by or on behalf of a domestic industry for the initiation of such investigation, they shall proceed only if they have sufficient evidence of dumping, injury and a causal link, to justify the initiation of an investigation.

Investigations shall, except under special circumstances, be concluded within 1 year, and in no case more than 18 months, after their initiation. Moreover, the authorities shall immediately terminate the investigation upon finding that the margin of dumping is minimus; or that the volume of dumped imports, actual or potential, or the injury, is negligible. The margin of dumping shall be considered to be minimus if it is less than 2 percent, expressed as a percentage of the export price. The volume of dumped imports shall normally be regarded as negligible if the volume of dumped imports from a particular country is found to account for less than 3 percent of imports of the like product in the importing country unless countries which individually account for less than 3 percent of the imports of the like product in the importing country collectively account for more than 7 percent of imports of the like product in the importing country.

3) Preliminary determination

The authorities shall make preliminary determination on the alleged dumping case after the investigation mentioned above. Where the preliminary determination affirms the dumping and the consequent injury to a domestic industry, the following provisional anti-dumping measures may be taken, such as to levy provisional anti-dumping tariffs, or to request the provision of cash deposits, etc. In any case an anti-dumping proceeding shall not hinder the procedures of customs clearance.

The application of provisional measures shall be limited to as short a period as possible, not exceeding 4 months or, on decision of the authorities concerned, upon request by exporters representing a significant percentage of the trade involved, to a period not exceeding 6 months. When authorities, in the course of an investigation, examine whether a duty lower than the margin of dumping would be sufficient to remove injury, these periods may be respectively 6 and 9 months.

4) Final determination

After preliminary determination, all interested parties may make further allegation or defences. The authorities shall accordingly further collect and examine the evidence and then make the final determination.

Once the final determination confirms the dumping and the consequent injury caused to the domestic industry, and the casual link between them, an anti-dumping duty may be imposed. The amount of the anti-dumping duty shall not exceed the margin of dumping and the anti-dumping duty shall remain in force only as long as and to the extent necessary to counteract dumping which is causing injury.

5) Judicial review

In light of the article 13 of the Anti-dumping Agreement, each contracting state whose national legislation contains provisions on anti-dumping measures shall maintain judicial, arbitral or administrative tribunals or procedures for the purpose, among other things, of the prompt review of administrative actions relating to final determinations. Such tribunals or procedures shall be independent of the authorities responsible for the determination or review in question.

Reading Material

China Imposes Anti-dumping Duties on Imports from India

Chinese importers of sulfamethoxazole have to pay anti-dumping duties as of the end of June, 2008 to offset damages caused by sulfamethoxazole producers in India.

The move followed the final determination made by the Ministry of Commerce which said sulfamethoxazole imports dumped from India have inflicted losses to local manufacturers.

The anti-dumping duty tax rates were set from 10.7% to 37.7%, and the tax would be in effect for 5 years.

Sulfamethoxazole is a sulfonamide bacteriostatic antibiotic, and also serves as an important material in producing other sulfonamides. It is commonly used to treat urinary tract infections.

China started its anti-dumping investigation on imported sulfamethoxazole from India in last June, and imposed temporary anti-dumping measures in February this year on the basis of its preliminary investigations.

8.1.3 Chinese Laws and Regulations on Anti-dumping
中国有关反倾销的法律法规

In China, the term anti-dumping was particularly prescribed for the first time in the article 30 of the Foreign Trade Law of the PRC[9] which was enacted in 1994. Three years later, in 1997, the Anti-dumping and Anti-subsidy Regulations of the PRC[10] was promulgated. In 2001, the Anti-dumping Regulation of the PRC[11] has been enacted, with most provisions conforming to those of the Agreement on Implementation of Article VI of GATT 1994. In light of the article 2 of this regulation, the meaning of anti-dumping was formulated as the circumstances where "imported products enter the market of PRC by way of dumping, and cause a material injury or constitute a threat of material injury to an already established domestic industry, or cause a material impediment to the establishment of a domestic industry".

8.2 Anti-subsidy Law
反补贴法

8.2.1 Subsidy and International Anti-subsidy Legislation
补贴及国际反补贴立法

1. Subsidy

In international trade, the meaning of subsidy is the financial contribution or any form of income or price support which is conferred by the government or any public body of the exporting country and which brings a benefit to the receiver. Export subsidy is a government policy to encourage export of goods and discourage sale of goods on the domestic market through low-cost loans or tax relief for exporters, or government financed international advertising or R&D. An export subsidy may artificially reduce the cost of exports and distort the competition.

2. International anti-subsidy legislation

Subsidy is considered disadvantageous to international trade and easy to result in unfair trade. In order to protect domestic market, almost every importing country confronts subsidy with countervailing measures. In order to harmonize the anti-subsidy measures of different countries, the original members of GATT constituted Art VI, Art XVI of GATT 1947. But the two articles are too brief to be applied in practice.

The Subsidy and Anti-subsidy Regulations Rules[12] was reached at the end of the Tokyo Round in 1979. This rule is the first international treaty on anti-subsidy. It provided for the investigation procedure and classified the export subsidy. Later, at the Uruguay Round in 1994, the Agreement on Subsidies and Countervailing Measures (SCM)[13] was signed and came into effect on Jan. 1st, 1995. It has 11 parts, 32 provisions and 7 annexes (substantial and procedural problems) and is more definite and practicable than the 1979 rules.

8.2.2 Major Principles of SCM 补贴与反补贴措施协议的主要原则

The Agreement on Subsidies and Countervailing Measures (SCM) first defines subsidy in particular and establishes three categories of subsidies: prohibited subsidy, actionable subsidy and non-actionable subsidy[14].

1. Definition of subsidy

In light of the article 1 of SCM, a subsidy exists if there is a financial contribution, income or price support by a government or any public body within a territory of a member to domestic producers and exporters, or any form of income or price support in the sense of Article XVI of GATT 1994; or if a benefit is thereby conferred.

The goal of a subsidy is to promote the competitive ability of domestically produced goods in both domestic and international market, and therefore may hinder import and encourage export.

2. Classification of subsidies

The SCM classifies subsidies into three categories, that is, prohibited subsidy, actionable subsidy and non-actionable subsidy.

1) Prohibited subsidy

This type of subsides is specifically designed to distort international trade, and likely to hurt the trade of other countries. Therefore a signatory of SCM shall neither grant nor maintain such subsidies. According to SCM, except certain agricultural subsidies, there are two types of subsidies being prohibited.

The first type prohibited subsidy consists of subsidies contingent, in law or in fact, whether wholly or as one of several conditions, on export performance. This type of subsidies is export subsidies. Hence, any subsidy whose payment to the recipient is directly linked to its export performance is a prohibited subsidy. According to the Annex I of SCM, export subsidies may be: a) the provision by governments of direct subsidies to a firm or an industry contingent upon export performance; b) currency retention schemes or any similar practices which involve a bonus on exports; c) internal transport and freight charges on export shipments, provided or mandated by governments, on terms more favorable than for domestic shipments; d) the provision by governments or their agencies either directly or indirectly through government-mandated schemes, of imported or domestic products or services for use in the production of exported goods; e) the full or partial exemption, remission, or deferral specifically related to exports, of direct taxes or social welfare charges paid or payable by industrial or commercial enterprises; f) the allowance of special deductions directly related to exports or export performance, over and above those granted in respect to production for domestic consumption, in the calculation of the base on which direct taxes are charged; g) the exemption or remission, in respect of the production and distribution of exported products, of indirect taxes in excess of those levied in respect of the production and distribution of like products when sold for domestic consumption; h) the exemption, remission or deferral of prior-stage cumulative indirect taxes on goods or services used in the production of exported products in excess of the exemption, remission or deferral of like prior-stage cumulative indirect taxes on goods or services used in the production of like products when sold for domestic consumption; i) the remission or drawback of import charges in excess of those levied on imported inputs that are consumed in the production of the exported product (making normal allowance for waste); j) the provision by governments of export credit guarantee or insurance programmes, of insurance or guarantee programmes against increases in the cost of exported products or of exchange risk programmes, at premium rates which are inadequate to cover the long-term operating costs and losses of the programmes; k) the grant by governments of export credits at rates below those which they actually have to pay for the funds so employed, or the payment by them of all or part of the costs incurred by exporters or financial institutions in obtaining credits, in so far as they are used to secure a material advantage in the field of export credit terms; l) any other charge on the public account constituting an export subsidy in the sense of Article XVI of GATT 1994.

The second type of prohibited subsidy consists of subsidies contingent, whether solely or as one of several other conditions, upon the use of domestic over imported goods. Such a subsidy sometimes is referred to as a local content subsidy[15] and will discriminate against the imported goods and hence impair the benefits that may have accrued to an importing country.

2) Actionable subsidy

Actionable subsidies are actionable and permitted in certain field. Through the use of subsidies, it may be cause adverse effects to the interests of other signatories, i.e.: a) injury to the domestic industry of another member; b) nullification or impairment of benefits accruing directly or indirectly to other members under GATT 1994 in particular the benefits of concessions bound under Article II of GATT 1994; c) serious prejudice to the interests of another member.

Whenever a member has reason to believe that an actionable subsidy, granted or maintained by another member, results in injury to its domestic industry, nullification or impairment or serious prejudice, it may request consultations with the other member. In the event that it is determined that such adverse effects exist, the subsidizing member must withdraw the subsidy or remove the adverse effects.

3) Non-actionable subsidy

For the first time, the SCM defines and explains the term of non-actionable subsidy. Such subsidies cannot be challenged in the WTO's dispute settlement procedure, and countervailing duty cannot be imposed on those imports so subsidized. According to SCM, non-actionable subsidies could either be non-specific subsidies, or specific subsidies involving assistance to industrial research and pre-competitive development activity, assistance to disadvantaged regions, or certain type of assistance for adapting existing facilities to new environmental requirements imposed by law and/or regulations.

Where another member believes that an otherwise non-actionable subsidy is resulting in serious adverse effects to a domestic industry, it may seek a determination and recommendation on the matter.

3. Procedural requirements on countervailing measures

The SCM allows members to take countervailing measures against subsidies. It also makes detailed procedural requirements on countervailing measures for the purpose of ensuring such measures to be right and fair.

1) Initiation and Investigation

An investigation to determine the existence, degree and effect of any alleged subsidy shall be initiated upon a written application by or on behalf of the domestic industry. An application shall include sufficient evidence of the existence of a subsidy, injury and a causal link between the subsidized imports and the alleged injury. Besides, an investigation shall not hinder the procedures of customs clearance, and investigations shall, except in special circumstances, be concluded within 1 year, and in no case more than 18 months, after their initiation.

2) Consultations

As soon as possible after an application is accepted, and in any event before the initiation of any investigation, the subsidizing member shall be invited to consultations with the aim of clarifying the situation. Furthermore, throughout the period of investigation, the subsidizing member shall be afforded a reasonable opportunity to continue consultations, with a view to clarifying the factual situation and to arriving at a mutually agreed solution.

3) Imposition of a countervailing duty

After reasonable efforts have been made to complete consultations, if a member makes a final determination of the existence and amount of the subsidy and that, through the effects of the subsidy, the subsidized imports are causing injury, it may impose a countervailing duty in accordance with the provisions of SCM.

4) Judicial review

The SCM requires members to create an independent tribunal to review the consistency of determinations of the investigating authority under domestic laws.

8.2.3 Chinese Laws and Regulations on Anti-subsidy
中国有关反补贴的法律法规

In China, like anti-dumping, anti-subsidy is also first prescribed in the Foreign Trade Law of the PRC in 1994. Then in 1997 Anti-dumping and Anti-subsidy Regulations of the PRC was promulgated. With the China'entry into WTO, Chinese government enacted the Countervailing Regulation of the PRC[16] in 2002, and revised it in 2004. The article 2 of this regulation states that "in case that imported products are subsidized and cause material injury or constitute a threat of material injury to an already established domestic industry, or cause a material impediment to the establishment of a domestic industry, an investigation shall be conducted and countervailing measures shall be taken in accordance with this Regulation".

 Group Discussion ▶▶▶

1. Why does WTO make detailed legal rules on anti-dumping and anti-subsidy?
2. Discuss some important international legal rules on anti-dumping and anti-subsidy.
3. Try to compare Chinese legal rules on anti-dumping and anti-subsidy with those international rules.

NOTES ▶▶▶

1 like product   同类产品

2 Agreement on Implementation of Article VI of GATT 1994   《关于执行＜1994 年关贸总协定＞第 6 条的协议》（通常简称为《反倾销协议》，即 Anti-dumping Agreement）

3 Customs Tariff Act   （加拿大）《海关关税法》

4 Kennedy Round   《关税与贸易总协定》的"肯尼迪回合"多边贸易谈判

5 Agreement on Implementation of Article VI of GATT   《关于执行＜关贸总协定＞第 6 条的协议》（通常简称为《反倾销守则》，即 Anti-dumping Code）

6 Tokyo Round   《关税与贸易总协定》的"东京回合"多边贸易谈判

7 Uruguay Round   《关税与贸易总协定》的"乌拉圭回合"多边贸易谈判

8 margin of dumping   倾销幅度，倾销差价

9 Foreign Trade Law of the PRC   《中华人民共和国对外贸易法》

10 Anti-dumping and Anti-subsidy Regulations of the PRC   《中华人民共和国反倾销和反补贴条例》

11 Anti-dumping Regulation of the PRC   《中华人民共和国反倾销条例》

12 Subsidy and Anti-subsidy Regulations Rules   《补贴与反补贴守则》

13 Agreement on Subsidies and Countervailing Measures (SCM)   《补贴与反补贴措施协议》

14 prohibited subsidy   禁止性补贴；actionable subsidy   可申诉补贴；non-actionable subsidy   不可申诉补贴

15 local content subsidy   当地含量补贴

16 Countervailing Regulation of the PRC   《中华人民共和国反补贴条例》

Anti-dumping Duties Imposed by European Council on Electronic Weighing Scales Exported by a Chinese Company

欧洲理事会对某中国公司出口的电子秤征收反倾销税

Following a complaint lodged by European Community producers of electronic weighing scales accounting for the majority of the total Community production of that product, the Commission initiated an anti-dumping proceeding pursuant to art 5 of Council Regulation (EC) 384/96 (on protection against dumped imports from countries not Members of the European Community) (the basic regulation) in respect of imports of certain electronic weighing scales originating in China, South Korea and Chinese Taiwan. The applicant was a company incorporated under Chinese law which produced such scales and exported them to the Community. Following further investigation, the Council imposed anti-dumping duties of 12.8% on the products exported by the applicant. The applicant applied for annulment of that regulation. It alleged four pleas in support of its action: (i) a manifest error of assessment in the application of art 2(7) of the basic regulation; (ii) infringement of art 3(2), (3), (5) and (8) of the basic regulation in that no injury to Community industry had been shown; (iii) infringement of art 3(6) of the basic regulation in respect of a manifest error of assessment when determining causation; and (iv) infringement of the procedural rules laid down in the basic regulation.

The Court of First Instance of the European Communities (CFI) held that there was no merit in any of the applicant's complaints and the action for annulment would be dismissed in its entirety. The applicant had failed: (i) to produce sufficient evidence to show that it had charged different prices to different customers and that its economic decisions had been taken in response to market signals reflecting supply and demand; (ii) to show that it did not sell its products at a loss in China or that there were purely commercial reasons for its conduct; and (iii) to show that it had maintained the identified ratio of sales on the Chinese domestic market to exports for purely commercial reasons. It followed that the Community institutions had committed no manifest error when concluding that the applicant had not fulfilled the criteria under art 2(7) of the basic regulation that it had operated in market economy conditions. Moreover, in the circumstances, the Council had made no error in evaluating the economic indicators relating to market shares, sales prices and profitability of the Community industry and there had been no manifest error of assessment when determining causation, so that it had therefore been established that injury had been caused to Community markets. Finally, there had been no procedural errors in the way in which the Community institutions had reached their decisions.

US Anti-dumping and Countervailing Duty Cases against Imports of Canadian Wheat
美国对加拿大小麦的反倾销及反补贴税案件

Sept. 13, 2002, the North Dakota Wheat Commission and the US Durum Growers Association file petitions seeking anti-dumping and countervailing duties on imports of durum and hard red spring wheat from Canada.

Oct. 23, 2002, the US Department of Commerce (DOC) initiates countervailing and anti-dumping investigations. Nov. 25, 2002, the US International Trade Commission (ITC) makes a preliminary determination that Canadian imports of durum and hard red spring wheat cause injury to US farmers. Mar. 4, 2003, the DOC makes a preliminary determination that two Canadian programs represent countervailable subsidies: provision of government railcars and the government guarantees to the Canadian Wheat Board. Provisional countervailing duties of 3.94% are imposed on durum and hard red spring wheat.

May 2, 2003, the DOC makes a preliminary determination in the anti-dumping case, resulting in provisional duties of 8.15% on durum and 6.12% on imports of Canadian hard red spring wheat.

Aug. 29, 2003, the DOC makes final determinations. In the countervail case, the DOC identifies what it calls "comprehensive financial risk coverage" and the provision of government railcars as subsidies. It sets a countervail rate of 5.29 % for both durum and hard red spring wheat. In the anti-dumping cases, it decides dumping is occurring and sets dumping margins of 8.26% for durum and 8.87 % for hard red spring wheat.

Oct. 3, 2003, the ITC determines that imports of durum wheat from Canada do not injure US durum producers, but is split 2–2 on whether imports of Canadian hard red spring wheat injure the US wheat sector. The split decision favors the plaintiff and, as a result, a 14.2% tariff continues to apply to imports of hard red spring wheat, while the tariff on durum is lifted.

Nov. 3, 2003, the Canadian Wheat Board (CWB) joins the Government of Canada and provincial governments of Saskatchewan and Alberta in filing an appeal for a NAFTA review panel to examine the DOC countervailing duty determination. Nov. 24, 2003, the CWB files a request for a NAFTA panel review of the injury decision on the grounds that the ITC decision is unsupported by substantial evidence. Dec. 23, 2003, the North American Millers' Association files complaints with NAFTA, also citing lack of substantial evidence. July 9, 2004, the NAFTA panel is selected to review the DOC countervail decision, following appeals by the CWB and governments of Canada, Saskatchewan and Alberta.

July 30, 2004, the US Court of International Trade dismisses an appeal by the North Dakota Wheat Commission of the ITC determination that Canadian durum imports are not injuring the US durum industry. Aug. 3, 2004, the NAFTA panel is selected to review the ITC injury decision, after an appeal by the CWB. Oct. 26, 2004, NAFTA panel holds hearings regarding appeal of countervailing duties.

Mar. 10, 2005, the NAFTA panel reviewing the DOC countervail determination announces its decision. The panel agreed with the CWB arguments and rejected the DOC's treatment of the three CWB government guarantees as a single program under the heading of "financial risk coverage". The panel has required each guarantee to be separately evaluated, which could lead to reduction or removal of the duties. After being granted a time extension, the DOC has until Aug. 8, 2005 to respond.

Mar. 9, 2005, NAFTA panel holds hearings regarding appeal of injury determination. June 7, 2005, the NAFTA panel concludes that the ITC determination on injury was not supported by substantial evidence. The panel remands this decision back to the ITC for resolution, attaching nine specific conditions that must be satisfied. The ITC has 90 days to respond.

August 8, 2005, the DOC responds to the first NAFTA panel directive by lowering the countervailing duty rate to 2.54% from 5.29%. The total tariff is now 11.4%.

October 5, 2005, the ITC reverses its injury decision, paving the way for tariff removal.

Dec. 12, 2005, the NAFTA panel issues its final decision. Jan. 2, 2006, duty liability is removed on Canadian wheat imports to the US Feb. 24, 2006, the tariff is lifted.

Chinese Firm Wins Anti-dumping Case on Lighters Brought by the EU
中国公司打赢欧盟针对打火机的反倾销案件

In recent years, many Chinese enterprises have lost anti-dumping cases brought by foreign companies. However, there was a successful counter-case against the powerful EU by a dozen companies producing cigarette lighters in Wenzhou city. What were the reasons for this, and what does it mean?

After China's entry to the WTO in late 2001, the Chinese economy merged with the world economy to a greater extent. At the same time, many Chinese enterprises suffered greatly from a lack of knowledge concerning trade exchanges between countries. However, some Chinese companies have begun to pay more attention to self-protection through legal means. An anti-dumping case which took place in Wenzhou city in eastern China may bring some enlightenment in this regard.

Statistics show that China is the biggest victim of anti-dumping cases in the world. The Chinese suffer tens of billions of dollars of financial losses. Given this severe reality, the winning case of Chinese lighter companies offers much valuable experience for other domestic enterprises. To take up the weapons of law and regulation in defense of our business interests turns out to be a proper way towards joining the world economic community.

In an office of a cigarette lighter company in Wenzhou city in eastern China, a special fax made the managing director Su Shangxi very pleased.

Managing Director of Wenzhou Oriental Lighter Corp, Ltd. Su Shangxi explains: "This is the symbol of the EU, and this is the signature of the official who is in charge of anti-dumping in the Trade Department of the EU Commission. The main content of the fax is an announcement issued by the EU Commission. It states that the European Lighter Manufacturers Association, on behalf of the European Economic Community's disposable gas-filled lighter industry, has withdrawn its anti-dumping counterclaim on July 14, 2002. It means that we've won completely the lighter case. "

Since 2001, some European lighter manufacturers have been creating trade barriers through the EU to stop the entry of Chinese products.

In September 2001, the EU began to draft regulations creating barriers for Chinese lighter companies who sold cheap products. The regulation provided that imported lighters under 2 Euros must include an operation lock function for children. This was clearly designed to target foreign companies producing comparatively cheap lighters, including a great number of lighter factories in China's Wenzhou city. Because these companies had to purchase the patent for the lighter safety lock at a high cost, they were likely to lose their past competitive edge in price over the products made in the EU.

Domestic anti-dumping experts pointed out that nearly all lighters under 2 Euros exported to European countries were made in China, so the EU's regulation was a discriminatory measure targeting Chinese companies. In early 2002, some lighter companies in Wenzhou managed to go to Europe for negotiations with the parties involved in the drafting of the discriminatory regulation. However, when they set foot on the European soil, they felt it was too late to win back their rights.

Li Zhongjian, the vice chairman of Wenzhou Lighters Association says: "They said that they'd received no response at all from the Chinese lighter industry long after discussion of the regulation. This didn't work against the announcement of the regulation, because our companies went to Europe to discuss this matter till they finally decided to make it take effect from 2004. But during the months ahead, they might make some revisions. "

Although the regulation was passed as scheduled, Wenzhou's businessmen still felt optimistic about their fate in the future. Because of the somewhat mild response from the EU officials to their first visit to Europe, they became aware that the EU threshold was not too high to cross. Soon after their return, Wenzhou's lighter manufacturers urged the EU to initiate the revision procedure as promised to the delegation from the Chinese enterprises. Meanwhile, they suggested that the Chinese government set up a dispute resolution system after China's entry to the WTO. Their pleas for help received strong government support. As a counter measure, the EU issued a report in June of 2002, which said that if Chinese lighter companies' dumping behavior was confirmed, they would impose high tariffs on Chinese lighters.

Li Zhongjian also says: "If our exported lighters had a 150 percent tariff imposed, it would become impossible for Chinese products to enter the European market." Chinese enterprises could not afford to give up.

Li explains: "if the EU succeeds in the anti-dumping case, other countries will follow suit. It is likely that such cases will extend from the lighter industry to many other sectors, such as leather shoes, glasses and clothes."

Zhou Dahu, the chairman of Wenzhou Lighters Association tells us: "Through the organization and arrangement by our association, we made a final decision that 15 lighter companies should raise a harmless plea and one should try to win market economy status."

Right after being informed of the EU's charges, the association played a very important role in mobilizing all forces in the lighter industry in Wenzhou city. They worked in coordination, raised fund and invited lawyers for some months. Meanwhile, they punctually reported the situation of the anti-dumping case to the relevant government departments. Some EU officials even came to Wenzhou to make on-site investigations of the enterprises involved in the case.

When these companies cooperated with the EU investigators, the Chinese government was trying all means at a different level to win benefits for Chinese lighter enterprises. In October of 2002, Wenzhou Oriental Lighter Corp, Ltd was exclusively entitled to take part in the "Sino-European Anti-dumping Forum" to be held in Brussels, the headquarters of the EU. On October 7, Li Zhongjian delivered a speech at the forum on behalf of the Chinese lighter industry.

"The day after the forum, they sent the approval for Market Economy Status to our lawyer's office in Brussels. I was welcomed by fireworks when I walked off the plane. All people concerned agreed that we had won the first victory," Li says.

The EU for the first time bestowed market economy status on Wenzhou Oriental Lighter Corp, Ltd. and 4 other Chinese companies.

Professor, Yang Ruilong from China Renmin University comments: "It is a signal for the great number of Chinese enterprises and entrepreneurs that it's time for us to take measures. If this is correct, we'll probably be the winners. With the increasing internationalization of our country, trade friction of this kind will continue. So our enterprises should first gain sufficient awareness: don't be afraid but meet it positively."

Chapter 9

Competition Law
竞争法

Learning Objectives

☑ To understand the meaning of competition law

☑ To learn the general rules of the competition laws of major countries in the present world

☑ To know about the Chinese laws and regulations on competition

Opening Vignette

History of Competition Law

Competition law, referred to as antitrust law in the US, commonly has three main elements.

- Prohibiting agreements or practices that restrict free trading and competition between business entities. This includes in particular the repression of cartels.
- Banning abusive behavior by a firm dominating a market, or anti-competitive practices that tend to lead to such a dominant position. Practices controlled in this way may include predatory pricing, tying, price gouging, refusal to deal, and many others.
- Supervising the mergers and acquisitions of large corporations, including some joint ventures. Transactions that are considered to threaten the competitive process can be prohibited altogether, or approved subject to "remedies" such as an obligation to divest part of the merged business or to offer licenses or access to facilities to enable other businesses to continue competing.

The earliest record of competition law traces back to the efforts of Roman legislators to control price fluctuations and unfair trade practices. Through the middle ages in Europe, Kings and Queens repeatedly cracked down on monopolies, including those created through state legislation. The English common law doctrine of restraint of trade became the precursor to modern competition law. This grew out of the codifications of US antitrust statutes, which in turn had considerable influence on the development of European competition laws after the World War II.

Modern competition law begins with the US legislation of the Sherman Act of 1890[1] and the Clayton Act of 1914[2]. While other, particularly European, countries also had some form of regulation on monopolies and cartels, the US codification of the common law position on restraint of trade had a widespread effect on subsequent competition law development. Both after World War II and after the fall of the Berlin wall, competition law has gone through phases of renewed attention and legislative updates around the world. Increasingly the focus has moved to international competition enforcement in a globalized economy.

The WTO members have been recently discussing how future global competition law could look. Competition law has already been substantially internationalized along the lines of the US model by nation states themselves, however, the involvement of international organizations has been growing. Increasingly active at all international conferences are the United Nations Conference on Trade and Development (UNCTAD)[3] and the Organization for Economic Co-operation and Development (OECD)[4], which is prone to making neo-liberal recommendations about the total application of competition law for public and private industries. Chapter 5 of the post war Havana Charter[5] contained an Antitrust code but this was never incorporated into the WTO's forerunner, the GATT. At the ongoing Doha round[6] of trade talks, discussion includes the prospect of competition law enforcement moving up to a global level.

 Warm-up Questions

1. What are the functions of competition law?
2. Why is competition law necessary for modern societies?
3. Give some examples of anti-competitive practices.

9.1   An Overview of Competition Law
竞争法概述

9.1.1   A Brief Introduction to Competition Law   竞争法简介

Competitive law (antitrust law) is the law that prohibits anti-competitive behavior (monopoly) and unfair business practices. Anti-unfair competition law and anti-monopoly law are in the category of competition law, and both of them must comply with the fair competition rules of competition law. These competition laws make illegal certain practices deemed to hurt businesses or consumers or both, or generally to violate standards of ethical behavior.

The legislation of competition law differs from one country to another. The name or the content of the law are appreciably different. Some countries, such as the United States, Hungary do not distinguish the conduct of unfair competition and monopoly, and do not legislate separately. On the contrary, other countries, such as German and Japan, distinguish these two concepts and legislate separately (i. e., there are both anti-unfair competition law and anti-monopoly law in these countries).

In the present world, the US antitrust law and the EU competition law are the two largest and most influential systems of competition law.

9.1.2　Unfair Competition　不正当竞争

1. Meaning of unfair competition

Economic fairness is traditionally a topic for political debate and may be thought to be the heart of welfare judgments in economics. While unfairness in a business environment is much less widely discussed, unfair competition comes along with the common competitive action.

Unfair competition may be defined as any act or conduct in carrying out economic activity which is contrary to bone fide trade practice and harms or threatens to harm the interests of competitors. This covers activities such as false advertising, trademark infringement, and restrictions on the ability of ex-employees of an enterprise to be engaged by another enterprise in the same line of activity. Under many nations' laws, unfair competition is the basis for a legal action (suit) for damages and/or an injunction to halt the deceptive practices against an unfair competitor if the practices tend to harm one's business.

2. Features of unfair competition conducts

Competitions in commerce should abide by the law, while unfair competition, whose harm is deemed outweighs its benefits, is characterized by elude or directly against the law, in order to maximize the profits.

Any actions in the course of industrial or commercial activities that are contrary to honest practices may amount to a conduct of unfair business practice and may give rise to a claim in damages. An unfair competition conduct usually has the following features.

1) Causing confusion

Conduct or practice which causes confusion, or is likely to confusion with respect to another's enterprise or its activities, especially, the products or services offered by such enterprise, may constitute an unfair practice. This could occur particularly concerning a trademark, a trade name, or the appearance, presentation and association of a product.

2) Damaging another's goodwill or reputation

A conduct or practice which damages or is likely to damage, the goodwill or reputation of another person's enterprise, may constitute an unfair practice, regardless of whether such conduct or practice causes confusion. Damages to goodwill or reputation result from the dilution of the goodwill or reputation attached to any of the following:

(1) A trade mark, whether it is registered;

(2) A business identifier other than a trademark or trade name;

(3) The appearance of a product;

(4) The presentation of products or services;

(5) A celebrity or a well-known fictional character.

3) Misleading the public

A conduct or practice which misleads, or is likely to mislead the public concerning an enterprise or its activities may constitute an unfair practice. For this purpose, misleading the public may arise from an advertisement or promotion, and concerning any of the following conditions:

(1) The manufacturing process of a product;

(2) The suitability of a product or service for a particular purpose;

(3) The quality or quantity or other characteristics of products or services;

(4) The geographical origin of products or services;

(5) The conditions on which products or services are offered or provided;

(6) The price of products or services or the manner in which it is calculated.

4) Violation of trade secret

A conduct or practice which results in the disclosure, acquisition or use by others of secret information without the consent of the person lawfully in control of such information and in a manner contrary to honest commercial practices, may constitute an unfair practice. It may result from industrial or commercial espionage, or from breach of contract, breach of confidence, inducement to commit any of such breaches, or from acquisition.

Trade secrets are types of information that set one business distinguished from their competitors. It may be product formulas, pattern designs, compilation of data, or other business secrets and do not have to be patented, copyrighted, or trademarked to be protected. Therefore, any information shall be considered a "trade secret" if:

(1) It is not, as a body or in the precise configuration and assembly of its components, generally known among or readily accessible to persons that normally would have knowledge of or access to the kind of information in question;

(2) It has commercial value because it is a secret;

(3) The rightful holder has taken responsible steps under the circumstances to keep it secret.

In addition, any practice or other conduct that consists of, or results in an unfair commercial use by a competent authority, or by other persons as a result of the improper disclosure by a competent authority; of secret tests or other data concerning pharmaceutical, agricultural or chemical products that utilize new chemical entities the origination of which requires considerable effort and which data have been submitted to the competent authority for the purpose of obtaining approval of the marketing of such products.

5) Discrediting competitors

Any false or unjustifiable allegation, in the course of industrial or commercial activities, that discredits, or is likely to discredit, another enterprise or activities, products or services offered by such enterprise, may constitute an unfair practice. Discrediting may arise out of an advertisement or promotion and may, in particular, occur with respect to any of the following:

（1）The manufacturing process of a product;

（2）The suitability of a product or service for a particular purpose;

（3）The quality or quantity or other characteristics of products or services;

（4）The conditions on which products or services are offered or provided;

（5）The price of products or services or the manner in which it is calculated.

Besides, in some countries, commercial bribery, tying[7] and sale with prizes[8], are also deemed as unfair competition conducts.

9.1.3　Monopoly　垄断

1. Dominance and monopoly

Dominance and monopoly refer to the market power of firms to raise prices, restrict production, and decrease the quality of goods and services. Together these issues have led legislature to establish laws protecting the consumers. Dominance and monopoly problems form the focus of much attention in competition (antitrust) law.

A dominant position in a market is a question of what degree of market power a firm holds. A firm may be considered dominant in a market with a small number of powerful players. This situation is termed an oligopoly, and that together firms have collective dominance. If there is only one major player in a market, the word monopoly is used.

However, the term "monopoly power" often refers to the wider phenomenon, involving collusion and cartel, and/or excessive concentration of market power.

2. Abuse of dominant position

In law, having a dominant position or a monopoly in the market is not illegal in itself. However certain categories of behavior will, when a business is dominant, be considered abusive and be met with legal sanctions. Such abusive behaviors mainly include tying, predatory pricing, exclusive dealing[9], market restriction and price squeezing[10].

1）Tying

Tying occurs where a supplier, as a condition of supplying a good or service, requires a customer to acquire another good from the supplier or his nominee. Tying also occurs where a supplier requires that a dealer refrain from using or distributing in conjunction with the supplied good any other good that is not of the particular brand. An example of tying would be the case of a manufacturer supplying a small shop upon the condition that the shop agrees to purchase other goods or services from the manufacturer.

2）Predatory pricing

Predatory pricing, may be also called predatory dumping, means that an large enterprise sets its prices very low, often below the costs of production, with the intention of forcing competitors out of the market so that is can establish a monopoly and charge higher price in the future to gain supernormal profits.

3）Exclusive dealing

Exclusive dealing occurs where a supplier requires that as a condition for supplying goods or services to an independent dealer, that dealer must sell or deal only in goods supplied by the supplier or a nominee of the supplier. An example of this would be where a dominant supplier as a condition of supplying raw material (flour) to a bakery, demands that the bakery only source additional inputs (sugar) from an affiliated enterprise identified by the supplier.

4) Market restriction

Market restriction occurs where a supplier, as a condition for supplying the goods, requires an independent dealer to supply the goods only in a specified market. For example, an enterprise supplying agricultural products may demand, as a condition of supplying, that a retailer only retails those products in a limited prescribed area.

5) Price squeezing

Price squeezing refers to such a situation where unreasonable or inflated purchase prices are imposed by a dominant manufacturer upon independent dealers with whom the manufacturer may be competing through an affiliate enterprise. Such price squeezing will result in a restriction of competition in the retail or derived product market. This occurs where a supplier inflates the price of the raw material it supplies to a manufacturer forcing the manufacturer to retail the derived product at prices higher than competitive prices. This may be done because the raw material supplier is itself a competing retailer of the derived product.

3. Collusion and cartel

In some countries, collusion and cartel are also regarded as particular forms of monopoly.

In the study of economics and market competition, collusion takes place within an industry when rival companies cooperate for their mutual benefit. Collusion most often takes place within the market form of oligopoly, where the decision of a few firms to collude can significantly impact the market as a whole. The aim of collusion is to increase individual member's profits by reducing competition. Collusion may be explicit (overt) or implicit (tacit). Cartel is a special case of explicit collusion, which is based on a formal agreement among the colluding parties.

Collusions often involve price fixing, wage fixing, kickbacks, output determination, market division[11], bid rigging[12], division of profits and establishment of common sales agencies between the colluding parties.

4. Excessive concentration of market power

Excessive concentration of market power is considered as a special form of monopoly in some countries. However, it is difficult for legislators to define the meaning of excessive concentration of market power. What is more practicable is closely supervising the mergers and acquisitions of big firms for the purpose of preventing from excessive concentration of market power. Therefore, some countries make detailed provisions on mergers and acquisitions in competition law, or enacted specific laws regulating mergers and acquisitions.

9.2 Competition Laws of Some Countries or Regions
　　　某些国家或地区的竞争法

9.2.1 Antitrust Law of the US　美国的反托拉斯法

The American term antitrust law arose not because the US antitrust statutes had anything to do with ordinary trust law, but because the large American corporations used trusts to conceal the nature of their business arrangements. Big trusts became synonymous with big monopolies, the perceived threat to the free market these trusts represented led to the Sherman and Clayton Acts. These laws, in part, codified past American and English common law of restraints of trade.

The Sherman Act of 1890 is the first US federal statute of antitrust, and also the pathbreaker of modern competition law in the world. This act provides that every contract, combination in the form of trust or otherwise, or conspiracy, in restraint of trade or commerce among states, or with foreign nations, is deemed to be illegal. The act also provides that every person who shall monopolize, or attempt to monopolize, or combine or conspire with any other person or persons, to monopolize any part of the trade or commerce among states, or with foreign nations, shall be deemed guilty of a felony.

The Clayton Act of 1914 was enacted to add further substance to the US antitrust law regime by seeking to prevent anti-competitive practices in their incipiency. Notably, the act prohibits: a) price discrimination between different purchasers if such discrimination substantially lessens competition or tends to create a monopoly in any line of commerce; b) exclusive dealings, or tying but only when these acts substantially lessen competition; c) mergers and acquisitions where the effect may substantially lessen competition; d) any person from being a director of two or more competing corporations.

The Federal Trade Commission Act of 1914[13] established the Federal Trade Commission (FTC). The FTC consists of five members appointed by the president and has the power to investigate persons, partnerships, or corporations in relation to antitrust acts. Examples of unlawful trade practices include misbranding goods quality, origin, or durability; using false advertising; mislabeling to mislead consumer about product size; and advertising or selling rebuilt goods as new. The act also gave the FTC the power to institute court proceedings against alleged violators and provided the penalties if found guilty.

In practice, the US courts have developed two principles of antitrust law: rule of reason[14] and per se rule[15]. The rule of reason means that only combinations and contracts unreasonably restraining trade are subject to actions under antitrust law, and that possession of monopoly power are not illegal. Per se rule means that categories of anti-competitive behavior in antitrust law are conclusively presumed to be an "unreasonable restraint on trade" and thus anti-competitive and illegal per se. In the past decades, the US Supreme Court has determined the following activities to be illegal per se regardless of the reasonableness of such actions:

(1) Price fixing;

(2) Group boycott[16];

(3) Geographic market division;

(4) Resale price maintenance[17];

(5) Tying;

(6) Other abuse patent right of restrictive business practice, such as various permit trading of restrictive clause.

9.2.2 Competition Law of the EU 欧盟的竞争法

Besides the antitrust law of the US, the competition law of EU (European Union) is also one of the most perfect legal systems of competition law.

In 1957 six Western European countries signed the Treaty, establishing the European Economic

Community (EEC Treaty or Treaty of Rome)[18], which over the last fifty years has grown into a European Union of nearly half a billion citizens. Healthy competition is seen as an essential element in the creation of a European common market free from restraints on trade. The EC Treaty makes important provisions on competition which have been followed as basic principles by later EU legislators of competition law.

The first provision is the article 85, which deals with cartels and restrictive vertical agreements. According to this article, all agreements between undertakings, decisions by associations of undertakings and concerted practices which may affect trade between members and which have as their object or effect the prevention, restriction or distortion of competition within the common market, are prohibited. This article then gives examples of restrictive practices such as price fixing or market sharing and confirms that any of such agreements are automatically void. However, this article creates exemptions, if the collusion is for distributional or technological innovation, gives consumers a "fair share" of the benefit and does not include unreasonable restraints that risk eliminating competition anywhere.

The article 86 deals with monopolies, or more precisely firms who have a dominant market position and abuse that position. Unlike the US antitrust law, EC law has never been used to punish the existence of dominant firms, but merely imposes a special responsibility to conduct oneself appropriately. Specific categories of abuse listed in this article include price discrimination and exclusive dealing, much the same as the relevant provisions of the US Clayton Act. Also under this article, the European Council was empowered to enact a regulation to control mergers between firms, in order to test whether a concentration (i. e. merger or acquisition) with a community dimension (i. e. affects a number of EU member states) might significantly impede effective competition, again, similar to the US Clayton Act's "substantial lessening of competition".

9.2.3   Competition Law of China   中国的竞争法

1. The Anti-Unfair Competition Law of the PRC

The Anti-Unfair Competition Law of the PRC[19] was adopted in 1993. This is the first law of china which aims to encourage and promote a healthy market economy by prohibiting unfair business activities. The term "unfair competition" in this law refers to a business operator's conducts infringing upon the legal rights and interests of another business operator and disturbing the social and economic order.

This law lists the following unfair competition activities:

(1) Feigning the others' registered trade mark;

(2) Using the specific name, package, decoration of the famous or noted commodities, or using a similar one which may confuse consumers distinguishing the commodities to the famous or noted commodities;

(3) Using the name of other enterprise or personal name without consent of such enterprise or person, and making the public confuse this commodity to the other's commodity;

(4) Feigning the certificate of attestation, mark of fame and high qualification, or the certificate of origin of the commodities, which makes others to misunderstand the qualification of the commodities because of the false certificates;

(5) Abuse of administrative power or administrative monopoly;

(6) Commercial bribery;

(7) Advertisement or propaganda which is false or liable to be misunderstood;

(8) Infringement upon trade secret;

(9) Selling commodity at the price lower than the commodity's cost in order to put the other competitors out of the competition, except for selling fresh or live commodities, quickly selling commodities before their expiration or the other overstock commodities, cutting prices or on sale in season, or cutting prices to sell commodity for cleaning debts, changing or suspending business;

(10) Selling commodity attached with unreasonable condition or force the consumers to unwillingly purchase any additional commodity that come together with the product that the consumer buys;

(11) Selling commodity with lottery fraudulently or with prize valued more than ¥5000;

(12) Fabricating or spreading false facts to damage the business reputation or commodity fame of the other competitor;

(13) Collusion for bidding or colluding with the company inviting bidding for the purpose of putting the other bidders out of the competition.

The scope of unfair competition activities are so wide in this law that some of them are further regulated by the Anti-Monopoly Law of the PRC[20] that just entered into force on August 1, 2008 and some by the Chinese laws of intellectual property right.

Reading Material

Chinese Anti-Monopoly Law Took Effect on August 1, 2008

Upholding fair competition, China's first anti-monopoly law, that took effect on August 1, 2008, ushered in a new chapter in the development of Chinese market economy. The new law will be a real boon to Chinese consumers by putting various monopoly practices under control.

As a basic framework for building a fair, uniform and national legal system for competition, the new law lays out only certain principles guiding anti-monopoly work. Lack of specific regulations and guidelines for practice will make it hard to enforce the law efficiently. Hence, law-makers should press ahead with follow-up legislation to bring into full play the role of the anti-monopoly legislation in protecting consumers.

A full-fledged anti-monopoly law is particularly needed as the country makes big strides to develop its market economy after three decades of remarkable economic reforms and opening-up. On the one hand, the law will help create a level playing field for all enterprises by preventing dominating companies from abusing their superior market positions.

---

2. The Anti-Monopoly Law of the PRC

The Anti-monopoly Law of the PRC shall be applicable to monopolistic conducts in economic activities within the PRC, and the conducts outside the territory of the PRC if they eliminate or have restrictive effect on competition in the domestic market of the PRC.

In light of the article 3 of this law, the term "monopolistic conduct" is defined as the following conducts:

（1）Monopolistic agreements among undertakings；

（2）Abuse of dominant market positions by undertakings；

（3）Concentration of undertakings that eliminates or restricts competition or might be eliminating or restricting competition.

9.3   International Legislation Relating to Competition
与竞争有关的国际立法

In the present world, there are three most important international conventions and rules relating to competition, which involves protection of the fair competition in international markets. They are the Paris Convention for the Protection of Industrial Property (Paris Convention)[21], the Agreement on Trade-Related Aspects of Intellectual Property Rights (TRIPs)[22] and the UN Set of Multilaterally Agreed Equitable Principles and Rules for the Control of Restrictive Business Practices[23] (the UN Set).

9.3.1   Provisions on Competition of Paris Convention
《巴黎公约》中有关竞争的规定

The Paris Convention for the Protection of Industrial Property signed in Paris, France, in 1883, entered into force in 1884, and was revised for many times, which takes the first step in defining the act (conduct) of unfair competition. The convention takes repression of unfair competition as an important method to protect industry property and require the members to assure effective protection against unfair competition.

The Paris Convention deems any act of competition contrary to honest practices in industrial or commercial matters unfair competition as an act of unfair competition. In particular, the following acts are prohibited by the convention：

（1）All acts of such a nature as to create confusion by any means whatever with the establishment, the goods, or the industrial or commercial activities, of a competitor；

（2）False allegations in the course of trade of such a nature as to discredit the establishment, the goods, or the industrial or commercial activities, of a competitor；

（3）Indications or allegations the use of which in the course of trade is liable to mislead the public as to the nature, the manufacturing process, the characteristics, the suitability for their purpose, or the quantity, of the goods.

The three categories of acts are important examples of unfair competition and may cover many of unfair competition acts committed in practice. However, there exist in practice some other unfair competition conducts, such as imitation or copying and violation of trade secret, do not fall into any of these three categories.

9.3.2   Provisions on Competition of TRIPs
《与贸易有关的知识产权协议》中有关竞争的规定

The Agreement on Trade-Related Aspects of Intellectual Property Rights (TRIPs), which was negotiated in 1994, is an international agreement administered by the WTO. It sets down minimum standards for many forms of intellectual property protection, which relates to the protection of fair competition, such as the protection of know-how and geographical indications.

According to TRIPs, trade secrets and know-how which have commercial value must be protected against breach of confidence and other acts contrary to honest commercial practices. Test data submitted to governments in order to obtain marketing approval for pharmaceutical or agricultural chemicals must also be protected against unfair commercial use.

In respect of geographical indications, the agreement lays down that all parties must provide means to prevent the use of any indication which misleads the consumer as to the origin of goods, and any use which would constitute an act of unfair competition. A higher level of protection is provided for geographical indications for wines and spirits, which are protected even where there is no danger of the public's being misled as to the true origin. Exceptions are allowed for names that have already become generic terms, but any country using such an exception must be willing to negotiate with a view to protecting the geographical indications in question. Furthermore, provision is made for further negotiations to establish a multilateral system of notification and registration of geographical indications for wines.

Besides, the agreement also concerns anti-competitive practices in contractual licenses. It provides for consultations between governments, where there is reason to believe that licensing practices or conditions pertaining to intellectual property rights constitute an abuse of these rights and have an adverse effect on competition, and also gives remedies against such abuse.

9.3.3　The UN Set
联合国《关于控制限制性商业做法的公平原则和规则的一揽子多边协议》

Under the auspices of the UNCTAD, the Set of Multilaterally Agreed Equitable Principles and Rules for the Control of Restrictive Business Practices was approved by the United Nations Conference on Restrictive Business Practices in April, 1980. Then in December, 1980, the General Assembly[24] adopted it.

Since the adoption of the UN Set in 1980, four United Nations Conferences to Review All Aspects of the Set have taken place under the auspices of UNCTAD, in 1985, 1990, 1995 and 2000 respectively. The Fourth Review Conference adopted a resolution which contains the words of reaffirming the validity of the UN Set and recommending to the General Assembly to subtitle the Set for reference as "UN Set of Principles and Rules on Competition", and calling upon all member states to implement the provisions of the UN Set.

The main contents of the UN Set are to be briefed as follows.

1. Objectives

Taking into account the interests of all member states, particularly those of developing countries, the UN Set are framed in order to achieve the following major objectives:

(1) To ensure that restrictive business practices do not impede or negate the realization of benefits that should arise from the liberalization of tariff and non-tariff barriers affecting world trade, particularly those affecting the trade and development of developing countries;

(2) To attain greater efficiency in international trade and development, particularly that of developing countries, in accordance with national aims of economic and social development and existing economic structures;

(3) To protect and promote social welfare in general and, in particular, the interests of consumers in

both developed and developing countries;

(4) To eliminate the disadvantages to trade and development which may result from the restrictive business practices of transnational corporations or other enterprises, and thus help to maximize benefits to international trade and particularly the trade and development of developing countries.

2. Definition of restrictive business practices

The "restrictive business practices" in the UN Set means acts or behavior of enterprises which, through an abuse or acquisition and abuse of a dominant position of market power, limit access to markets or otherwise unduly restrain competition, having or being likely to have adverse effects on international trade, particularly that of developing countries, and on the economic development of these countries, or which through formal, informal, written or unwritten agreements or arrangements among enterprises, have the same impact.

3. Scope of application

The UN Set applies to restrictive business practices occurring in the course of transactions of good or service, including those of transnational corporations, adversely affecting international trade, particularly that of developing countries and the economic development of these countries. It applies irrespective of whether such practices involve enterprises in one or more countries.

However, the UN Set shall not apply to intergovernmental agreements, nor to restrictive business practices directly caused by such agreements.

4. Major provisions

The UN Set prescribes the principles and rules for the states at national, regional and sub-regional levels and for enterprises, and also provides for the international measures and international institutional machinery aiming to deal with restrictive business practices.

According to the UN Set, in general, the enterprises shall refrain from the following restrictive business practices:

(1) Agreements fixing prices, including as to exports and imports;

(2) Collusive tendering;

(3) Market or customer allocation arrangements;

(4) Allocation by quota as to sales and production;

(5) Collective action to enforce arrangements, for example, by concerted refusals to deal;

(6) Concerted refusal of supplies to potential importers;

(7) Collective denial of access to an arrangement, or association, which is crucial to competition;

(8) Predatory behavior towards competitors, such as using below cost pricing to eliminate competitors;

(9) Discriminatory, i. e. unjustifiably differentiated, pricing or terms or conditions in the supply or purchase of goods and services;

(10) Mergers, takeovers, joint ventures or other acquisitions of control, whether of a horizontal, vertical or a conglomerate nature;

(11) Fixing the prices at which goods exported can be resold in importing countries;

(12) Restrictions on the importation of goods which have been legitimately marked abroad with a trademark identical with or similar to the trademark protected as to identical or similar goods in the

importing country where the trademarks in question are of the same origin, i. e. belong to the same owner or are used by enterprises between which there is economic, organizational, managerial or legal interdependence and where the purpose of such restrictions is to maintain artificially high prices.

Besides, the enterprises shall not, when not for ensuring the achievement of legitimate business purposes, engage in such following conducts:

(1) Partial or complete refusals to deal on the enterprise's customary commercial terms;

(2) Making the supply of particular goods or services dependent upon the acceptance of restrictions on the distribution or manufacture of competing or other goods;

(3) Imposing restrictions concerning where, or to whom, or in what form or quantities, goods supplied or other goods may be resold or exported;

(4) Making the supply of particular goods or services dependent upon the purchase of other goods or services from the supplier or his designee.

The UN Set requires the member states to seek appropriate remedial or preventive measures to prevent and/or control the use of restrictive business practices within their competence when it comes to the attention of states that such practices adversely affect international trade, especially, the trade and development of the developing countries. Where for the purposes of the control of restrictive business practices, a state obtains information from enterprises containing legitimate business secret, it should accord such information reasonable safeguards normally applicable in this field, particularly to protect its confidentiality.

However, in practice, many enterprises may not abide by the regulations of the UN Set, since it is not a formal international convention and does not have the legal effect.

Group Discussion

1. Discuss the concept of competition with your partner.
2. Explain the relation between monopoly and competition.
3. Try to compare the Chinese competition law with the US antitrust law.

NOTES

1　Sherman Act of 1890　（美国）《1890 年谢尔曼法案》
2　Clayton Act of 1914　（美国）《1914 年克莱顿法案》
3　United Nations Conference on Trade and Development (UNCTAD)　联合国贸易与发展会议
4　Organization for Economic Co-operation and Development (OECD)　经济合作与发展组织
5　Havana Charter　《哈瓦那宪章》
6　Doha round　世界贸易组织"多哈回合"多边贸易谈判
7　tying　搭售（亦用 tying in contract, tying arrangement, tied selling）
8　sale with prizes　有奖销售
9　exclusive dealing　独家交易

10 price squeezing 价格压榨，价格挤压

11 market division 瓜分市场（有时也用 market sharing）

12 bid rigging 串通投标

13 Federal Trade Commission Act of 1914   （美国）《1914 年联邦贸易委员会法案》

14 rule of reason 合理原则

15 per se rule 本身（违法）原则

16 group boycott 集体抵制

17 resale price maintenance 维持转售价格，控制转售价格（有时缩写为 RPM）

18 Treaty of the European Economic Community（EEC Treaty or Treaty of Rome）《欧洲经济共同体条约》（又称为《罗马条约》）

19 Anti-Unfair Competition Law of the PRC 《中华人民共和国反不正当竞争法》

20 Anti-Monopoly Law of the PRC 《中华人民共和国反垄断法》

21 Paris Convention for the Protection of Industrial Property（Paris Convention）《保护工业产权巴黎公约》（简称为《巴黎公约》）

22 Agreement on Trade-Related Aspects of Intellectual Property Rights（TRIPs）《与贸易有关的知识产权协议》

23 UN Set of Multilaterally Agreed Equitable Principles and Rules for the Control of Restrictive Business Practices   （联合国）《关于控制限制性商业做法的公平原则和规则的一揽子多边协议》（可简称为 the UN Set）

24 General Assembly 联合国大会

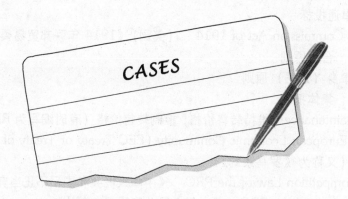

European Union Microsoft Competition Case
欧盟对微软公司的竞争诉讼

The case was brought by the European Commission of the European Union (EU) against Microsoft for abuse of its dominant position in the market (according to competition law). It started as a complaint from Novell over Microsoft's licensing practices in 1993, and eventually resulted in the EU ordering Microsoft to divulge certain information about its server products and release a version of Microsoft Windows without Windows Media Player.

1. Initial Complaints

In 1993, Novell said that Microsoft was blocking its competitors out of the market through anti-competitive practices. The complaint centred on the license practices at the time which required royalties from each computer sold by a supplier of Microsoft's operating system, whether or not the unit actually contained the Windows operating system. Microsoft reached a settlement in 1994, ending some of its license practices.

Sun Microsystems joined the fray in 1998 when it complained about the lack of disclosure of some of the interfaces to Windows NT. The case widened even more when the EU started to look into how streaming media technologies were integrated with Windows.

2. Judgment

Citing ongoing abuse by Microsoft, the EU reached a preliminary decision in the case in 2003 and ordered the company to offer both a version of Windows without Windows Media Player and the information necessary for competing networking software to interact fully with Windows desktops and servers. In March 2004, the EU ordered Microsoft to pay €497 million ($613 million or £381 million), the largest fine ever handed out by the EU at the time, in addition to the previous penalties, which included 120 days to divulge the server information and 90 days to produce a version of Windows without Windows Media Player.

The next month Microsoft released a paper containing scathing commentary on the ruling including: "The commission is seeking to make new law that will have an adverse impact on intellectual property rights and the ability of dominant firms to innovate." Microsoft paid the fine in full in July 2004.

3. Follow-up

Microsoft has a compliant version of its flagship operating system without Windows Media Player available under the negotiated name "Windows XP N". In response to the server information requirement, Microsoft released the source code, but not the specifications, to Windows Server 2003 service pack 1 to members of its Work Group Server Protocol Program (WSPP) on the day of the original deadline. Microsoft also appealed the case, and the EU had a week-long hearing over the appeal which ended in April 2006.

In December 2005 the EU announced that it believed Microsoft did not comply fully with the ruling, stating that the company did not disclose appropriate information about its server programs. The EU said that it would begin to fine Microsoft €2 million (US $3.04 million or £1.53 million) a day until it did so. Microsoft stated in June 2006 that it had begun to provide the EU with the requested information, but according to the BBC the EU stated that it was too late.

On 12 July 2006, the EU fined Microsoft for an additional €280.5 million (US $427.47 million), €1.5 million (US $2.29 million) per day from 16 December 2005 to 20 June 2006. The EU threatened to increase the fine to 3 million ($4.57 million) per day on 31 July 2006 if Microsoft did not comply by then.

On 17 September 2007, Microsoft lost their appeal against the European Commission's case. The €497 million fine was upheld, as were the requirements regarding server interoperability information and bundling of Media Player. In addition, Microsoft has to pay 80 percent of the legal costs of the Commission, while the Commission has to pay 20 percent of the legal costs by Microsoft. However, the appeal court rejected the Commission ruling that an independent monitoring trustee should have unlimited access to internal company organization in the future. On 22 October 2007, Microsoft announced that it would comply and not appeal the decision any more, and Microsoft did not appeal within the required two months as of 17 November 2007.

Microsoft announced that it will demand 0.4 percent of the revenue (rather than 5.95 percent) in patent-licensing royalties, only from commercial vendors of interoperable software and not from open source developers. The interoperability information is available for a one-time fee of €10,000 (US $15,275).

On 27 February 2008, the EU fined Microsoft an additional €899 million (US $1.4 billion) for failure to comply with the March 2004 antitrust decision. This represents the largest penalty ever imposed in 50 years of EU competition policy. This latest decision follows a prior €280.5 million fine for non-compliance, covering the period from June 21, 2006 until October 21, 2007.

On 9 May 2008 Microsoft lodged an appeal in the European Court of First Instance seeking to overturn the €899 million fine, officially stating that it intended to use the action as a "constructive effort to seek clarity from the court".

United States Microsoft Antitrust Case
美国对微软公司的反托拉斯诉讼

This case was a set of consolidated civil actions filed against Microsoft Corporation on May 18, 1998 by the US Department of Justice (DOJ) and twenty US states.

The plaintiffs alleged that Microsoft abused monopoly power in its handling of operating system sales and web browser sales. The issue central to the case was whether Microsoft was allowed to bundle its flagship Internet Explorer (IE) web browser software with its Microsoft Windows operating system. Bundling them together is alleged to have been responsible for Microsoft's victory in the browser wars as every Windows user had a copy of Internet Explorer. It was further alleged that this unfairly restricted the market for competing web browsers (such as Netscape Navigator or Opera) that were slow to download over a modem or had to be purchased at a store. Underlying these disputes were questions over whether Microsoft altered or manipulated its application programming interfaces (APIs) to favor Internet Explorer over third party web browsers, Microsoft's conduct in forming restrictive licensing agreements with OEM computer manufacturers, and Microsoft's intent in its course of conduct.

Microsoft stated that the merging of Microsoft Windows and Internet Explorer was the result of innovation and competition, that the two were now the same product and were inextricably linked together and that consumers were now getting all the benefits of IE for free. Those who opposed Microsoft's position countered that the browser was still a distinct and separate product which did not need to be tied to the operating system, since a separate version of Internet Explorer was available for Mac OS. They also asserted that IE was not really free because its development and marketing costs may have kept the price of Windows higher than it might otherwise have been.

The case was tried before the US District Court Judge Thomas Penfield Jackson. Judge Jackson issued his findings of fact on November 5, 1999, which stated that Microsoft's dominance of the personal computer operating systems market constituted a monopoly, and that Microsoft had taken actions to crush threats to the monopoly, including Apple, Java, Netscape, Lotus Notes, Real Networks, Linux, and others. Then on April 3, 2000, he issued a two-part ruling: his conclusions of law were that Microsoft had committed monopolization, attempted monopolization, and tying in violation of Sections 1 and 2 of the Sherman Act, and his remedy was that Microsoft must be broken into two separate units, one to produce the operating system, and one to produce other software components.

On September 26, 2000, after Judge Jackson issued his findings of fact, the plaintiffs attempted to send Microsoft's appeal directly to the US Supreme Court. However, the Supreme Court declined to hear the appeal and sent the case to a federal appeals court.

The D. C. Circuit Court of Appeals overturned Judge Jackson's rulings against Microsoft but did not overturn the findings of fact. The D. C. Circuit Court remanded the case for consideration of a proper remedy under a more limited scope of liability. Judge Colleen Kollar-

Kotelly was chosen to hear the case. The DOJ announced on September 6, 2001 that it was no longer seeking to break up Microsoft and would instead seek a lesser antitrust penalty.

On November 2, 2001, the DOJ reached an agreement with Microsoft to settle the case. The proposed settlement required Microsoft to share its application programming interfaces with third-party companies and appoint a panel of three people who will have full access to Microsoft's systems, records, and source code for five years in order to ensure compliance. However, the DOJ did not require Microsoft to change any of its code nor prevent Microsoft from tying other software with Windows in the future. On August 5, 2002, Microsoft announced that it would make some concessions towards the proposed final settlement ahead of the judge's verdict.

On November 1, 2002, Judge Kollar-Kotelly released a judgment accepting most of the proposed DOJ settlement. Nine states (California, Connecticut, Iowa, Florida, Kansas, Minnesota, Utah, Virginia and Massachusetts) and the District of Columbia (which had been pursuing the case together with the DOJ) did not agree with the settlement, arguing that it did not go far enough to curb Microsoft's anti-competitive business practices. On June 30, 2004, the US appeals court unanimously approved the settlement with the DOJ, rejecting objections from Massachusetts that the sanctions were inadequate.

Protecting Goodwill and Reputation of a Business in the UK: The Law of Passing Off
英国对企业信誉和声望的保护：仿冒法

An action for passing off is made out when a person makes a misrepresentation which is calculated to deceive and cause damage to the business or goodwill of the other person, and that other person has accumulated goodwill in respect to the a trade mark, sign, name or trade dress. Passing off is sometimes referred to as the "law of unregistered trade marks", although it may also relate to a registered trade mark and as such, an infringement of a registered trade mark may also be actionable as a passing off.

Thus to succeed in an action for passing off, a claimant must show three essential elements: goodwill, misrepresentation and damage.

1. Goodwill

Passing off protects the goodwill of a claimant's business which is an established property right. It was defined by Lord Macnaghten in the case of *IRC v. Muller & Co's Margarine Ltd.* (*1901*) as:

"... a thing very easy to describe, very difficult to define. It is the benefit and advantage of the good name, reputation and connection of a business. It is the attractive force which brings in custom. It is the one thing which distinguishes an old-established business from a new business at its first start. The goodwill of a business must emanate from a particular centre or source. However widely extended or diffused its influence may be, goodwill is worth nothing unless it has power of attraction sufficient to bring customers home to the source from which it emanates."

Goodwill is established through use of a mark, name, get-up or any other sign which is distinctive of a business. Passing off does not protect these marks, names, get-up or other signs per se, but protects the goodwill of the business that uses them, as it is that goodwill accumulated through use that is the property right it is protected.

There is no particular time frame within which goodwill must be created. It is possible for a business to create goodwill within a very brief period of trading, although the trading activity would be required to be intensive. Provided the claimant is able to show that they have the requisite goodwill, it is irrelevant how long they have been trading for. In exceptional circumstances it is possible for goodwill to be created by pre-launch activity. However, there are circumstances in which a claimant may have been trading for some time, but they have not generated any goodwill. This is usually the case when the name of a business is descriptive. In the case of *County Sound PLC v. Ocean Sound Ltd.* (*1991*), the plaintiff's use of the name "The Gold AM" for over six months for a radio station which played "golden oldies" was held not to have acquired the requisite goodwill. In any event, whether goodwill has actually been created will depend on the individual circumstances of each case. The essence of goodwill is how well the business is known, either directly or indirectly as a result of exposure of the trade name or trade dress to the relevant public.

Goodwill is not the same as reputation for the purposes of passing off. While the two are very closely related, they may be distinguished from one another. It is true to say that a business which has established goodwill is also likely to have a reputation. However the existence of a reputation in a mark, name, get-up or other sign is not necessarily indicative of the presence of goodwill. In the case of *Harrods v. Harrodian School* (*1996*), Millett L J stated that: "Damage to goodwill is not confined to loss of custom, but damage to reputation without damage to goodwill is not sufficient to support an action for passing off."

An action for passing off does not confer monopoly rights in a name as such. In theory, there is nothing preventing one party from using the name of another party provided the relevant market can be distinguished from each other. This is illustrated in the case of *Harrods v. Harrodian School* (*1996*) where even the "Harrods" name, which is highly distinctive, was not protected and the defendants were entitled to use it as the name of their school. It was held that the goodwill in the department store of the claimant would not be damaged:

"It is well settled that (unless registered as a trade mark) no one has a monopoly in his brand name or get-up, however familiar these may be. Passing off is a wrongful invasion of a right of property vested in the plaintiff but the property which is protected by an action for passing off is not the plaintiff's proprietary right in the name or get-up which the defendant has misappropriated but the goodwill and reputation of his business which is likely to be harmed by the defendant's misrepresentation."

To be successful in an action for passing off in the UK, the claimant must have goodwill in this country which relates to the claimant carrying on his business. As goodwill is local in character, where a claimant has goodwill in various countries, he will have goodwill in each country. In UK based proceedings, it is only UK goodwill that is relevant. However, section 56 of the Trade Marks Act 1994, does offer some form of protection to trade marks which are extremely well known, even of the proprietor of mark does not do business in the UK or have any form of goodwill.

2. Misrepresentation

There must be a misrepresentation, whether intentional or not, as to the goods or services offered by the other party which leads to confusion in the minds of members of the public. The misrepresentation must be a material one, creating a real, tangible risk of damage to the claimant. The misrepresentation must be believed by those to whom it is addressed and they must act in reliance upon it. In the case of *Spalding v. Gamage* (*1915*), Lord Parker stated that:

"The basis of a passing off action being a false representation by the defendant, it must be proved in each case as a fact that the false representation was made. Of course, it may have been made in express words, but cases of express misrepresentation of this sort are rare. The more common case is where the representation is implied in the use or imitation of a mark, trade name or get-up with which the goods of another are associated in the minds of the public. In such cases the point to be decided is whether, having regard to all the circumstances of the case ... the defendant's use of such mark, name or get-up is calculated to deceive."

This derives from the proposition that "nobody has any right to represent his goods as the goods of someone else".

The fact that there may be confusion in the minds of members of the public does not necessarily mean that the misrepresentation is material. As Lloyd J stated in the case of *HFC Bank plc v. HSBC Bank PLC* (*2000*):

"Even actual confusion does not show that there has been a misrepresentation by anyone; all that it shows is that people make assumptions, jump to unjustified conclusions and put two and two together to make five."

Misrepresentation can occur in a number of ways and according to Lord Parker in *Spalding v. Gamage*, it would be impossible to classify each and every way in which a misrepresentation could occur. However, the most common forms of misrepresentation are: a) where the defendant represents that his goods or services are those of the claimant; b) where the defendant represents that the claimant's goods or services are of a particular type of quality; c) where the defendant represents that the businesses of the defendant and claimant are one and the same or in some way affiliated with one another.

However, even where a representation is true, it may still be misleading in the sense that it is calculated to deceive, which is not a defence.

A misrepresentation may be implied where both parties businesses share a common field of activity. However, it is not a requirement that there necessarily be a common field of activity between the parties. Although where this is the case, it will be easier to demonstrate the existence of a misrepresentation.

It is possible for one party to use another party's mark, name, get-up or other sign, if he does so in a way which is not calculated to deceive. Where one party makes use of the other party's name, while at the same time making it unambiguously clear, that the goods or services to be supplied are not connected in any way with the other party, there will be no passing off by way of misrepresentation.

3. Damage

If a claimant is to succeed in an action for passing off it is essential that the alleged misrepresentation is likely to cause damage to the goodwill of the business. It is not necessary to prove actual damage. Proving the likelihood of damage is sufficient.

There will be no cause of action for passing off where there is no damage or prospect of damage to the goodwill of the claimant's business.

The type of damage which may occur as a result of passing off includes the following.

1) Direct loss of sales

This is where parties are in actual competition with each other and the defendant holds his goods out as those of the claimant, although they do not need to appeal to the same type of customer for damage to occur. Damages are likely to be awarded for "depriving (the plaintiff) of the profit he might have made by the sale of the goods which, ex hypothesi, the purchaser intended to buy". (*Lord Cranworth LC in Seixo v. Provezende (1866)*) This is the most common head of damage for passing off.

2) Inferiority of defendant's goods and services

This is where the defendant's goods and services, which are inferior to the claimant's, are in fact passed off as the claimant's. This head of damage is not essential to an action for passing off where the parties are in actual competition with each other, but may still be relevant if the claimant wishes to apply for injunctive relief.

When the defendant passes off the claimant's goods or services as being of an inferior quality, it is necessary that these goods or services are a different quality to those actually offered by the claimant. In the case of *Combe v. Scholl (1977)*, the defendants misrepresented that their goods were just as good as the claimant's but this was untrue. The defendant's product was actually inferior and an injunction was granted as it was thought that the claimant's reputation could suffer if the public purchased the defendant's product under the assumption it was the claimant's.

Damage under this head is difficult to quantify compared with loss of sales. The case of *Rolls-Royce Motors Ltd. v. Zanelli (1979)* demonstrated this point: "The damage that may be done to the plaintiffs, if inferior work is put out as being the work of Rolls-Royce, is quite incalculable and of very great financial harm to Rolls-Royce. On this aspect of the case they are certainly in a very unusual position, in that a large part of the goodwill of Rolls-Royce does depend on their reputation for immaculate finish and engineering".

3) "Injurious association" with the claimant

Even where the defendant and claimant are not in actual competition with each other, it is still possible for there to be damage caused to the claimant. According to Warrington L J in *Ewing v. Buttercup Margarine Co. Ltd.* (*1917*):

"To induce the belief that my business is a branch of another man's business may do that other man damage in all kinds of ways. The quality of goods I sell; the kind of business I do; the credit or otherwise which I might enjoy — all those things may immensely injure the other man who is assumed wrongly to be associate with me. "

Damage under this head usually occurs where one business is mistaken for another. Where the defendant is an honest trader with an established reputable business, there is not likely to be a prospect of damage to the claimant.

If the claimant is to prove damage under this head, he must show one of the following:

(1) That the defendant's business is one which is generally held in low regard, which will in turn have an effect on the reputation of the claimant;

(2) That the defendant may personally have a bad reputation, despite his trade being reputable;

(3) That the defendant provides goods or services which are of a poor quality;

(4) The defendant may break the law;

(5) The defendant's business may fail or face difficulties which may also damage the claimant's credit.

It is essential that if a claimant is to succeed in an action for passing off, that all three elements stated above are satisfied, otherwise the action will fail.

Passing off is a catch area all area of law that entitles a business to prevent other businesses from unfairly using its goodwill. Goodwill is the attractive force that brings in customers and is the essence of what passing off protects. Otherwise, known as the law of common law trade marks, it protects against all activities of a business that may lead the public into believing that they are the actual trader. It is therefore a flexible and adaptable area of law (in contrast to registered trade marks), geared to protect what might be called the reputation and association of goods or services to a particular business. It is undoubted that protecting the goodwill of a business is important to maintain the fairness of market competition.

Chapter 10

Other laws Relating to International Business

其他与国际商务有关的法律

Learning Objectives

- ☑ To understand the meaning of intellectual property
- ☑ To understand the contents and characteristics of an intellectual property right
- ☑ To learn about the important international laws of intellectual property
- ☑ To know about the important international laws of Ecommerce

Opening Vignette

Development of International Intellectual Property Laws

Intellectual property (IP) protection, as one of the newest concepts in modern societies, first became an important issue at an international level in the end of 19th century, and has remained so ever since.

One of the first international treaties relating to intellectual property in the broadest sense was the Paris Convention for the Protection of Industrial Property (the Paris Convention). Written in 1883, the treaty created under the Paris Convention provided protection for such properties as patents, industrial models and designs, trademarks, and trade names. Over 100 countries have signed the Paris Convention treaty, and it has been modified several times. Two of the most important provisions of the treaty relate to the rights of national treatment and priority. The right of national treatment ensures that those individuals seeking a patent or trademark in a foreign country will not be discriminated against and will receive the same rights as a citizen of that country. The right of priority provides an inventor 1 year from the date of filing a patent application in his or her home country (six months for a trademark or design application) to file an application in a foreign country. The legal, effective date of application in the foreign country is then retroactively the legal, effective filing date in the home country, provided the application is made within the protection period. If the invention is made public prior to filing the home country application, however, the right of priority in a foreign country is no longer applicable.

Enforcement and protection of intellectual property at the international level has historically been extremely complex. Laws have varied significantly from country to country, and the political climate within each country has influenced the extent of protection available. Separate legislation and treaties specifically addressed relevant procedures, conventions, and standards for each area within the scope of intellectual property, such as copyright or trade secrets.

Many international laws relating to intellectual property were significantly altered with the 1994 passage of the General Agreement on Tariffs and Trade (GATT). In fact, the member nations that signed the GATT committed themselves to a higher degree of intellectual property protection than had been provided under any earlier multinational treaties.

Under the guidance of the World Trade Organization (WTO), all member nations were required to adopt specific provisions for the enforcement of rights and settlement of disputes relating to intellectual property. Under these provisions, trademark counterfeiting and commercial copyright piracy are subject to criminal penalties.

Intellectual property allows individuals who come up with a new idea to enjoy the exclusive use of that idea for a certain period of time, which can be a significant monetary incentive for entrepreneurs. But intellectual property law is extraordinarily complex, so small business owners interested in IP issues should consult a legal expert in order to protect themselves to the full extent of the law. "The law on intellectual property ... is everywhere both comparatively new and in flux," observed *The Economist* (US). It is also important for would-be entrepreneurs to be aware of the legal rights of others as they prepare to engage in business activities. After all, few small companies can withstand the rigors of defending themselves from patent infringement lawsuits (especially if the charge is legitimate).

Today, the strong protections of intellectual property are recognized as one of the cornerstones of the formation and growth of small businesses, especially since the advent of the Internet and other new technologies have placed a premium on new ideas and innovations. On the other hand, with the increasing prevailing of the Internet, there are some new problems arising in intellectual property laws. For example, whether should one pay for watching a film through Internet? If pay, whom should he pay to? How and how much to pay?

 Warm-up Questions

1. What do you think the intellectual property is?
2. What are the purposes of intellectual property laws?
3. Give some examples of international conventions or agreements on intellectual property.

10.1 Law of Intellectual Property
知识产权法

10.1.1 An Overview 概述

When discussing intellectual property laws, it should be noted that, almost under all jurisdictions, national or international, intellectual property laws and competition laws overlap each other in many areas. However, there are still certain features which can distinguish competition laws from intellectual property laws. For instance, anti-monopoly is the heart of most competition laws but hardly involved in intellectual property laws.

Nevertheless, some authors prefer classifying competition law into the system of intellectual property laws while others argue that protection of intellectual property is one of the most important means to protect fair competition.

Regardless of the controversy, those concepts and rules which most closely relates to intellectual property will be discussed in the next sections.

1. What is intellectual property

Intellectual property, is a legal concept referring to creations of the mind. It is covered by intellectual property laws which give the inventors, authors or holders exclusive right[1] to control reproduction or adaptation of such works for a certain period of time. Under intellectual property law, the holder of one of these abstract "properties" has certain exclusive rights to the creative work, commercial symbol, or invention by which it is covered.

Traditional intellectual property is divided into two categories: industrial property and copyright.

1) Industrial property

The article 1 of the Paris Convention for the Protection of Industrial Property states that the protection of industrial property has as its object patents, utility models, industrial designs, trademarks, service marks, trade names, indications of source or appellations of origin, and the repression of unfair competition. Among them, the patent and trademarks are the most important ones.

- Patent

A patent right is a set of exclusive rights granted by a state to an inventor or his assignee for a fixed period of time in exchange for a disclosure of an invention. In practice, the procedure for granting patents, the requirements placed on the patentee and the extent of the exclusive rights may vary very much from one country to another.

Generally speaking, a patent application must include one or more claims defining the invention which must be new, inventive, and useful or industrially applicable. The content of patent right involves several rights, such as the exclusive rights, the assigning right[2], and so on. The exclusive right granted to a patentee, in most countries, is the right to prevent or exclude others from making, using, selling, offering to sell or importing the invention. Therefore, the exclusive right is the basic right of patent.

In modern societies, the patent laws are enacted to protect patent rights for inventions-creations, encourage inventions-creations, foster the spreading and application of inventions-creations, and promote the development of science and technology.

- Trademark

A trademark is a word, symbol, or phrase, used to identify a particular manufacturer or seller's products and distinguish them from the products of another. Trademark right usually arises out of the use and/or registration of a mark in connection only with a specific type or range of products or services. The content of trademark right consists of the exclusive right, the renewal right[3], the assigning right, and etc. Like patent right, the exclusive rights are also the basic right of trademark. Other rights extend from exclusive rights.

Trademark laws are formulated for the purposes of improving the administration of trademarks, protecting the right to exclusively use of trademarks, and encouraging producers and operators to guarantee the quality of their goods and services and maintain the reputation of their trademarks, so as to protect the interests of both consumers, and sellers, and to promote the healthy development of the market economy.

2) Copyright

Copyright refers to the rights to literary, artistic and scientific works.

In narrow sense, copyright shall include personal rights and property rights. The former include the right of publication[4], the right of authorship[5], the right of alternation[6], the right to integrity of the work[7], and etc. The latter include the right to license and the right to get compensation. In other words, a copyright owner has the right to reproduce, distribute, exhibit, perform, broadcast, adapt, translate, or compile the work, and the right to license another to do any of these things, and to get compensation in accordance with law if someone did one of these things without his consent.

In broad sense, copyright also include related rights[8] which include those of performing artists in their performances, producers of phonograms in their recordings, and those of broadcasters in their radio and television programs. Moreover, the Agreement on Trade-Related Aspects of Intellectual Property Rights also stipulated that layout-designs (topographies) of integrated circuits[9] and undisclosed information are involved in the scope of protection of intellectual property rights.

Copyright laws are legislated to protect the copyright of authors of literary, artistic and scientific works and their related rights in most countries.

2. Characteristics of intellectual property rights

Typically, an intellectual property right shall be exclusive, regional and having a time limitation.

The exclusivity of intellectual property right refers to that the owner of an intellectual property shall have the right to prevent all third parties, without having the owner's consent, from using the property in the course of trade. With regard to copyright, it grants a copyright holder a negative right to exclude others from exploiting their artistic or creative work. In case of any acts of infringement upon an intellectual property happen, the owner shall have the right to request compensation, cease of the infringement, or even the right to sue.

The regionality of intellectual property right means that when an owner is granted a protection of an intellectual property in one country, he shall not automatically obtain a protection of the intellectual property in another country, unless the two countries have concluded an international convention or agreement to that effect. Where there is no such convention or agreement, the owner has to go through the formalities of application or registration according to the relevant laws of the other country if he wants the intellectual property to be protected by law in another country.

The time limitation of intellectual property right refers to that the protection by law of the intellectual property is not timeless and shall be ended after a fixed period. The time limitation of the protection by law of the intellectual property shall not be too long or else the development of science and technology may be hampered.

10.1.2　WIPO　世界知识产权组织

1. Origin of WIPO

The term "intellectual property" is formally defined for the first time in the Convention Establishing the World Intellectual Property Organization of 1967 which established the World Intellectual Property Organization (WIPO).

In 1883, the Paris Convention for the Protection of Industrial Property was signed. In 1886, the Berne Convention for the Protection of Literary and Artistic Works[10] was entered into. Both of the Conventions had created a framework for international integration of the various types of intellectual property. The United International Bureaux for the Protection of Intellectual Property[11] (also known as its French acronym BIRPI), which was the predecessor of the WIPO, was established in 1893 to administer the Paris Convention and the Berne Convention.

In 1967, the WIPO was formally created to replace the BIRPI by the Convention Establishing the World Intellectual Property Organization which was signed at Stockholm in 1967.

In 1974, WIPO became a specialized agency of the UN system of organizations, with a mandate to administer intellectual property matters recognized by the member states of the UN. WIPO expanded its role and further demonstrated the importance of intellectual property protection in the management of globalized trade in 1996 by entering into a cooperation agreement with the WTO. By now, almost all UN members as well as Vatican City are members of WIPO.

2. Role of WIPO

The WIPO is a self-governed organization, i. e. , it is a separate legal entity. According to the Convention Establishing the World Intellectual Property, the legal capacity of WIPO includes the following aspects:

(1) The organization shall enjoy on the territory of each member state, in conformity with the laws of that state, such legal capacity as may be necessary for the fulfillment of the organization's objectives and for the exercise of its functions;

(2) The organization may conclude bilateral or multilateral agreements with the other member states with a view to the enjoyment by the organization, its officials, and representatives of all member states, of such privileges and immunities as may be necessary for the fulfillment of its objectives and for the exercise of its functions;

(3) On matters within its competence, the organization may make suitable arrangements for consultation and cooperation with international nongovernmental organizations and, with the consent of the governments concerned, with national organizations, governmental or nongovernmental.

WIPO is dedicated to developing a balanced and accessible international intellectual property system, which rewards creativity, stimulates innovation and contributes to economic development while safeguarding the public interest.

10.1.3 The Paris Convention 《巴黎公约》

The Paris Convention, concluded in 1883, is the first major international treaty designed to help the people of one country obtain protection in other countries for their intellectual creations in the form of industrial property rights. The Paris Convention entered into force in 1884 within 14 member states and it is open to all states for accession. China entered into the convention in 1985.

1. Scope of industrial property

In light of article 1 of the Paris Convention, the scope of industrial property includes patents, utility models, industrial designs, trademarks, service marks, trade names, indications of source or appellations of origin (geographical indications), and the repression of unfair competition. Furthermore, in broad sense, industrial property may not be limited to industrial and commercial properties but likewise to agricultural and extractive industries and to all manufactured or natural products, such as wines, grain, tobacco leaf, fruit, cattle, minerals, mineral waters, beer, flowers, and flour.

2. Main principles

The Paris Convention is the first and most important international convention for the protection of industrial property, and established the most significant principles of international protection of industrial properties. These principles are largely divide into the following two categories.

1) **National treatment**

National treatment[12] is an important principle. It requests the member states treated other members in nondiscrimination[13]. Under the articles 2 and 3 of the Paris Convention, with regard to the protection of industrial property, each member must grant the same protection to nationals of the other member as it grants to its own nationals.

2) **Priority right**

In light of the article 4 of the Paris Convention, the meaning of the priority right[14] is that an applicant from one member shall be able to use its first filing date (in one of the member) as the effective filing date in another member, provided that the applicant files another application within 6 months (for industrial designs and trademarks) or 12 months (for patents and utility models) from the first filing.

10.1.4 The Berne Convention 《伯尔尼公约》

The Berne Convention was signed at Berne in 1886 and came into force in 1887. China entered into the Convention in 1992.

1. The aims and scope of application

The Berne Convention is aiming to help nationals of its members, being equally animated by the desire to protect, in as effective and uniform a manner as possible, the rights of authors in their literary and artistic works.

According to article 2 of the Convention, the "literary and artistic works" shall include every production in the literary, scientific and artistic domain, whatever may be the mode or form of its expression, such as:

(1) Books, pamphlets and other writings;

(2) Lectures, addresses, sermons and other works of the same nature;

(3) Dramatic or dramatic-musical works;

(4) Choreographic works and entertainments in dumb show;

(5) Musical compositions with or without words;

(6) Cinematographic works to which are assimilated works expressed by a process analogous to cinematography;

(7) Works of drawing, painting, architecture, sculpture, engraving and lithography;

(8) Photographic works to which are assimilated works expressed by a process analogous to photography;

(9) Works of applied art;

(10) Illustrations, maps, plans, sketches and three-dimensional works relative to geography, topography, architecture or science.

2. Main principles

1) National treatment

The Berne Convention desires to establish a system of equal treatment in the internationalized copyright amongst signatories. It requires its signatories to recognize the copyright of works of authors from other signatory countries, in the same way it recognizes the copyright of its own nationals.

2) Automatic protection

The meaning of the automatic protection[15] is that the protection of copyright, under the Berne Convention, must be automatic, i. e., no formality shall be required to get the protection. The article 5 of the convention provides that authors shall enjoy, in respect of works for which they are protected under this convention, in member countries, the rights which their respective laws do now or may hereafter grant to their nationals, as well as the rights specially granted by this convention. In this regard, it is different from the protection of patent.

3) Independency

The convention provides that the enjoyment and the exercise of the rights which belong to of the author shall be independent of the existence of protection in the country of origin of the work.

In light of the paragraph 4 of the article 5, the country of origin of the work shall be considered to be:

(1) In the case of works first published in a member, that country;

(2) In the case of works published simultaneously in several members which grant different terms of protection, the member whose legislation grants the shortest term of protection;

(3) In the case of works published simultaneously in a non-member and in a member, the latter country;

(4) In the case of unpublished works or of works first published in a non-member, without

simultaneous publication in a member, the member of which the author is a national, provided that: when these are cinematographic works the maker of which has his headquarters or his habitual residence in a member, the country of origin shall be that country; and when these are works of architecture erected in a member or other artistic works incorporated in a building or other structure located in a member, the country of origin shall be that country.

4) Minimum standards of protection

The Berne Convention required member states to provide strong minimum standards of protection[16] for other signatory countries. The minimum standards of protection, according to the Berne Convention, include: the right of authorship, the right to integrity of the work, the right of translation, the right of reproduction, the right of broadcast, the right of public recitation, the right of adaptation, the right of production, the right of record, and the right of public performance, and so on.

The Berne Convention also provides that all works except photographic and cinematographic works shall be copyrighted for at least 50 years after the author's death, but parties are free to provide longer terms. For photographic works the Berne Convention sets a minimum term of 25 years from the year the photograph was created, and for cinematographic works, 50 years after the first showing, or 50 years after creation if it hasn't been shown within 50 years after the creation.

10.1.5   TRIPs 《与贸易有关的知识产权协议》

International policies towards protecting intellectual property rights have taken place great changes over the past two decades. Rules on how to protect patents, copyright, trademarks and other forms of intellectual property have become a standard component of international trade agreements. Most significantly, during the Uruguay Round of multilateral trade negotiations, the Agreement on Trade-Related Aspects of Intellectual Property Rights (TRIPs) was concluded.

As the important component of GATT, TRIPs is an international agreement administered by the WTO and binding on all the WTO members, which sets down minimum standards for many forms of intellectual property regulation and most of the world's economies have to respect. It establishes legal compatibility between member jurisdictions by requiring the harmonization of applicable laws.

Reading Material

The Requirements of TRIPS

TRIPS requires member states to provide strong protection for intellectual property rights. For example, under TRIPS:

Copyright terms must extend to 50 years after the death of the author, although films and photographs are only required to have fixed 50 and 25 year terms, respectively.

Copyright must be granted automatically, and not based upon any "formality", such as registrations or systems of renewal.

Computer programs must be regarded as "literary works" under copyright law and receive the same terms of protection.

National exceptions to copyright (such as "fair use" in the US) must be tightly constrained.

Patents must be granted in all "fields of technology", although exceptions for certain public interests are allowed and must be enforceable for at least 20 years.

Exceptions to patent law must be limited almost as strictly as those to copyright law.

Since TRIPs came into force it has received a growing level of criticism from developing countries, academics, and non-governmental organizations. Some of this criticism is against the WTO as a whole, but many advocates of trade liberalization also dislike TRIPs. TRIPs' wealth redistribution effects (moving money from people in developing countries to copyright and patent owners in developed countries) and its imposition of artificial scarcity on the citizens of countries that would otherwise have had weaker intellectual property laws, are a common basis for such criticisms.

1. The relationship between TRIPs and the Berne Convention, the Paris Convention

TRIPs introduces intellectual property law into the international trading system for the first time and remains the most comprehensive international agreement on intellectual property so far. Many of the TRIPs provisions on trademark and patent were imported from the Paris Convention and many of them on copyright were imported from the Berne Convention. Therefore, it can be said that TRIPs is drafted on the basis of both the Paris Convention and the Berne Convention.

2. Scope of intellectual property

The paragraph 2 of article 1 of TRIPs stipulated the scope of intellectual property as follows: copyright and related rights, trademarks, geographical indications, industrial designs, patents, layout-designs (topographies) of integrated circuits, undisclosed information.

Compared with its forerunners, TRIPs enlarged the scope of intellectual property, such as the undisclosed information.

3. Main principles

1) National treatment

The national treatment principle of TRIPs has similar meaning to those of the Paris Convention and the Berne Convention.

2) Most-favored-nation treatment

TRIPs, for the first time, put up the principle of most-favored-nation treatment in intellectual property laws. This principle means that, with regard to the protection of intellectual property, any advantage, favor, privilege or immunity granted by a member to the nationals of any other country shall be accorded immediately and unconditionally to the nationals of all other members, unless exempted from this obligation in accordance with the provisions of the agreement.

4. Particular provisions on intellectual property rights

TRIPs makes particular and detailed provisions on protection of each type of the right falling into the scope of intellectual property rights it defined, which will be briefed as follows.

1) Copyright and related rights

TRIPs follows the Berne Convention's criterion about the protection of copyright (except the personal rights); and extend copyright protection to expressions but not to ideas, procedures, methods of operation or mathematical concepts as such. With the development of communication technology and Internet, the TRIPs enlarged the scope of protection in computer programs and compilations of data, as well as the related rights to protection of performers, producers of phonograms (sound recordings) and broadcasting organizations.

- Computer programs and compilations of data

Computer programs shall be protected as literary works under the Berne Convention (1971 Revision). Compilations of data or other material, whether in machine a readable or other forms, which by reason of the selection or arrangement of their contents constitutes intellectual creations, shall be protected as such. Such protection, which shall not extend to the data or material itself, shall be without prejudice to any copyright subsisting in the data or material itself.

For computer programs and cinematographic works, a member shall provide authors and their successors in title the right to authorize or to prohibit the commercial rental to the public of originals or copies of their copyright works. In respect of computer programs, this obligation does not apply to rentals where the program itself is not the essential object of the rental.

- Related rights to protection of performers, producers of phonograms and broadcasting organizations

According to the article 14 of TRIPs, performers, producers of phonograms (sound recordings) and broadcasting organizations, also take some related rights, which involve the following.

(1) In respect of a fixation of their performance on a phonogram, performers shall have the possibility of preventing the following acts when undertaken without their authorization: the fixation of their unfixed performance and the reproduction of such fixation, or the broadcasting by wireless means and the communication to the public of their live performance.

(2) Producers of phonograms shall enjoy the right to authorize or prohibit the direct or indirect reproduction of their phonograms.

(3) Broadcasting organizations shall have the right to prohibit the following acts when undertaken without their authorization: the fixation, the reproduction of fixations, and the rebroadcasting by wireless means of broadcasts, as well as the communication to the public of television broadcasts of the same. Where members do not grant such rights to broadcasting organizations, they shall provide owners of copyright in the subject matter of broadcasts with the possibility of preventing the above acts, subject to the provisions of the Berne Convention (1971 Revision).

(4) The term of the related rights protection available to performers and producers of phonograms shall last at least until the end of a period of 50 years computed from the end of the calendar year in which the fixation was made or the performance took place. The term of related rights protection to broadcasting organizations shall last for at least 20 years from the end of the calendar year in which the broadcast took place.

2) Trademarks

- Protectable subject matter

As to the protection of trademarks, the basic principle of TRIPs is the same as that of the Paris Convention. The article 15 of TRIPs requires that any sign, or any combination of signs, capable of distinguishing the goods or services of one undertaking from those of other undertakings, shall be capable of constituting a trademark. Such signs, in particular words including personal names, letters, numerals, figurative elements and combinations of colors as well as any combination of such signs, shall be eligible for registration as trademarks.

Where signs are not inherently capable of distinguishing the relevant goods or services, members may make registration depending on distinctiveness acquired through use. Members may require, as a condition of registration, that signs be visually perceptible. However, actual use of a trademark shall not be a condition for filing an application for registration.

- Rights conferred

The paragraph 1 of article 16 of the TRIPs provides that the owner of a registered trademark shall have the exclusive right to prevent all third parties, without having the owner's consent, from using in the course of trade identical or similar signs for goods or services which are identical or similar to those in respect of which the trademark is registered where such use would result in a likelihood of confusion.

In case of the use of an identical sign for identical goods or services, a likelihood of confusion shall be presumed. The rights described above shall not prejudice any existing prior rights, nor shall they affect the possibility of members making rights available on the basis of use.

On the other hand, the TRIPs allows members to provide limited exceptions to the rights conferred by a trademark, such as fair use of descriptive terms, provided that such exceptions take account of the legitimate interests of the owner of the trademark and of third parties.

- Well-known trademark

The paragraph 2 of article 16 of the TRIPs stipulates that in determining whether a trademark is well-known, members shall take account of the knowledge of the trademark in the relevant sector of the public, including knowledge in the member concerned which has been obtained as a result of the promotion of the trademark.

- Time limit of protection

The article 18 of the TRIPs requires that initial registration and each renewal of registration, of a trademark shall be for a term of no less than 7 years. The registration of a trademark shall be renewable indefinitely.

3) Protection of geographical indications

Compared with the Paris Convention, TRIPs places more emphasis on the protection of geographical indications, in particular, the protection for geographical indications for wines and spirits. The article 22 of TRIPs provides that geographical indications are indications which identify a good as originating in the territory of a member, or a region or locality in that territory, where a given quality, reputation or other characteristic of the good is essentially attributable to its geographical origin.

Members shall provide the legal means for interested parties to prevent misleads the public, or any use which constitutes an act of unfair competition within the meaning of article 10bis of the Paris Convention (1967 Revision).

4) Industrial designs

In light of the articles 25 and 26 of TRIPs, members shall provide for the protection of independently created industrial designs (including textile designs) that are new or original. The duration of protection available shall amount to at least 10 years.

5) Patents

- Patentable subject matter

According to the article 27 of TRIPs patents shall be available for any inventions, whether products or processes, in all fields of technology, provided that they are new, involve an inventive step and are capable of industrial application.

Patents shall be available and patent rights enjoyable without discrimination as to the place of invention, the field of technology and whether products are imported or locally produced. Members may exclude from patentability of inventions if the prevention within their territory of the commercial exploitation of which is necessary to protect public order or morality, including to protect human, animal or plant life or health or to avoid serious prejudice to the environment, provided that such exclusion is not made merely because the exploitation is prohibited by their law. Members may also exclude diagnostic, therapeutic and surgical methods for the treatment of humans or animals from patentability. Moreover, plants and animals other than micro-organisms, and essentially biological processes for the production of plants or animals other than non-biological and microbiological processes, may also be excluded from patentability.

- Rights conferred

The article 28 of TRIPs stipulates that a patent shall confer on its owner the following exclusive rights:

(1) Where the subject matter of a patent is a product, to prevent third parties not having the owner's consent from the acts of making, using, offering for sale, selling, or importing for these purposes that product;

(2) Where the subject matter of a patent is a process, to prevent third parties not having the owner's consent from the act of using the process, and from the acts of using, offering for sale, selling, or importing for these purposes at least the product obtained directly by that process.

Besides, patent owners shall have the right to assign, or transfer by succession, the patent and to conclude licensing contracts.

- Conditions on patent applicants

In order to apply a patent, members shall require an applicant to disclose the invention in a manner sufficiently clear and complete for the invention to be carried out by a person skilled in the art and may require the applicant to indicate the best mode for carrying out the invention known to the inventor at the filing date or, where priority is claimed, at the priority date of the application.

- Time limit of protection

The article 33 of the TRIPs provides that the term of protection available shall not end before the expiration of a period of 20 years counted from the filing date.

6) Layout-designs (topographies) of integrated circuits

The articles 35 to 38 of TRIPs provides that:

(1) Members shall consider unlawful the following acts if performed without the authorization of the right holder: importing, selling, or otherwise distributing for commercial purposes a protected layout-design, an integrated circuit in which a protected layout-design is incorporated, or an article incorporating such an integrated circuit only in so far as it continues to contain an unlawfully reproduced layout-design;

(2) Layout-designs shall be protected for a term of no less than 10 years.

7）Undisclosed information

• Elements of undisclosed information

In light of the article 39 of TRIPs, undisclosed information indicates know-how（trade secret）which must possess the following three conditions:

（1）Information is secret in the sense that it is not, as a body or in the precise configuration and assembly of its components, generally known among or readily accessible to persons within the circles that normally deal with the kind of information in question;

（2）Information has commercial value because it is secret;

（3）Information has been subject to reasonable steps under the circumstances, by the person lawfully in control of the information, to keep it secret.

• Protection of undisclosed information

In light of the article 39 of the TRIPS, undisclosed information and data is brought into the scope of anti-unfair competition, which involves:

（1）In the course of ensuring effective protection against unfair competition as provided in the Paris Convention（1967 Revision）, members shall protect undisclosed information in accordance with the relevant provisions of this agreement;

（2）Natural and legal persons shall have the possibility of preventing information lawfully, within their control, from being disclosed to, acquired by, or used by others without their consent in a manner contrary to honest commercial practices so long as such information is secret in the sense that it is not, as a body or in the precise configuration and assembly of its components, generally known among or readily accessible to persons within the circles that normally deal with the kind of information in question; or has commercial value because it is secret; and has been subject to reasonable steps under the circumstances, by the person lawfully in control of the information, to keep it secret;

（3）Members, when requiring, as a condition of approving the marketing of pharmaceutical or of agricultural chemical products which utilize new chemical entities, the submission of undisclosed test or other data, the origination of which involves a considerable effort, shall protect such data against unfair commercial use; In addition, members shall protect such data against disclosure, except where necessary to protect the public, or unless steps are taken to ensure that the data are protected against unfair commercial use.

• Remedies

Provided that the undisclosed information was used without the authorization of the right holder, that the judicial authorities of members shall have the authority to order a party to desist from an infringement, among other things, to prevent the entry into the channels of commerce in their jurisdiction of imported goods that involve the infringement of an intellectual property right, immediately after customs clearance of such goods. Members may limit the remedies available against use to payment of remuneration. In other cases, the remedies shall apply or, where these remedies are inconsistent with a member's domestic law, declaratory judgments and adequate compensation shall be available.

10.1.6 Chinese Intellectual Property Laws 中国的知识产权法

After implementing the policy of reform and open-up, China has gradually enacted a number of laws and regulations relating to intellectual property protection, such as the Patent Law of the People's

Republic of China, the Trademark Law of the People's Republic of China, the Copyright Law of the People's Republic of China, the Regulations on the Protection of Computer Software, the Regulations on the Protection of Layout Designs of Integrated Circuits, and etc. Moreover, China has taken part in most international conventions and agreements on intellectual property, as well as the World Intellectual Property Organization; and has been trying best to coordinate domestic intellectual property laws with the relevant international rules.

The three most important Chinese intellectual property law will be briefed as follows.

1. Patent law

The Patent Law of the PRC was promulgated in 1984 and amended in 1992 and 2000.

This law is enacted to protect patent rights for inventions-creations. According to this law, "inventions-creations" are defined as inventions, utility models and exterior designs. The duration of patent right for inventions shall be 20 years, the duration of patent right for utility models and patent right for exteriors designs shall be 10 years, counted from the date of filing the application.

At present, the State Intellectual Property Office[17] is in charge of the application, examination and approval in China.

2. Trademark law

The Trademark Law of the PRC was formulated in 1982 and amended in 1993 and 2001.

This law is enacted for the purposes of improving the administration of trademarks, protecting the right to exclusive use of trademarks and encouraging producers and operators to guarantee the quality of their goods and services and maintain the reputation of their trademarks, so as to protect the interests of consumers, producers and operators, and to promote the development of the socialist market economy.

The Trademark Office of the State Administration for Industry and Commerce[18] is in charge of the trademark registration and administration throughout the country. Any natural person, legal person or other organization that needs to acquire the right to exclusive use of a trademark for the commodities it produces, manufactures, processes, selects or markets, or services it offers, shall file an application for trademark registration with the Trademark Office.

The period of validity of a registered trademark shall be 10 years, counted from the day the registration is approved.

3. Copyright law

The Copyright Law of the PRC was enacts in 1990 and amended in 2001.

This law aims to protect the copyright of authors in their literary, artistic and scientific works and rights and interests related to copyright. Such works in this law are defined as literature, art, natural science, social science and engineering technology created in the following forms:

(1) Writings works;

(2) Oral works;

(3) Music, dramatic, quyi, dance and acrobatic works;

(4) Painting and architectural works;

(5) Photographic works;

(6) Cinematographic works and works created by virtue of the analogous method of film production;

(7) Graphic works such as diagrams of project design, drawings of product design, maps and sketches as well as works of their model;

(8) Computer software;

(9) Other works set out by laws and administrative regulations.

This Law does not apply to:

(1) Laws, regulations, resolutions, decisions and decrees of state authorities and other documents of legislative, administrative or judicial nature, as well as their official translations;

(2) News on current events;

(3) Calendar, numerical tables, general tables and formulas.

In addition, the measures for protecting the copyright in folk literary and artistic works shall be formulated by other laws.

According to this law, copyright includes the following personal rights and property rights: right of publication, right of authorship, right of alternation, right to integrity of the work, right of reproduction, right of distribution, right of lease, right of exhibition, right of performance, right of show, right of broadcast, right of information network dissemination, right of production, right of adaptation, right of translation, right of compilation, and other rights that shall be enjoyed by copyright owners.

Term of protection for the right of authorship, the right of alteration and the right to integrity of the work of authors shall not be restricted. For other rights, term of protection shall be the life of the author and 50 years after his death, and expires on December 31 of the 50th year after the death of the author; in relation to a collective work, term of protection expires on December 31 of the 50th year after the death of the last of the authors.

10.2 Model Law on Electronic Commerce
电子商务示范法

10.2.1 An Overview of Electronic Commerce 电子商务概述

Electronic commerce, as the newest aspect of modern business, commonly known as ecommerce or e-commerce, consists of the buying and selling of products or services over electronic systems such as the Internet and other computer networks.

The amount of trade conducted electronically has grown extraordinarily since the spread of the internet. The meaning of electronic commerce has changed over the last 30 years. Originally, electronic commerce meant the facilitation of commercial transactions electronically, using technology such as Electronic Data Interchange (EDI)[19] and Electronic Funds Transfer (EFT)[20]. These were both introduced in the late 1970s, allowing businesses to send commercial documents like purchase orders or invoices electronically. The growth and acceptance of credit cards, ATM and telephone banking in the 1980s were also forms of electronic commerce. Since the 1990s, electronic commerce has been considered to additionally including enterprise resource planning systems, data mining as well as data warehousing.

With the fast development of electronic commerce, it is increasing necessary to legislate relevant laws to protect it. However, the electronic commerce is a so new thing that, up to now, few laws have been enacted to regulate it in most countries.

Notably, in 1996, the United Nations Commission on International Trade Law (UNCITRAL) formulated the Model Law on Electronic Commerce that has been taken as the pillar of electronic commerce laws since its birth.

10.2.2　Model Law on Electronic Commerce　《电子商务示范法》

1. A brief introduction

The Model Law on Electronic Commerce was adopted by the UNCITRAL in 1996. The Model Law was prepared in response to a major change in the means by which communications are made between the UN members using computerized or other modern techniques in doing business (sometimes referred to as "trading partners"). It is intended to serve as a model to countries for the evaluation and modernization of certain aspects of their laws and practices in the field of commercial relationships involving the use of computerized or other modern communication techniques, and for the establishment of relevant legislation where none presently exists.

Under the guidance of UNCITRAL Model Law on Electronic Commerce, the EU, the US, Japan, and some other countries have enacted Electronic Commerce Laws. In the US, a Framework for Global Electronic Commerce[21] was promulgate in 1997 and the Electronic Signatures in Global and National Commerce Act (E-Sign Act)[22] was passed in the Capitol Hill in 2000. The EU put forward European Initiative in E-commerce[23] in 1997 and enacted the EU Directive on a Community Framework for Electronic Signatures[24] in 1999. In China, the Electronic Signature Law of the PRC began to be drafted in 2004.

2. Sphere of application

The article 1 of the Model Law on Electronic Commerce says that this law applies to any kind of information in the form of a data message[25] used in the context of commercial activities. In light of the article 2, the term "data message" refers to information generated, sent, received or stored by electronic, optical or similar means including, but not limited to, electronic data interchange, electronic mail, telegram, telex or telecopy. The meaning of "electronic data interchange" is the electronic transfer from computer to computer of information using an agreed standard to structure the information.

3. Particular provisions

Generally speaking, the Model Law stipulated the validity of a date message which is used in the formation of a contract. The stipulations may be summarized as follows.

(1) The force adeffect of a data message is equal to the writing's force adeffect.

(2) With regard to the validity of a data message signature, where the law requires a signature of a person, that requirement is met in relation to a data message if: a) a method is used to identify that person and to indicate that person's approval of the information contained in the data message; and b) that method is as reliable as was appropriate for the purpose for which the data message was generated or communicated, in the light of all the circumstances, including any relevant agreement.

(3) As to the original of contract, it is legitimate if only the information to be presented or retained in its original.

(4) In any legal proceedings, nothing in the application of the rules of evidence shall apply so as to

deny the admissibility of a data message in evidence as to the evidential weight of data messages.

（5）As to the retention of data messages, the information contained force adeffect so long as which is met by retaining data messages and is accessible so as to be usable for subsequent reference.

（6）In the context of contract formation, unless otherwise agreed by the parties, either an offer or the acceptance of an offer, or both, may be expressed by means of data messages. Where a data message is used in the formation of a contract, that contract shall not be denied validity or enforceability on the sole ground that a data message was used for that purpose.

（7）As to the recognition by parties of data messages, the parties shall not be denied legal effect, validity or enforceability solely on the grounds that it is in the form of a data message.

It should be noted that, however, as to the time and place of formation of contracts in cases where an offer and/or the acceptance of an offer is expressed by means of a data message, no specific rule has been included in the Model Law in order not to interfere with national law applicable to contract formation.

 **Group Discussion** ▶▶▶

1. Try to differentiate intellectual property from intellectual property rights.
2. Discuss the contents of the major types of intellectual property rights.
3. Make some remarks on Chinese intellectual property laws.
4. Give some examples of electronic commerce.

 NOTES ▶▶▶

1　exclusive right　专有权
2　assigning right　转让权
3　renewal right　续展权
4　right of publication　发表权
5　right of authorship　署名权
6　right of alternation　修改权
7　right to integrity of the work　保护作品完整权
8　related rights　邻接权
9　layout-designs (topographies) of integrated circuits　集成电路布图设计（拓扑图）
10　Berne Convention for the Protection of Literary and Artistic Works　《保护文学和艺术作品伯尔尼公约》(简称为 the Berne Convention)
11　United International Bureaux for the Protection of Intellectual Property　保护知识产权联合国际局
12　national treatment　国民待遇
13　nondiscrimination　非歧视待遇
14　priority right　优先权

15   automatic protection   自动保护

16   minimum standards of protection   最低保护标准

17   State Intellectual Property Office   国家知识产权局

18   Trademark Office of the State Administration for Industry and Commerce   国家工商行政管理总局商标局

19   Electronic Data Interchange（EDI）   电子数据交换

20   Electronic Funds Transfer（EFT）   电子资金转账

21   Framework for Global Electronic Commerce   《全球电子商务框架文件》

22   Electronic Signatures in Global and National Commerce Act（E-Sign Act）   《全球和国内商业电子签名法案》

23   European Initiative in E-commerce   《欧洲电子商务行动方案》

24   EU Directive on a Community Framework for Electronic Signatures   《欧盟关于建立电子签名共同法律框架的指令》

25   data message   数据电文

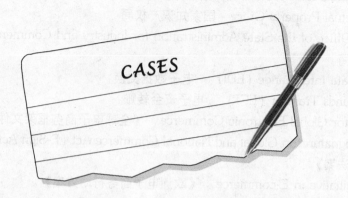

CASES

Frosty Treats, Inc. v. Sony Computer Entertainment America, Inc.
冰冻盛宴公司诉美国索尼电脑娱乐公司案

Frosty Treats, Inc. is the name of "one of the largest ice cream truck street vendors" in the United States. Their trucks uniformly feature a "Frosty Treats" logo, typically surrounded by the logos of various frozen snacks sold by the vender. Another feature of the trucks is the "Safety Clown", an image of a clown pointing children towards the back of the vehicle.

In the mid 1990s, Sony Computer Entertainment America released a video game that allows players to wreak havoc on simulated streets with a variety of vehicles, including an ice cream truck prominently featuring a logo that says "Frosty Treats". In the video game ice cream truck is driven by a crazed clown known as "Sweet Tooth", one of many featured in the game.

Frosty Treats, Inc. filed a lawsuit against Sony contending that the game infringed on the company's trademarks through the use of the phrase, "Frosty Treats", as well as similarities between the video game clown and the company's own safety clown. The US District Court for the Western District of Missouri granted summary judgement to Sony and dismissed the case, holding that the name could not be protected because it was generic. Frosty Treats appealed the dismissal to the Eighth Circuit Court of Appeals on June 15, 2005.

The Eighth Circuit affirmed the dismissal, holding that the name was indeed generic and held that the safe clown of Frosty Treats lacked distinctiveness in the marketplace such that it would merit protection. Furthermore, the Court noted such striking dissimilarities between the company's clown and the game clown that no consumer would be likely to confuse the two.

Perfect 10 v. Google, Inc
完美 10 诉谷歌公司案

One of the rights accorded to the owner of copyright is the right to reproduce or to authorize others to reproduce the work in copies or phonorecords. This right is subject to certain limitations found in sections 107 through 118 of the US Copyright Act. One of the more important limitations is the doctrine of "fair use". Although fair use was not mentioned in the previous copyright law, the doctrine has developed through a substantial number of court decisions over the years. Section 107 contains a list of the various purposes for which the reproduction of a particular work may be considered "fair", such as criticism, comment, news reporting, teaching, scholarship, and research. Section 107 also sets out four factors to be considered in determining whether or not a particular use is fair:

(1) The purpose and character of the use, including whether such use is of commercial nature or is for nonprofit educational purposes;

(2) The nature of the copyrighted work;

(3) Amount and substantiality of the portion used in relation to the copyrighted work as a whole;

(4) The effect of the use upon the potential market for or value of the copyrighted work.

The distinction between "fair use" and infringement may be unclear and not easily defined. There is no specific number of words, lines, or notes that may safely be taken without permission. Acknowledging the source of the copyrighted material does not substitute for obtaining permission.

The following case may help to understand the "fair use".

The plaintiff, Perfect 10 (P10), sold a magazine that featured sexually provocative images of women. It also operated a website featuring such images and leased some of these images to other businesses. The defendant operated a commercial service on Internet to find images, created thumbnails of them, and indexed them; when a user then entered a search term that Google's search algorithms matched to an image, Google displayed that image's thumbnail amongst a grid of other thumbnails, and if the user clicked on a thumbnail, it displayed the page that the full image came from "framed" within but clearly distinguished from the Google site. Google did not store or physically transmit the full images, only their thumbnails.

On November 19, 2004, P10 filed suit against Google asserting copyright and trademark infringement claims. After settlement discussions lasting several months, P10 filed for a preliminary injunction for Google to cease linking to and distributing its images.

Later, in February 2006, District Judge A. Howard Matz ordered that P10 and Google jointly propose a wording for a preliminary injunction to halt Google's distribution of thumbnails of P10's works.

Following the district court's decision, both sides cross-appealed to the US Court of Appeals for the Ninth Circuit.

P10's claims of direct infringement were twofold. First, it argued that Google's framing of infringing websites constituted direct infringement by Google itself, and requested that Google be enjoined from so framing websites infringing its content; second, it argued that Google's creation and distribution of thumbnails was direct infringement, and requested that Google be enjoined from creating and distributing thumbnails of its images.

The court found that the relevant question in whether Google was guilty of displaying and distributing the full-sized images due to framing others' content was whether it hosted and physically transmitted the content itself, rejecting P10's argument that the relevant question should be whether the content is visually incorporated into the site. Since on the physical level, Google only provided an instruction for the user's computer to fetch the infringing pages from servers not under its control, the court found that P10 was unlikely to succeed on this point, and so denied its request for injunction.

Google did not dispute that it displayed and distributed protected derivative works of the plaintiff's images. However, it argued that such thumbnails were protected under the copyright doctrine of fair use, which is generally considered as being of four factors mentioned in the first paragraph.

On the fair use issue, the court held: the first, second, and fourth fair use factors weigh slightly in favor of P10. The third weighs in neither party's favor. Accordingly, the Court concludes that Google's creation of thumbnails of P10's copyrighted full-size images, and the subsequent display of those thumbnails as Google Image Search results, likely do not fall within the fair use exception. The Court reaches this conclusion despite the enormous public benefit that search engines such as Google provide. Although the Court is reluctant to issue a ruling that might impede the advance of Internet technology, and although it is appropriate for courts to consider the immense value to the public of such technologies, existing judicial precedents do not allow such considerations to trump a reasoned analysis of the four fair use factors.

Therefore, the court ruled that P10 was entitled to injunctive relief for Google's use of thumbnails.

Questions Raised by Yoga Copyright
瑜珈著作权引发的问题

Bikram Choudhury, the self-proclaimed Hollywood "yoga teacher to the stars," incensed his native country, India, by getting a US copyright on his style of yoga 4 years ago.

In response, India has put 100 historians and scientists to work cataloging 1,500 yoga poses recorded in ancient texts written in Sanskrit, Persian and Urdu. India will use the catalogue to try to block anyone from cornering the market on the 5,000-year-old discipline of stretching, breathing and meditating.

Bikram, who goes by one name like Bono and Beyoncé, says he sought legal protection for his yoga because "it's the American way."

"You cannot drive the car if you do not have a driver's license," he explains. "You cannot do brain surgery if you are not a brain surgeon. You cannot even do a massage if you don't have a license." And, he says, "you shouldn't be able to teach his Bikram Yoga unless you pay him for a license."

India wants to thwart anyone who tries to profit from the nation's so-called "traditional knowledge," from yoga to 150,000 ancient medical remedies. India already has successfully challenged one US patent granted to two Indian-born Americans who used the spice turmeric in a wound-healing product. That patent was revoked by the US Patent and Trademark Office.

"Practically every Indian housewife knows (turmeric) and uses it to heal wounds," says an official of India's National Institute of Science Communication and Information Resources, which is developing the Traditional Knowledge Digital Library. When completed, perhaps as soon as December, the digital library will be translated into English, French, German, Spanish and Japanese and sent to copyright, patent and trademark offices around the world.

That way, when someone such as Bikram tries to get a copyright on yoga moves or patents on ancient medicinal cures, those offices could say: "No, that's not original. They've been doing it in India for thousands of years."

Typically, patents are given only to those who invent or discover something new. In general, copyrights go on written works; trademarks go on company and product names.

India has no plans to challenge Bikram in court, Gupta says. But it hopes the digital library will stop others from following him.

Some of Bikram's fellow yoga teachers are skeptical of India's efforts to protect yoga. "It's a little late in the game," says Beth Shaw, president of YogaFit in Hermosa Beach, California, which developed a yoga program for health clubs. "They should have done it 30 years ago."

In the world of yoga, Bikram, is something of a star. A collector of Bentleys and Rolls-Royces, he teaches his classes of up to 100 students with flamboyant style. He began teaching yoga in the 1970s after immigrating to America. Bikram obtained his first US copyright in 1979 for a book he wrote, Bikram's Beginning Yoga Class. He also got a trademark for the name of his company, Bikram's Yoga College of India.

In 2003, a group of yoga teachers sued Bikram, saying he couldn't copyright yoga. He fought back. A federal judge ruled in April 2005 that Bikram's copyright was legitimate and enforceable. Having a copyright protects Bikram's style and, more significantly, the income he derives from the global yoga empire he's built.

As corporations and researchers scour the globe for medical cures from plants or animals, or materials to use for genetic engineering, countries are beginning to try to protect their traditional knowledge. They want a new definition of the term "intellectual property" to be sure they'll profit from any uses of their knowledge and resources.

The WIPO administers and negotiates international treaties involving patents and may mediate disputes. Most challenges are made to the patent offices of individual countries, and are decided through its courts.

In 2005, India's National Institute randomly selected 762 US patents that had been granted for medicinal products using plants; it found that 49 percent were based on traditional Indian knowledge. It is estimated that about 2,000 patents each year based on India's traditional medicine are taken out somewhere in the world.

Negotiations are underway at the WIPO on ways to protect traditional knowledge. But there's no consensus yet.

As its popularity has exploded, yoga has become a big business, with licensing and certification from yoga schools, consolidation and takeovers. As a result, yoga copyrights and trademarks are sure to increase, says Stephen Russell, president of the Yoga Alliance, which registers training programs for yoga schools. That's because there needs to be a "barrier to entry" in the business, Russell says, so people can "protect their niche".

Americans spend about $3 billion one year on yoga classes and products, including clothes, vacations, DVDs and books, according to Yoga Journal magazine. The magazine's 2004 poll of 4,700 Americans estimated that 16.5 million people practice yoga. That's an increase of 43 percent from 2002. An additional 25 million said they intend to try yoga.

Bikram says his copyright is essential to protecting his business, which he predicts — with his usual flair for the dramatic — to be the answer to all of America's woes: bad health from too much drinking, too much smoking, too much stress. "I guarantee you, yoga will compete with computers, automobiles, sports, music, and the drug industry," Bikram says, "Yoga will take over the world!"

Glossary
专业词汇表

A

abnormal use, misuse or abuse of the product　非正常使用、误用或滥用产品

absolute acceptance　单纯承兑，无条件承兑

acceptance by intervention　参加承兑

acceptance for honor　参加承兑

acceptor for honor　参加承兑人

accumulation fund　公积金

actionable subsidy　可申诉补贴

administrative law　行政法

agency by estoppel　不容否认的代理

agency by ratification　追认的代理

agency of necessity　客观必需的代理

agent　代理人

Anglo-American Law System　英美法系

anticipatory breach（of contract）　预期违约

appointed agency　指定代理

Articles of Association　（英国英语）公司内部细则

Articles of Incorporation　（美国英语）公司组织大纲

artificial person　法人

assigning right　转让权

assumption of the risk　自担风险

Attorney General　（美国）州检察长

authorized capital system　授权资本制

authorized capital　授权资本

automatic protection　自动保护

B

bad cheque　空头支票

bearer draft 无记名汇票

bearer stock 无记名股

bid rigging 串通投标

bill of exchange 汇票

bill of sale 卖方继续保持占有的动产权益转让合同

bill relationship 票据关系

blank endorsement 空白背书，无记名背书

board of directors 董事会

board of supervisors 监事会

bona fide 善意的

breach of condition 违反条件，违反要件

breach of implied warranty of authority 违反有代理权的默示担保

breach of warranty 违反担保

Bylaws （美国英语）公司内部细则

C

capital stock （美国英语）股份资本，股本

case law 判例法

cash cheque 现金支票

causing relationship of instrument 票据的原因关系

cheque （英国英语）支票

CISG（United Nations Convention on Contracts for the International Sale of Goods） 《联合国国际货物销售合同公约》

civil capacity 民事行为能力

Civil Law System 民法法系

civil partnership 民事合伙

clean acceptance 单纯承兑，无条件承兑

clear acceptance 单纯承兑，无条件承兑

commercial partnership 商业合伙，商事合伙

Common Law System 普通法系

common law 普通法，习惯法

common stock 普通股

company charter 公司章程

comparative negligence 相对疏忽

conclusive evidence 确证，决定性证据

conditional endorsement 附条件背书

confirming agent 保付代理人

confirming bank （信用证）保兑行

confirming house 保付商行

constitutional law 宪法

Continental Law System 大陆法系

contract for brokerage　行纪合同

contract for commission　委托合同

contract for intermediation　居间合同

Contracting States　缔约国

contributory negligence　承担疏忽

convertible corporate bond　可转换公司债

corporate constitution　公司章程

county court　郡法院

Court of Appeals　（英国）上诉法院

court of first instance　一审法院

court of second instance　二审法院

courts of chancery　（英国）枢密大臣法庭、大法官法庭

criminal law　刑法

crossed cheque　划线支票

Crown Court　（英国）王冠法院

D

damages　损害赔偿

data message　数据电文

dead freight　空舱费

deed contract under seal　签字蜡封合同

defective title　权利瑕疵

del credere agent　信用担保代理人

delay in performance　给付延迟

deposit　提存

direct agency　直接代理

disclaimer or limitation of warranty　担保的排除或限制

discretionary accumulation fund　任意公积金

doctrine of most significant contact　最密切联系原则

Doha round　世界贸易组织"多哈回合"多边贸易谈判

dormant partnership　隐名合伙

draft　汇票

drawee　受票人，付款人

drawer　（汇票或支票）出票人

droit coutumier　（法语）法律汇编

E

ECU（European Currency Unit）　欧洲货币单位

EDI（Electronic Data Interchange）　电子数据交换

EFT（Electronic Funds Transfer） 电子资金转账

endorsee 被背书人

endorsement for collection 委托取款背书

endorsement of pledge 质权背书，设质背书

endorser 背书人

entrusted agency 委托代理

equity 衡平法，平衡法

establishment by public share offer 募集设立

establishment by sponsorship 发起设立

exclusive dealing 独家交易

exclusive right 专有权

export house 出口商行

express appointment 明示的指定

F

fault liability 过错责任，过失责任

fictitious person 法人

formal security 要式证券

forwarding agent 运输代理人

freight forwarder 运输代理人

full endorsement 完全背书，完整背书

fundamental breach（of contract） 根本性违约

funding relationship of instrument 票据的资金关系

G

GATT（General Agreement on Tariffs and Trade） 《关税与贸易总协定》

general acceptance 普通承兑

General Assembly 联合国大会

general crossed cheque 普通划线支票

general endorsement 空白背书，无记名背书

general jurisdiction court 普通管辖权法院

general meeting of shareholders 股东大会

general partnership 普通合伙

group boycott 集体抵制

guarantor 保证人

H

hardship 艰难情形，履行艰难

Havana Charter　《哈瓦那宪章》
High Court　（英国）高等法院
holder in due course　正当持票人
holder　持票人
House of Lords　（英国）上议院

I

implied authority　默示的授权
INCOTERMS（International Commercial Terms）　《国际贸易术语解释通则》
indirect agency　间接代理
individual proprietorship　个人企业，个人独资企业，独资经营企业
INGO（International Non-governmental Organization）　国际非政府间组织
injunction　禁令
instrument relationship　票据关系
insurance broker　保险经纪人
interdicted person　禁治产者
interim general meeting of shareholders　临时股东大会
invitation for offer　要约邀请
invitation to treat　要约邀请
issued capital　发行资本

J

joint and several liability　连带责任，共同责任
judge-made law　判例法
juridical person　法人
juristic person　法人
jury trial　陪审团
justice court　低级法院

K

Kennedy Round　《关税与贸易总协定》的"肯尼迪回合"多边贸易谈判
kiting cheque　空头支票

L

late acceptance　逾期接受
law merchant　商业习惯法，商人法
law of nations　万国公法，国际法

Law of Restitution　偿还法

layout-designs（topographies）of integrated circuits　集成电路布图设计（拓扑图）

legal capacity　法律行为能力

legal person　法人

legal relationships of international business　国际商事法律关系

lex mercatoria　（拉丁语）商业习惯法，商人法

like product　同类产品

limitation of action　诉讼时效

limited jurisdiction court　有限管辖权法院

limited liability company　有限责任公司

limited liability partnership　有限责任合伙

limited partnership　有限合伙，两合公司

liquidated damages　违约金，约定的赔偿金

listed company　上市公司

local content subsidy　当地含量补贴

Lord Chancellor　英国封建时代的枢密大臣（今指大法官）

lord chief justice　最高法院的首席法官

M

magistrate court　治安法院

mail-box rule　投邮主义

magistrate court　治安法院

maker　（本票）出票人

margin of dumping　倾销幅度，倾销差价

market division　瓜分市场

market sharing　瓜分市场

material breach　重大违约

Memorandum of Association　（英国英语）公司组织大纲

merger by absorption　吸收合并

merger by consolidation　新设合并

merger　混同

minimum contact　最低限度的接触

minimum standards of protection　最低保护标准

minor breach　轻微违约

monetary restitution　金钱上的恢复原状

N

national treatment　国民待遇

negative prescription　消灭时效

negligence 疏忽

negotiable instrument 票据

no-fault liability 无过错责任，无过失责任

non par value stock 无票面金额股

non-actionable subsidy 不可申诉补贴

nondiscrimination 非歧视待遇

non-instrument relationship 非票据关系

notice of dishonor 拒付通知

O

obligation cause 债之约因

OECD（Organization for Economic Co-operation and Development） 经济合作与发展组织

offer and acceptance 发盘与接受

open endorsement 空白背书，无记名背书

order draft 记名汇票

P

par value stock 有票面金额股

payee 收款人

payer for honor 参加付款人

payment by intervention 参加付款

payment for honor 参加付款

payment 清偿

pecuniary restitution 金钱上的恢复原状

per se rule 本身（违法）原则

personal jurisdiction 对人的管辖权

PICC（Principles of International Commercial Contracts） 《国际商事合同通则》

positive law 成文法，制定法

positive prescription 取得时效

power of attorney 委任书，授权书

preferred stock 优先股

presentment for acceptance 承兑提示

presentment for payment 付款提示

price squeezing 价格压榨，价格挤压

prima facie evidence 初步证据

principal 本人，委托人

principle of informality 不要式原则

prior holder 前手

priority right 优先权

private international law　国际私法

private law　私法

privity of contract　合同关系

procedural laws　诉讼法，程序法

product with unavoidable dangerous feature　产品带有不可避免的不安全性

prohibited subsidy　禁止性补贴

promissory note　本票

promoter　发起人

protest for dishonor　（汇票）拒付证书

public international law　国际公法

public law　公法

public welfare organization　公益组织

putting in default　催告

Q

qualified acceptance　附有限制条件的承兑，非单纯承兑

qualified endorsement　无追索权背书

quasi contract　准合同

quasi-judicial　准司法性的

Queen's Bench Division　王座庭

R

registered stock　记名股

related rights　邻接权

release　免除

renewal right　续展权

resale price maintenance　维持转售价格，控制转售价格

rescission　解除合同

reserve fund　公积金

restrictive endorsement　限制转让背书

right of alternation　修改权

right of authorship　署名权

right of publication　发表权

right to integrity of the work　保护作品完整权

Romano-Germanic Law System　罗马－日耳曼法系

rubber cheque　空头支票

rule of reason　合理原则

S

sale with prizes　有奖销售

SCM（Agreement on Subsidies and Countervailing Measures）　《补贴与反补贴措施协议》

secured corporate bond　担保公司债

set-off　抵销

share capital　（英国英语）股份资本，股本

simple contract　简式合同

sole proprietorship　个人企业，个人独资企业，独资经营企业

special crossed cheque　记名划线支票

special endorsement　特别背书，记名背书

special general partnership　特殊的普通合伙

specific performance　实际履行

state court　（美国）州法院

Statute of Frauds　欺诈法

statute　制定法

statutory accumulation fund　法定公积金

statutory agency　法定代理

statutory agent　法定代理人

statutory capital system　法定资本制

statutory law　制定法

stock limited company　股份有限公司

strict liability　严格责任

subject matter　标的物

subsequent alteration　擅自改动产品

subsequent holder　后手

superior court　高级法院

supervening impossibility of performance　给付不能

T

tenants-in-chief　总佃户，领主

time bill of exchange　远期汇票，定期汇票

Tokyo Round　《关税与贸易总协定》的"东京回合"多边贸易谈判

tort　民事侵权行为

transfer cheque　转账支票

tying　搭售

U

UCP（Uniform Customs and Practice for Documentary Credits）　《跟单信用证统一惯例》

UNCITRAL 联合国国际贸易法委员会

UNCTAD 联合国贸易与发展会议

UNIDROIT 国际统一私法协会

unjust enrichment 不当得利

unlimited liability 无限责任

unwritten law 不成文法，习惯法

unsecured corporate bond 无担保公司债

Uruguay Round 《关税与贸易总协定》的"乌拉圭回合"多边贸易谈判

US Circuit Court 美国联邦巡回法院

US court 美国联邦法院

US District Court 美国联邦地方法院

US Supreme Court 美国联邦最高法院

V

voluntary agency 意定代理

W

written law 成文法，制定法

References
参考文献

［1］冯大同. 国际商法. 北京：对外贸易教育出版社，1991.

［2］全国国际商务专业人员职业资格考试用书编委会. 国际商务专业知识. 北京：中国商务出版社，2005.

［3］姜作利. 国际商法. 北京：法律出版社，2004.

［4］曹祖平. 新编国际商法. 北京：中国人民大学出版社，2004.

［5］沈四宝. 国际商法教学案例（英文）选编. 北京：法律出版社，2007.

［6］马齐林. 新编国际商法. 广州：暨南大学出版社，2004.

［7］袁绍岐. 国际商法. 广州：暨南大学出版社，2006.

［8］向嫣红. 国际商法. 北京：北京交通大学出版社，2004.

［9］朱羿锟. 中国商法. 北京：法律出版社，2003.

［10］莫世健. 国际商法. 北京：中国法制出版社，2004.

［11］SEALY L S. Commercial law：text，cases and materials. London：Butterworth，1999.

［12］CARR I. International trade law. London：Cavendish Publishing Ltd. ，2005.